Unraveling Dyslexia

SPECIAL EDUCATION LAW, POLICY, AND PRACTICE

Series Editors

Mitchell L. Yell, PhD, University of South Carolina
David F. Bateman, PhD, American Institutes for Research

The *Special Education Law, Policy, and Practice* series highlights current trends and legal issues in the education of students with disabilities. The books in this series link legal requirements with evidence-based instruction and highlight practical applications for working with students with disabilities. The titles in the *Special Education Law, Policy, and Practice* series are designed not only to be required textbooks for general education and special education preservice teacher education programs but are also designed for practicing teachers, education administrators, principals, school counselors, school psychologists, parents, and others interested in improving the lives of students with disabilities. The *Special Education Law, Policy, and Practice* series is committed to research-based practices working to provide appropriate and meaningful educational programming for students with disabilities and their families.

Titles in Series

Developing Educationally Meaningful and Legally Sound IEPs by Mitchell L. Yell, David F. Bateman, and James G. Shriner

Sexuality Education for Students with Disabilities by Thomas C. Gibbon, Elizabeth A. Harkins Monaco, and David F. Bateman

Creating Positive Elementary Classrooms: Preventing Behavior Challenges to Promote Learning by Stephen W. Smith and Mitchell L. Yell

Service Animals in Schools: Legal, Educational, Administrative, and Strategic Handling Aspects by Anne O. Papalia, Kathy B. Ewoldt, and David F. Bateman

Evidence-Based Practices for Supporting Individuals with Autism Spectrum Disorder edited by Laura C. Chezan, Katie Wolfe, and Erik Drasgow

Special Education Law Annual Review 2021 by David F. Bateman, Mitchell L. Yell, and Kevin P. Brady

Dispute Resolution Under the IDEA: Understanding, Avoiding, and Managing Special Education Disputes by David F. Bateman, Mitchell L. Yell, and Jonas Dorego

Advocating for the Common Good: People, Politics, Process, and Policy on Capitol Hill by Jane E. West

Related Services in Special Education: Working Together as a Team by Lisa Goran and David F. Bateman

The Essentials of Special Education Advocacy by Andrew M. Markelz, Sarah A. Nagro, Kevin Monnin, and David F. Bateman

Disability and Motor Behavior: A Handbook of Research by Ali S. Brian and Pamela S. Haibach-Beach

You're Hired! Practical Strategies for Guiding Individuals with Autism Spectrum Disorder to Competitive Employment by Patricia S. Arter, Tammy B. H. Brown, and Jennifer Barna

Unraveling Dyslexia: A Guide for Teachers and Families by Kristin L. Sayeski

For a full list of books in this series, visit https://rowman.com/Action/SERIES/_/RLSELPP/Special-Education-Law,-Policy,-and-Practice.

Unraveling Dyslexia

A Guide for Teachers and Families

Kristin L. Sayeski
University of Georgia

ROWMAN & LITTLEFIELD
Lanham • Boulder • New York • London

Executive Acquisitions Editor: Nathan Davidson
Assistant Acquisitions Editor: Hollis Peterson
Sales and Marketing Inquiries: textbooks@rowman.com

Published by Rowman & Littlefield
An imprint of The Rowman & Littlefield Publishing Group, Inc.
4501 Forbes Boulevard, Suite 200, Lanham, Maryland 20706
www.rowman.com

86-90 Paul Street, London EC2A 4NE

Copyright © 2024 by The Rowman & Littlefield Publishing Group, Inc.

Icons on page 22 in chapter 2 © DivVector/DigitalVision Vectors/Getty Images (bat), FingerMedium/DigitalVision Vectors/Getty Images (egg), and CSA Images/CSA Images/Getty Images (dog).

All rights reserved. No part of this book may be reproduced in any form or by any electronic or mechanical means, including information storage and retrieval systems, without written permission from the publisher, except by a reviewer who may quote passages in a review.

British Library Cataloguing in Publication Information Available

Library of Congress Cataloging-in-Publication Data

Names: Sayeski, Kristin L., author.
Title: Unraveling dyslexia : a guide for teachers and families / Kristin L. Sayeski, University of Georgia.
Description: Lanham, Maryland : Rowman & Littlefield, [2023] | Series: Special education law, policy, and practice | Includes bibliographical references and index.
Identifiers: LCCN 2023036645 (print) | LCCN 2023036646 (ebook) | ISBN 9781538170236 (cloth) | ISBN 9781538170243 (paperback) | ISBN 9781538170250 (epub)
Subjects: LCSH: Dyslexic children--Education--United States. | Reading--Remedial teaching--United States. | Reading disability. | Response to intervention (Learning disabled children)
Classification: LCC LC4709 .S39 2023 (print) | LCC LC4709 (ebook) | DDC 371.91/440973--dc23/eng/20230825
LC record available at https://lccn.loc.gov/2023036645
LC ebook record available at https://lccn.loc.gov/2023036646

Contents

1	Dyslexia and the Complex Behavior of Reading	1
2	Creating the Code: Understanding English Orthography	17
3	Reading Instruction in the United States	31
4	Reading Science and Individual Differences in Reading	61
5	Structured Literacy: Word Recognition	83
6	Structured Literacy: Language Comprehension	121
7	Advocacy and Action	161
Glossary		175
References		181
Index		209
About the Author		219

Chapter One

Dyslexia and the Complex Behavior of Reading

One of the first descriptions of dyslexia came from Adolph Kussmaul (1877), a German professor of medicine. Writing in a medical encyclopedia, Kussmaul described the condition of the word *blindness*. The purpose of his chapter, titled "Diseases of the Nervous System and Disturbances of Speech," was to differentiate between the condition of aphasia—difficulty with word expression—and a condition described in the medical literature in which patients could speak but were unable to read. The cases Kussmaul described were examples of acquired conditions (i.e., conditions developed after birth) within adults, but his description accurately described the phenomenon observed in young children who experience difficulty with reading. Specifically, to differentiate between aphasia and this unique phenomenon, Kussmaul described and named the condition:

> [Patients] were no longer able . . . although sight was perfect, to read the written words which they saw. This morbid inability we will style, in order to have the shortest possible names at our disposition, . . . *word blindness*. (p. 770)

Despite the observations of intact vision within the medical literature, this difficulty with reading was studied most frequently by ophthalmologists. In fact, it was an ophthalmologist, Rudolf Berlin (1884), who first used the term *dyslexia* to describe the condition. For Berlin, the Greek *dys-* (difficulty) with *-lexia* (words) captured the topography or surface features of the condition characterized in medical case studies: Individuals with dyslexia experienced difficulty sounding out and recognizing printed words.

Despite the early interest and identification of the condition by Kussmaul, Berlin, and others, whose interest focused on clinical etiology (i.e., the medical cause of the difficulty), it was the work of British physicians, beginning in the 1890s, that shaped our understanding of what dyslexia is today (Kirby, 2020). These physicians documented what would be considered *developmental dyslexia*, difficulty with reading that was not caused by stroke, disease, or injury to the head but was manifested during the course of learning to read. One of the earliest descriptions came from W. Pringle Morgan in 1896. Morgan, a school physician, published a case study in the *British Medical Journal* detailing the perplexing characteristics of one of his students:

> Percy F.—a well grown lad, aged 14—is the eldest son of intelligent parents . . . He has always been a bright and intelligent boy, quick at games, and in no way inferior to others of his age. His greatest difficulty has been—and is now—his inability to learn to read. This inability is so remarkable, and so pronounced, that I have no doubt it is due to some congenital defect.

Further, when Morgan asked Percy F. to read a simple children's book, what Morgan observed is consistent with many observations of students with dyslexia today. Morgan noted:

> The result was curious. He did not read a single word correctly, with the exception of *and, the, of, that,* etc.; the other words seemed to be quite unknown to him, and he could not even make an attempt to pronounce them. . . . He says that he is fond of arithmetic and has no difficulty with it, but that printed or written words "have no meaning for him," and my examination of him quite convinces me that he is correct in that opinion. Words written or printed seem to convey no impression to his mind, and it is only after laboriously spelling them that he is able, by the sounds of the letters, to discover their import. . . . The schoolmaster who has taught him for some years says that he would be the smartest lad in the school if the instruction were entirely oral. . . . His father informs me that the greatest difficulty was found in teaching the boy his letters, and they thought never would he learn them. No doubt he was originally letter blind, but by dint of constant application, this defect has been overcome. (p.1378)

Perhaps Morgan's description of Percy F. is so often referenced because of its hauntingly familiar illumination of a condition easily recognized today by parents, teachers, educational psychologists, and individuals who experience dyslexia first-hand. What was happening in the brain that allowed Percy to solve mathematical computations quickly and easily but rendered him unable to read a word? How did his spelling of a word, even if that spelling was conducted *laboriously*, provide some kind of support for determining the pronunciation and meaning of the word? Why could Percy read words like *and*, *of*, and *that* quickly and automatically but still struggle with words that followed standard phonics patterns? Finally, and most important, could the principles of *constant application* that allowed Percy to overcome his inability to learn his letters be applied to the teaching of reading?

DEBATES OVER THE USE OF THE TERM *DYSLEXIA*

Berlin introduced the term *dyslexia* when most physicians were using the term *word blindness*. However, ophthalmologists studying the condition began to realize the difficulties with reading being observed did not appear to be an issue with visual accuracy. As James Hinshelwood (1900), a British ophthalmologist, pointed out: "The difficulty in learning to read was due not to any lowering of the visual acuity, but to some congenital deficiency of the visual memory for words" (p. 1507). As ophthalmologists were stepping away from the term *word blindness*, interest in the phenomenon by other professionals was growing. Specifically, a new branch of science—psychology—had taken an interest in the condition. Psychologists were less interested in etiology (i.e., the root cause of reading difficulty) and focused more on the treatment. That is, what are the best ways to remediate reading difficulty? The term *dyslexia* captured what psychologists could observe—students experiencing difficulty with words.

Since the first descriptions of the condition appeared in medical journals, there has been general agreement that *reading disability* exists. Most debate about dyslexia does not focus on the existence of reading difficulty; it has been established that a subset of individuals experiences persistent difficulty learning to read, not accounted for by other explanatory variables (Elliott & Grigorenko, 2014). Even though we know much more today about the cognitive, neurological, and environmental conditions surrounding reading difficulties, historical arguments about dyslexia endure. Before we move on to contemporary definitions of *dyslexia*, we will examine several recurring concerns. As you will soon learn, concerns about dyslexia are rooted in social, political, and educational contexts (Kirby, 2020). Understanding these contexts can help frame productive conversations about prevention, support, and intervention that practitioners, families, and individuals with reading difficulty ultimately seek.

One argument frequently used as a rationale as to why the concept of reading disability should not be named and assigned a label of *dyslexia* is the notion that reading is a social construct (Kabuto, 2016). Of course, writing is a human invention. In alphabetic languages like English, humans created symbols to represent speech sounds (e.g., the sound /b/ is represented by the letter *b*; the long *a* sound, /ā/, can be spelled *eigh*). If one lived on a remote island without access to print, there would be no need for reading. In contrast, living in a literate society places a high demand on one's reading ability. This fact helps explain the sharp increase in attention to reading disability in the late 1800s. By the end of the 19th century, demands for a greater proportion of society to be literate had increased sharply (Campbell, 2011). As more students attended school and were expected to read, more students were identified as having reading difficulties. Because society created a demand for reading does not render the difficulties experienced by those with dyslexia any less important or valid. The demand simply highlighted the unique difficulties some students experience when learning the complex task of reading. In other words, even though reading is socially constructed, this does not make reading difficulty less real. Instead, it means learning to read is a social justice concern. Denying students access to reading denies students access to important opportunities and privileges available within a literate society.

Another component of resistance to the concept of dyslexia has been historical and contemporary associations between reading disability and affluence. Since the early days of Percy F.—Pringle Morgan's boarding student with intelligent and wealthy parents—the push for clinical identification of and educational support for students with dyslexia has come from families with social and economic capital (Kirby, 2020). Of course, who else would be in such a position for advocacy other than those with the means and time to seek help? This does not preclude the benefits of research and instructional advances related to dyslexia from being shared with those who do not have similar social and economic capital. Quite the contrary: The push for more research and a wider distribution of information in any area can serve as an important driver of change for a wider population.

Notwithstanding the critical role of advocacy as an impetus for awareness, research, and services, inequities due to economic differences do exist, particularly regarding access (Hettleman, 2003). Affluent families have the option of hiring tutors, sending their children to private schools that specialize in reading disabilities, living in areas with well-resourced public schools, or even securing the training they need to provide services directly to their children (Hanford, 2017). In addition, students in underperforming schools, which are more likely situated in lower-income areas, are less likely to be identified and receive appropriate services (Hibel et al., 2010). However, these inequities do not mean that dyslexia is an invention of the rich; instead, universal access to early identification and high-quality reading instruction and intervention should be viewed as a national health priority (DeWalt et al., 2004).

Finally, a third source of resistance comes from a disdain for what is characterized as a deficit-based orientation inherent within the conceptualization of dyslexia. Within a deficit-based orientation, also referred to as a medical model, the focus is on identifying what is wrong with an individual and determining a treatment or solution for the problem. In contrast to viewing differences in reading ability as a disability or difficulty that needs to be fixed, individuals who resist a deficit orientation advocate for a strengths-based perspective—focusing on an individual's unique gifts and abilities and the promotion of those abilities. Unfortunately, the consequences of not learning to read or experiencing difficulty in learning to read render resistance to such deficit-based orientations a *luxury belief* (McShane, 2023). Luxury beliefs are opinions held by individuals who have the luxury of not experiencing the situation first-hand. First-hand accounts of individuals with dyslexia point to the devastating social, emotional, and educational consequences of not having their learning needs met and the life-altering consequences of receiving the direct, targeted intervention they require (Gerber, 2011; Peterson & Pennington, 2015). Although the unique strengths and talents of individuals should be accounted for and built upon within an instructional program, the significant challenges associated with learning to read should not be dismissed, overlooked, or avoided.

What we do know about the construct of dyslexia is that social, political, and educational conditions change. We also know that few things are considered settled science, and what is known about dyslexia will also change as science sheds new light on reading acquisition. New information may also result in the need for a new term or additional terms. For now, though, the term *dyslexia* has particular utility for individuals, families, educators, and advocates, as it reflects the difficulty many people experience learning to read the written word. Terms like *learning difference* or even *reading difficulty* fail to capture the significant impact an inability to read accurately and fluently presents. Although some characterize the use of any disability label as limiting, for many individuals and their families, receiving a formal diagnosis of dyslexia is liberating and brings hope rather than despair (Ramus, 2014; Shaywitz, 2020). With formal recognition comes a shared community, greater opportunities for awareness and focused research, and, as will be discussed extensively in Chapters 5 and 6, a strong impetus for the educational community to understand features of effective reading instruction and ensure the timely delivery of reading intervention.

Therefore, despite historical and contemporary resistance to the term, *dyslexia* is internationally recognized and succinctly conveys the significant needs and consequences associated with reading difficulty. Contemporary definitions converge on several key characteristics of the condition. Most significant, rather than painting a picture of a condition that is *fait accompli*, these definitions describe a condition that demands direct and focused instructional attention. In other words, a diagnosis of dyslexia does not signal a fixed condition; instead, it signals that it is time to provide immediate instructional support.

Contemporary Definitions

Many definitions of *dyslexia* exist, reflecting various purposes (e.g., epidemiological, diagnostic, descriptive, and educational). Yet they all address the significant and persistent difficulty some individuals experience with word-level reading not accounted for by age, visual acuity, or inadequate schooling (American Psychiatric Association, 2013; Kearns et al., 2019; Rose, 2009; World Health Organization, 2019). Individuals experiencing this specific reading difficulty will not grow out of it—reading ability is not simply a result of maturation—nor is the difficulty trivial. Such reading difficulties will affect one's quality of life. Thus, the existence of multiple definitions underscores the various organizations' need to formally recognize the condition, systematically identify individuals with the condition within a community, and/or provide services for individuals experiencing the condition. As highlighted in several definitions, reading ability occurs along a continuum. As such, there is no bright line distinguishing reading difficulty from a reading disability; professional judgment and contextual factors will be part of a diagnostic process.

Further, given the complex nature of reading ability, multiple factors will play a role in the manifestation of reading disability—genetic, epigenetic, and environmental (American Psychiatric Association, 2013). This means that all individuals identified as having dyslexia will not reflect a monolithic group—there will be variation across reading profiles. What is true is that these individuals experience difficulty with word-reading accuracy and fluency, and these difficulties will substantially limit their ability to access written information.

Similarities and Differences across Definitions

Within this section, definitions from the *Rose Review* (2009), the *Diagnostic and Statistical Manual* (DSM-5; American Psychiatric Association, 2013), the *International Classification of Diseases* (ICD-10; World Health Organization, 2019), and the International Dyslexia Association (IDA, 2002) are presented. A comparison of these definitions highlights the similarities and reflects a consensus regarding the conceptualization of dyslexia, particularly in the context of learning English.[1] The definitions reflect a *developmental*

---

[1]. Learning English, an alphabetic language with a deep orthographic structure, differs from learning to read non-alphabetic languages or learning to read shallow orthographies (e.g., Spanish, Finnish, Serbian, Turkish). These differences will be addressed in Chapter 2.

rather than an *acquired* condition. Developmental conditions are disorders of the developing nervous system, manifested in infancy or early childhood, that result in limitations in reaching developmental milestones or the development of functional skills. In contrast, *acquired conditions*, such as those studied by Kussmaul, result from disease (e.g., stroke, high fever) or accident (e.g., traumatic brain injury). The definitions also reflect different purposes. As such, a definition developed for one purpose, such as diagnosis, may not be the same as one created for awareness and advocacy.

In 2008, the secretary of state for education in the United Kingdom commissioned Sir Jim Rose to make recommendations on how to improve the delivery of instruction for students with dyslexia. After an extensive examination, Rose published his review, commonly called the *Rose Review* or *Rose Report* (2009). The report included a working definition of dyslexia and recommendations for practice. As the purpose of the definition was to help teachers identify students in need of additional support, the definition reflects that aim:

> Dyslexia is a learning difficulty that primarily affects the skills involved in accurate and fluent word reading and spelling. Characteristic features of dyslexia are difficulties in phonological awareness, verbal memory, and verbal processing speed. Dyslexia occurs across the range of intellectual abilities. It is best thought of as a continuum, not a distinct category, and there are no clear cut-off points. Co-occurring difficulties may be seen in aspects of language, motor coordination, mental calculation, concentration and personal organisation, but these are not, by themselves, markers of dyslexia. A good indication of the severity and persistence of dyslexic difficulties can be gained by examining how the individual responds or has responded to well-founded intervention.

The *Rose Review* definition captured many elements addressed in other definitions of *dyslexia*. Namely, (a) dyslexia is specific—relating directly to reading and spelling difficulties; (b) difficulty with phonology and processing are characteristic of the condition, and (c) dyslexia can co-occur with other conditions that affect other areas such as attention, organization, mathematics, and coordination. What differentiated the *Rose Review* definition from many others was its rejection of the idea that dyslexia occurs only in individuals with high intelligence. Although dyslexia had historically been viewed through a discrepancy lens—that is, the presence of reading difficulty (i.e., low reading achievement) was incompatible or *discrepant* from an individual's intelligence as measured by IQ tests—a growing body of research in the late 20th century pointed toward core deficits in phonology (i.e., processing the sounds of oral language) that were irrespective of intelligence as a central feature of dyslexia (Snowling, Hulme, & Nation, 2020; Stanovich & Siegel, 1994).

In 2013, the American Psychiatric Association followed suit in dropping the IQ-achievement discrepancy requirement as a part of its updated diagnostic criteria for *specific learning disorder with impairment in reading* in the fifth edition of its *Diagnostic and Statistical Manual* (*DSM-5*; American Psychiatric Association, 2013). The *DMS-5* description reiterated the biological basis of dyslexia and the developmental nature of the impairment:

> *Specific learning disorder*, as the name implies, is diagnosed when there are specific deficits in an individual's ability to perceive or process information efficiently and accurately. This neurodevelopmental disorder first manifests during the years of formal schooling and is characterized by persistent and impairing difficulties with learning foundational academic skills in reading, writing, and/or math. The individual's performance of the affected academic skills is well below average for age, or acceptable performance levels are achieved only with extraordinary effort. Specific learning disorder may occur in individuals identified as intellectually gifted and manifest only when the learning demands or assessment procedures (e.g., timed tests) pose barriers that cannot be overcome by their innate intelligence and compensatory strategies. For all individuals, specific learning disorder can produce lifelong impairments in activities dependent on the skills, including occupational performance. (APA, 2013, 315.00 [F81.0], p. 32)

Although the IQ-achievement discrepancy was removed from the definition, the *DSM-5*'s requirements for identification reflected specific elements of the condition that separate it from being synonymous with general poor reading. The *DSM-5* diagnostic criteria preserved the concept of *unexpectedness* (i.e., dyslexia is unexpected in relation to other cognitive functions and the provision of adequate academic instruction) and an instructional history of *persistent difficulty* consistent with most conceptualizations of dyslexia. Specifically, to be diagnosed with a specific learning disorder in reading, writing, or mathematics, the following criteria must be met:

A. Difficulties learning and using academic skills, as indicated by the presence of at least one of the following symptoms that have persisted for at least 6 months, despite the provision of interventions that target those difficulties:

1. Inaccurate or slow and effortful word reading (e.g., reads single words aloud incorrectly or slowly and hesitantly, frequently guesses words, has difficulty sounding out words).
2. Difficulty understanding the meaning of what is read (e.g., may read text accurately but not understand the sequence, relationships, inferences, or deeper meanings of what is read).
3. Difficulties with spelling (e.g., may add, omit, or substitute vowels or consonants).

4. Difficulties with written expression (e.g., makes multiple grammatical or punctuation errors within sentences; employs poor paragraph organization; written expression of ideas lacks clarity).
5. Difficulties mastering number sense, number facts, or calculation (e.g., has poor understanding of numbers, their magnitude, and relationships; counts on fingers to add single-digit numbers instead of recalling the math fact as peers do; gets lost in the midst of arithmetic computation and may switch procedures).
6. Difficulties with mathematical reasoning (e.g., has severe difficulty applying mathematical concepts, facts, or procedures to solve quantitative problems).

B. The affected academic skills are substantially and quantifiably below those expected for the individual's chronological age, and cause significant interference with academic or occupational performance, or with activities of daily living, as confirmed by individually administered standardized achievement measures and comprehensive clinical assessment. For individuals age 17 years and older, a documented history of impairing learning difficulties may be substituted for the standardized assessment.

C. The learning difficulties begin during school-age years but may not become fully manifest until the demands for those affected academic skills exceed the individual's limited capacities (e.g., as in timed tests, reading or writing lengthy complex reports for a tight deadline, excessively heavy academic loads).

D. The learning difficulties are not better accounted for by intellectual disabilities, uncorrected visual or auditory acuity, other mental or neurological disorders, psychosocial adversity, lack of proficiency in the language of academic instruction, or inadequate educational instruction. (pp. 66–67)

Finally, within the DSM-5, it was noted that:

Dyslexia is an alternative term used to refer to a pattern of learning difficulties characterized by problems with accurate or fluent word recognition, poor decoding, and poor spelling abilities. If dyslexia is used to specify this particular pattern of difficulties, it is important also to specify any additional difficulties that are present, such as difficulties with reading comprehension or math reasoning. (p. 67)

Thus, although situated under the broader term *specific learning disorder*, the manual acknowledged the use of the term *dyslexia* to indicate specific word-level reading difficulty. Additionally, the *DSM-5* diagnostic criteria captured similar elements present in the Rose definition but added layers of specificity to facilitate the diagnosis of the condition by psychiatrists and licensed psychologists. The exclusionary factors, in particular, serve to separate dyslexia from other conditions—such as intellectual disability, visual or auditory impairments, or specific language disorder—and also differentiate the condition from those who experience reading difficulties due to poor instruction. Regarding inclusionary factors, diagnostic features include persistent difficulty, onset during the developmental period, and observable, descriptive behaviors (see A1-6). Like the *Rose Report* definition, the *DSM-5* also noted that academic skills are distributed along a continuum; thus, clinical judgment is required for diagnosis. But, to facilitate clinical identification, the manual did specify that at least 1.5 standard deviations below the population mean would provide diagnostic certainty.

Of particular importance is the distinction made within the *DSM-5* regarding the difference between learning an academic skill like reading, writing, or mathematics from achieving naturally developing milestones: "In contrast to talking or walking, which are acquired developmental milestones that emerge with brain maturation, academic skills (e.g., reading, spelling, writing, mathematics) have to be taught and learned explicitly" (p. 68). The need for the direct teaching of academic skills stated within the *DSM-5* is a concept that will be revisited frequently throughout this book.

Another diagnostic-based definition comes from the *International Classification of Diseases* (*ICD-11*; World Health Organization, 2019). The *ICD-11* is used by the World Health Organization (WHO) in its efforts to collect epidemiological data on health-related conditions. The WHO also classifies dyslexia as a developmental learning disorder. Expressly, their definition of *developmental learning disorder in reading* (6A03.0) reflects similar inclusionary and exclusionary factors as found in the *DSM-5*:

> *Developmental learning disorder with impairment in reading* is characterised by significant and persistent difficulties in learning academic skills related to reading, such as word reading accuracy, reading fluency, and reading comprehension. The individual's performance in reading is markedly below what would be expected for chronological age and level of intellectual functioning and results in significant impairment in the individual's academic or occupational functioning. Developmental learning disorder with impairment in reading is not due to a disorder of intellectual development, sensory impairment (vision or hearing), neurological disorder, lack of availability of education, lack of proficiency in the language of academic instruction, or psychosocial adversity. (WHO, 2019, 6A03.0)

Finally, one of the most widely employed definitions of *dyslexia* within the U.S. comes from IDA. IDA's definition of dyslexia is frequently used to inform research, practice, and policy. Initially developed in 1994 and revised in 2002 in partnership with the National Center for Learning Disabilities,

IDA's definition of *dyslexia* has continued to evolve to reflect knowledge gained from ongoing epidemiological, developmental, and neurobiological research. Many state-level laws on dyslexia incorporated this definition within their legislation (Gearin, et al., 2022). Furthermore, the definition is commonly used by researchers in neuroscience, cognitive psychology, and special education. IDA's definition is notable in that it acknowledged the biological underpinnings of the condition, preserved the notion of unexpectedness, and clarified a relationship between the primary and secondary effects of the condition:

> *Dyslexia* is a specific learning disability that is neurobiological in origin. It is characterized by difficulties with accurate and/or fluent word recognition and by poor spelling and decoding abilities. These difficulties typically result from a deficit in the phonological component of language that is often unexpected in relation to other cognitive abilities and the provision of effective classroom instruction. Secondary consequences may include problems in reading comprehension and reduced reading experience that can impede growth of vocabulary and background knowledge. (IDA, 2002)

In summary, the conceptualization of *specific learning disorder in reading* is remarkably consistent across definitions. The demand for the numerous organizations and agencies to generate a definition underscores the significant impact the condition has on individuals' quality of life and the need for such individuals to be formally identified, counted, and served.

INDIVIDUALS WITH DISABILITIES EDUCATION ACT AND DYSLEXIA

Within the U.S., students with dyslexia may be eligible for special education services required by the Individuals with Disabilities Education Act (IDEA, 2004) under the category of *specific learning disability*:

> *Specific learning disability* means a disorder in one or more of the basic psychological processes involved in understanding or in using language, spoken, or written, that may manifest itself in the imperfect ability to listen, think, speak, read, write, spell, or to do mathematical calculations, including conditions such as perceptual disabilities, brain injury, minimal brain dysfunction, dyslexia, and developmental aphasia. (§ 1401[30][B])

In contrast to the *DSM-5* definition, this federal education definition offered a description of the condition, not a set of diagnostic criteria. The differences in presentations of the condition reflect the different purposes of the organizations. The *DSM-5* is used by clinicians for diagnosis, whereas the broad parameters of the IDEA are used by states for establishing their processes to determine eligibility for education services. Further, the IDEA definition of *specific learning disability* is consistent with other federal definitions of disability categories. That is, the definitions are necessarily vague. Some argue that the ambiguity present within federal legislation and regulations is essential, as the inexactness of the law allows states to stipulate more specific interpretations, thus preserving states' rights within education and recognizing the role of professional judgment and context for decision-making (U.S. Department of Education, 2021). Others yearn for greater specificity, which may reduce variation in identification patterns across states (Cottrell & Barrett, 2016).

Within the definition, the IDEA makes clear that students with dyslexia may be eligible for special education services under the law. Although students whose reading difficulties fall on the higher end of the distribution of low reading performance may not have an educational need that warrants special education, students with moderate to severe dyslexia will likely demonstrate the educational need necessary to qualify for special education services. However, despite the inclusion of the term *dyslexia* within the federal definition, schools have been reluctant to use the term within evaluation processes and on individualized education program (IEP) documents. Some administrators and teachers even thought they were prohibited from mentioning the word *dyslexia* in schools (Mitchell, 2020). To clarify the U.S. Department of Education's position on the relationship between dyslexia and the IDEA, the assistant secretary of education issued a "Dear Colleague" letter reiterating to school personnel that the term was permissible for use:

> I write today to focus particularly on the unique educational needs of children with dyslexia, dyscalculia, and dysgraphia, which are conditions that could qualify a child as a child with a specific learning disability under the Individuals with Disabilities Education Act. The purpose of this letter is to clarify that there is nothing in the IDEA that would prohibit the use of the terms dyslexia, dyscalculia, and dysgraphia in IDEA evaluation, eligibility determinations, or IEP documents. (Yudin, 2015)

Therefore, when seeking eligibility for special education services, schools may prefer to use the language of the federal category, *specific learning disability*. Still, nothing prohibits schools from using the term *dyslexia* to describe the characteristics of students who experience persistent word-level reading difficulties or from using the term on IEP documents or in communication with families.

STATE DYSLEXIA LEGISLATION

Against the backdrop of growing consensus around the conceptualization of dyslexia, a concerted push for state-level legislative solutions began in the early 2000s. Families of students who had been historically under-identified and underserved increasingly had access to information on best practices in reading instruction and intervention, and a political appetite for greater school accountability fueled reform efforts (Gearin et al., 2020). As a result, over the past two decades, there has been a dramatic increase in the number of states passing dyslexia-specific legislation (Youman & Mather, 2018). As of 2023, all but one state (Hawaii) and Puerto Rico had passed laws relevant to the education of students with dyslexia (National Center on Improving Literacy, 2023). The range of issues addressed by the legislation varied—from the use of universal screeners for early identification to pre-service or inservice teacher training mandates to specific school-based intervention requirements—and differed from state to state.

The different elements addressed within the laws reflected the various challenges experienced by families of students with dyslexia. First, families and advocates sought recognition of the condition. As noted previously, with formal recognition comes specialized services and funding for research. Many advocates invoked the mantra "Say dyslexia" to express their frustration with the lack of formal recognition. Second, advocates sought to promote a specific type of instruction—namely, instruction that would systematically and directly address issues related to the phonological difficulties many students with dyslexia experience.[2] The demand for a structured approach to reading instruction was in particular a reaction to the type of mainstream instruction teachers were providing writ large within the schools. Specifically, advocates were frustrated by balanced literacy approaches that failed to address the alphabetic principle (i.e., the relationship between speech sounds and letters) that undergirds alphabet languages like English; Seidenberg, 2017).

Finally, many of the laws attempted to address serious gaps in teacher preparation and inservice teacher training related to the provision of reading instruction and intervention. Within the laws, requirements that teachers be provided with information related to dyslexia and the treatment of dyslexia were delineated. In addition, some states specified elements of intervention schools must provide to students recognized as dyslexic (Gearin et al., 2020).

---

[2]. The type of systematic and explicit instruction advocated for is addressed at length in Chapters 5 and 6.

MYTHS AND MISCONCEPTIONS

Public awareness campaigns, like those associated with state-level legislation, have resulted in greater knowledge within the general public, but many myths and misconceptions about dyslexia persist. The most prevailing and unfortunate of these myths is the idea that individuals with dyslexia read backward. Reversals—when students spell certain letters backward—are a commonly occurring phenomenon across all young children learning to write. Although reversals may persist beyond the age when most students have outgrown them, written reversals are not a sign of backward decoding (Dehaene, 2009). The backward-reading myth perpetuates the false belief that dyslexia is solely or primarily a vision problem, which may be addressed by eye-training, special glasses, colored overlays, or special fonts (Henderson et al., 2013). Scientific evidence does not support the use of such vision-correcting methods (American Academy of Ophthalmology, 2014), and the backward-reading myth belies the language-based foundations of dyslexia.

Other myths and misconceptions related to dyslexia stem from a lack of understanding of reading acquisition (e.g., learning to read is part of a natural development process) or confusion about the power of instruction and intervention to remediate reading difficulties. Lack of knowledge directly contributes to beliefs that early signs of reading difficulty are not causes for concern, as all students develop differently, and these students will catch up with their peers as they mature. Similarly, failure to understand how the brain processes written language also contributes to the misconception that all students learn differently; thus, there are different ways or paths to reading proficiency. In stark contrast to these beliefs, research has demonstrated that although the pace and intensity may differ, what students need to know (implicitly or explicitly) about the structure of written language is the same, and this knowledge is necessary for accessing written language.[3]

Contrary to these misconceptions, mounting evidence points to the efficacy of early identification, intensive intervention, and language-based remediation for students with or at risk for dyslexia (Connor et al., 2013; Lovett et al., 2021; Torgesen, 2005; Wanzek et al., 2013). An overarching purpose of this book is to provide the type of information teachers, families, and reading professionals need to understand the complexities and nuances associated with learning to read. With knowledge comes the insight required to address the significant and life-altering needs of those individuals with dyslexia.

---

3. Foundational principles of reading instruction will be explored in Chapter 3: Reading Instruction in the United States.

DYSLEXIA TODAY

Prevalence data indicate that dyslexia is one of the most common neurodevelopmental disorders, with a 5% to 12% prevalence rate (Snowling, 2013). Although individuals with dyslexia will have different profiles, all will experience difficulty with word-level reading and spelling (Catts et al., 2017; Pennington et al., 2012). Many students with dyslexia struggle with phonology, poor verbal short-term memory, and difficulties with word retrieval (Snowling, 2019). However, given the complexity of learning to read and the genetic and environmental influences that play a role in reading acquisition, phonological differences do not account for all instances of dyslexia (Snowling, Hulme, & Nation, 2020). For example, some students with a family history of dyslexia and early signs of phonological difficulty may not reach a clinical threshold for dyslexia due to protective factors such as strong language skills and an effective early reading environment.

Similarly, some students who do not demonstrate phonological difficulties may be identified as dyslexic (Pennington, 2006). Variations in the profiles of students with dyslexia are best explained by multifactorial models of reading that take into account what is required of the brain when reading (i.e., the phonological, orthographic, and semantic demands of reading) and how other internal and external factors interact in the course of reading development (Catts et al., 2017). All these factors will be explored throughout this book.

In response to the question, "Is dyslexia real?," research has converged on several points. Specifically, findings demonstrate: (a) there is a genetic component to dyslexia; (b) there is evidence of language-related differences present before reading instruction begins (i.e., reading disability is not simply a result of poor teaching); and (c) dyslexia is not a developmental delay, as students with the condition will not get better due to maturation; intervention is required for these students to learn to read (Willingham, 2019). Given these premises, attention to dyslexia is warranted. As stated previously, future research will continue to inform an understanding of reading disability, which may result in a more nuanced understanding of reading differences. But, for now, the acute needs of students who experience persistent, word-level reading difficulty are succinctly captured under the term *dyslexia*.

UNRAVELING A COMPLEX CONSTRUCT

Reading is a complex, knotty behavior. Internal and external conditions interact to influence a person's ability to read. Pinpointing why difficulty with reading occurs involves disentangling the interwoven strands of this complex behavior and the contexts that support or hinder reading development (e.g., early language environments, the type of reading instruction provided). Some may consider the conundrum of dyslexia a Gordian knot,[4] but I prefer to think of dyslexia as the knot in *Maniac Magee* (Spinelli, 1990). In that story, the main character, Maniac, attempts to untie Cobble's Knot, a knot with "more contortions, ins and outs, twists and turns and dips and doodles than the brain of Albert Einstein himself" (p. 69). Dyslexia can seem like Cobble's Knot to the families of struggling readers, the teachers attempting to help those readers, the scientists who study reading difficulty, and most important, the individuals who experience reading difficulty themselves. The purpose of this book is to loosen the interwoven strands of dyslexia. Within each chapter, we will explore various internal and external factors associated with reading acquisition, beginning with the history of writing—which will set up the first challenge in learning to read—and ending with the types of reading and writing instruction that will facilitate the unsnarling of literacy for so many individuals.

---

4. Gordian knot is a metaphor for a complex or unsolvable problem, which comes from an ancient Greek legend wherein Alexander the Great, rather than untying the unwieldy knot, cut the knot with his sword.

Chapter Two

Creating the Code: Understanding English Orthography

What is reading? Understanding the answer to this relatively straightforward question is critical to understanding why difficulty with reading can occur. To understand what reading is, we need to explore the intricate relationship between spoken language and the development of writing systems.

Reading is the ability to translate writing (i.e., printed words) into spoken language. Writing, in turn, is the translation of speech sounds into written form. In this chapter, you will discover why learning to read differs from learning to talk and how the development of the alphabetic writing system of English influences the way reading should be taught. Specifically, we will trace the history of English orthography. An orthography refers to how the sounds of a language are represented by written symbols. Therefore, *English orthography* is the spelling system of English. When teachers possess an incomplete understanding of English orthography, they can unknowingly make learning to read more difficult. These difficulties are exacerbated for students with dyslexia, whose language needs demand that teachers know enough about English orthography to recognize and remediate these students' specific instructional needs.

WHY LANGUAGE ACQUISITION DIFFERS FROM READING ACQUISITION

Most children acquire language naturally. Within an infant's babbling, the phonemes (i.e., speech sounds) of language can be heard. Researchers have found that all babies produce similar sounds regardless of which languages they have been exposed to (Lee et al., 2010). These single-syllable sounds, called canonical babbling, consist of one consonant (nasal consonants [/m/, /n/] or stop consonants [/b/, /p/, /d/, /t/, /k/, /g/]) and one vowel (e.g., /ă/, /ŭ/) to produce the familiar "dadada" and "muhmuhmuh" chains (Vihman, 2014). In addition, infants can perceive the speech sounds of all word languages. By 12 months of age, though, speech production becomes language-specific, as children hone in and begin to imitate only those speech sounds present in their environment.

Although language acquisition is aided by direct instruction—a mother points to a dog and says, "dog"—language acquisition is developed unconsciously. Children repeat what they hear, try out new words and syntactical combinations (e.g., "Me go bed"), and continually refine and expand their language by incidentally gathering information from their environment. Thus, the acquisition of spoken language is considered a natural process (Pinker, 1994). Children surrounded by a greater volume of language (i.e., more words spoken in the home, daycare, or other early childhood environments) will learn more words than children from language-poor environments. Still, children will acquire whatever language is available to them (Hoff, 2013). In addition, like any other ability, language acquisition will vary across the population. Some children will pick up on language more quickly than others, and some will have greater retention of word knowledge. Despite these variations in language acquisition, the manner in which young children learn to talk is the same: Language acquisition occurs naturally, over time, through environmental exposure. In contrast, reading does not (Moats, 2020b).

Reading Is a Code-Based Endeavor

Why is language acquired naturally, but reading is not? Because reading is a code-based endeavor. To crack the code, you must be taught the rules of the code. You cannot guess or intuit the code. Through trial and error, you may be able to solve part of the code, but you will most likely have errors in your thinking. Important, though, the process would be incredibly inefficient. Unfortunately, your love of solving mysteries or even a cash prize will not aid you in your ability to break the code. The only way to break the code is for someone to teach it to you. For example, see if you can decode this famous opening line of a popular children's book: Pg moy spnom hz moy thhg, u spmmsy ynn sue hg u syuz.[1]

Could you do it? Did you break the code? Let's return to our babbling infants. They did not have to break a code to learn to speak. They took advantage of modeling and association to develop that skill (Weizman & Snow, 2001). Consider other things that require knowledge of a code. A person who

---

1. "In the light of the moon, a little egg lay on a leaf." (Carle, 1969)

does not know how to read music may be able to listen to someone play the piano and replicate the same melody with minimal guidance or instruction. That same person, though, could not be handed a sheet of musical notation and asked to interpret it. Why the notes look the way they do and how they are arranged on the page are arbitrary. Musical notation evolved similarly to other writing systems—from early markings on cuneiform tablets to the eventual standardization of the code. Thus, the goal of all writing systems is the same: to create a visual representation of aural forms such as songs and speech. Learning these writing systems requires direct instruction in how specific symbols are used to represent the aural forms.

What the Code Represents

> Ours is a mongrel language which started with a child's vocabulary of three hundred words, and now consists of two hundred and twenty-five thousand; the whole lot, with the exception of the original and legitimate three hundred, borrowed, stolen, smouched from every unwatched language under the sun, the spelling of each individual word of the lot locating the source of the theft and preserving the memory of the revered crime. (Twain & Neider, 2000)

In his quote, Twain makes two excellent observations: (a) the complexity of English stems from its rich and varied history, and (b) knowing the spelling of a word reveals its origin (i.e., where it was stolen from). Indeed, *the memory of the crime is preserved in its spelling*. When viewed this way, English spelling is not haphazard or without logic. On the contrary, English is a series of patterns yearning to be discovered. Recently, Scripps National Spelling Bee officials reinstated a speller who had been denied root information about a word (Associated Press, 2022). The savvy participant knew that word origin reveals spelling mysteries. Thankfully, the depth of word origin knowledge possessed by the middle schoolers who compete in the Scripps Spelling Bee is not required to be a competent reader or teacher of reading, but a basic grasp of the underlying structure of English can fundamentally change the way reading is taught.

Of course, reading is easier than spelling (Bosman & Van Orden, 1997). People can read far more words than they can spell, but young children learning to read lack the internalized code experienced readers have that allows experienced readers to read words such as *bureaucrat* and *jeopardy* fluently even though they may have to pause or rely on spell-check to accurately spell the words. Thus, the task of early reading instruction is to take students step by step through the code and begin to build their understanding of the alphabetic principle. The *alphabetic principle* is the knowledge that words are composed of letters that represent speech sounds. Once students have established a strong understanding of sound-symbol relationships, they can begin to *de*-code the words they encounter in print.

The more teachers know about English orthography, the easier it is for them to competently guide beginning and struggling readers through the process of decoding words. Further, and more important, children's understanding of what reading is and how to go about decoding words is greatly influenced by their early reading experiences. Therefore, setting students off on the path to reading means knowing enough about the code, such that the role of the teacher is to thoughtfully scaffold students' engagement with print.

THE HISTORY OF WRITTEN LANGUAGE

Throughout history, inventors and arbiters of writing systems were well-intentioned. They undertook the task of creating a reliable and feasible way to produce a written record of speech. One of the earliest complete writing systems, cuneiform, comes from Sumer, in ancient Mesopotamia. Before cuneiform, people of that region used symbols or pictures—logographs—to represent whole words. As agriculture became an established practice, people needed a way to document the trade of goods and services. As such, the symbols were primarily used for accounting. For example, a recording of the exchange of sheep or barley could be recorded (see Figure 2.1). These early logographs did not represent a complete writing system, as their use did not reflect the syntax of spoken language (Woods et al., 2010). In other words, the writings did not reflect complete sentences, and word order did not matter.

The triumph of cuneiform was that it did reflect a complete writing system that, when read, would reflect speech. This was a significant breakthrough in the development of all early writing systems. Meaning-based, whole-word symbols had their limits in terms of what could be communicated. The use of writing to share ideas, in contrast to writing used for accounting purposes, necessitated the capacity of writing to capture abstractions. For example, symbols indicating *two* (quantity) and *sheep* (animal) could represent the following concepts: *I gave him two sheep; I will give him two sheep;* or *The exchange of sheep is good for our economy.*

To go beyond meaning-based symbols, the sounds of the language needed to be represented. As the Sumerian language was composed of a limited number of syllables (i.e., single vowels [e.g., /ă/, /á/, /ĭ/, /ú/], consonant + vowel combinations [e.g., /dí/, /gă/, /ké/], and vowel + consonant combinations [e.g., /ĭd/, /ăg/, /úl/]), symbols were created to represent sounds at the syllable level. Unfortunately for the Sumerians, these phonetic (sound-

Creating the Code: Understanding English Orthography

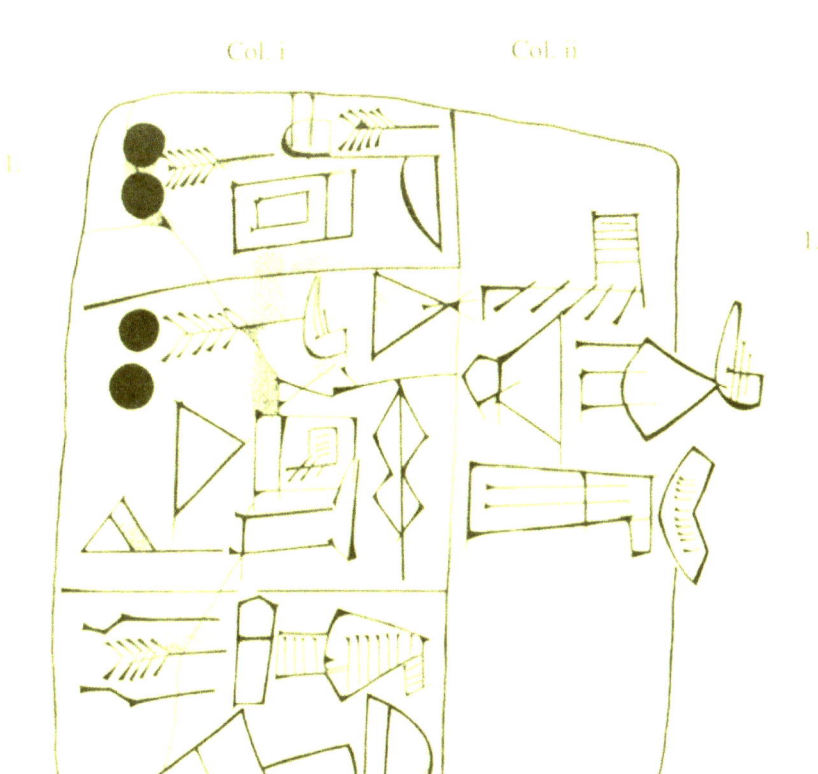

Figure 2.1. Proto-Cuneiform tablet reflecting an account of barley distribution

[Proto-Cuneiform tablet with seal impressions: administrative account of barley distribution with cylinder seal impression of a male figure, hunting dogs, and boars]. (ca. 3100-2900 BCE). Metropolitan Museum of Art, New York, NY, United States. https://www.metmuseum.org/art/collection/search/329081

based) symbols were layered with logographs (meaning-based, whole-word) symbols and additional symbols indicating the category of the word (e.g., trees/things made from wood, cities, people/professions, gods). As you can imagine, the sheer volume of symbols rendered the written language unwieldy and inaccessible to many.

The invention of alphabets, the use of symbols to represent individual spoken sounds, increased the utility and flexibility of writing as a platform for representing speech. The earliest alphabets consisted of mapping the initial sound of a word to a symbol representing that sound. In the Phoenician alphabet, for example, the word for *house* was "bet." Therefore, the symbol for *house* would represent the /b/ sound. Applying that logic to English, the word for *bed* may be spelled with a symbol for a bat 🦇, a symbol for an egg ○, and a symbol for a dog 🐕.

The Phoenician alphabet, generally considered the first, consisted only of letters representing consonants, leaving the reader to infer the appropriate vowel based on context. A consonantal alphabet fit the structure of the Semitic language of that region. For example, Semitic variations of the root word "to write" include *katab* (he wrote), *katabi* (I wrote), *katebu* (they wrote), *ketob* (write), *ketub* (being written) and were written as *ktb* (Olson, n.d.). Although consonantal writing systems alleviated the need to learn a multiplicity of spellings, readers were left to resolve which form of the word was being represented. In other words, an exact translation of text was not always possible. Consonantal systems worked well enough, though, for languages where consonant-vowel structures predominate.

It is important to recognize that writing systems evolved to reflect the unique attributes of the spoken language being represented. As such, there is congruence between a language and its orthography (Seidenberg, 2017). In addition, a writing system developed for one language will not work for another. Such was the case for the Greeks, whose language structure necessitated the inclusion of vowels within a writing system. Indo-European languages, such as Greek, have words that consist of only vowels, words that begin with vowels, and words with adjacent vowels (Powel, 1991). Therefore, the Greeks needed an alphabet that could represent these lexical contrasts. To build their alphabet, the Greeks adapted the Phoenician alphabet by aligning Phoenician-based symbols with Greek phonemes and by adding or modifying symbols. The process of alphabet adaptation and modification would continue as new languages, with their unique phonemes and phonetic structures, repurposed existing alphabets.

From the Phoenician Alphabet to the Standardization of English Spelling

To understand why some English words are spelled in seemingly unconventional ways, the history of the modern Latin alphabet, which is used for writing in English, offers great insight. Despite the hundreds of years it took to refine and standardize the Latin alphabet, some letter shapes look remarkably similar to the original Phoenician consonantal alphabet (see Figure 2.2). Like a game of telephone, the Phoenician alphabet was changed as it traveled from region to region and was shaped by the unique properties of the languages of the people who adopted it. The wheel, however, was not completely reinvented as new groups adopted and adapted it. Remember the

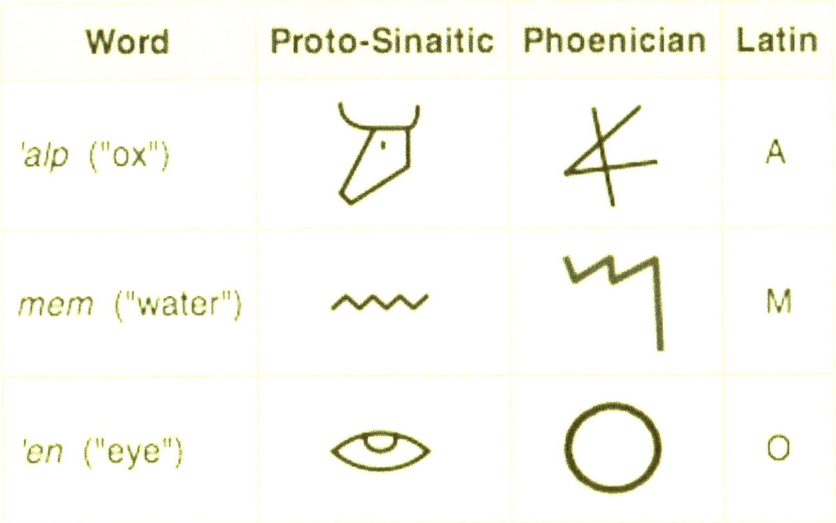

Word	Proto-Sinaitic	Phoenician	Latin
'alp ("ox")	(ox head symbol)	(Phoenician aleph)	A
mem ("water")	(wavy line)	(Phoenician mem)	M
'en ("eye")	(eye symbol)	O	O

Figure 2.2. Examples of symbol changes from Proto-Sinaitic symbols to the Latin alphabet

From "Proto-sinaitic-phoenician-latin-alphabet.jpg," by Rozemarijn vL, 2015, Wikimedia Commons (https://commons.wikimedia.org/wiki/File:Proto-sinaitic-phoenician-latin-alphabet.jpg). CC BY 4.0.

Greeks, who needed letters to represent vowel sounds? Rather than inventing new symbols, the Greeks repurposed a handful of letters from the Phoenician alphabet. To do this, they selected letters representing sounds not used in Greek. For example, the Phoenician letter A came from the word *alpu* (ox head), which represented a glottal consonant. In Greek, the *A*, named *alpha*, was used to represent a vowel. Similarly, the Phoenician *O* (for the word 'en or 'ayn) also represented a consonant in Semitic languages but became a vowel in the Latin alphabet.

Figure 2.3 presents a timeline of the Latin alphabet reflecting the changes and additions that occurred over thousands of years. We can clearly see traces of our modern alphabet in the Greek alphabet, established in the eighth century BC. Some consider the Greek alphabet to be the first true alphabet due to its inclusion of vowels (McCarter, 1974). By the third century, though, the Romans had conquered Greece, seized their script, and further modified the alphabet by adding the letters *S* and *F* and removing letters such as *J*, *V/U*, and *W*. By the fifth century, Roman occupation in Britain would bring numerous changes to the alphabet as different groups gained and lost influence within the region.

Specifically, after controlling Britain for about 400 years, the Romans were displaced when the Jutes, Saxons, and Angles (i.e., the Anglo-Saxons) invaded the region, bringing Old English, a Germanic language, with them. During the time that followed, Latin was the official language of the state used by the elite. Commoners, however, continued to use Old English. To

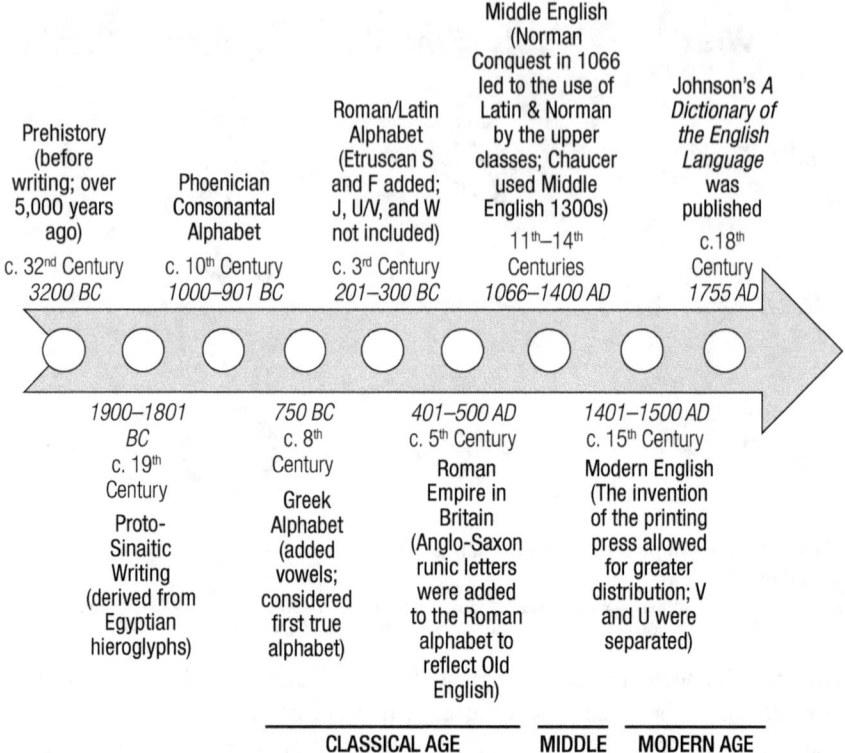

Figure 2.3. Timeline of the Latin (English) alphabet

accommodate sounds in Old English, letters were added to the Latin alphabet, such as the ligatures Æ and Ð and digraphs (two letters representing one sound; e.g., *th* and *sh*). If you attempted to read *Beowulf* in high school, you might be familiar with the script of Old English.

When the French Normans invaded Britain in A.D. 1066, the language and corresponding alphabet were again influenced. French words were adopted, and spelling conventions were created to account for new sounds (e.g., /zh/, /v/, /z/, /oy/) and newly adopted words containing vowel digraphs (e.g., *ai, au, ou*). But, by the 14th century, English regained its stature in Britain. By this time, spoken English reflected words and the unique phonemes of several languages. Letters of the Latin alphabet were used to represent the diversity of words spoken within the region, but the spelling of particular words was not consistent. Different writers would spell words differently, and even individuals would employ different spellings of the same word.[2]

---

2. William Shakespeare's name was not consistently spelled during his lifetime, 1564 to 1616. Variations included *Shakspere, Shakespear, Shaxspere,* and *Shaxper*, with the Bard himself employing several different spellings.

Two events would play a pivotal role in standardizing the spelling of English: the invention of the printing press in 1436 and the widespread adoption of Samuel Johnson's dictionary, *A Dictionary of the English Language,* in 1755. First, the printing press revealed the idiosyncratic nature of spelling. Different spellings of the same word might appear within the same text, across different texts composed by different writers, or even in the same sentence! Relatedly, now that a larger audience had access to printed materials, consistency in spelling would facilitate access (i.e., the specific spellings of words could be directly taught) and ensure information was communicated clearly (i.e., ambiguity in spelling could lead to misidentification of words and change the meaning of the text). Publishers, in particular, were keen to standardize the spelling of words. However, formal standardization of spelling would not come about until almost 300 years after the invention of the printing press.

In 1746, a group of booksellers commissioned Samuel Johnson to create an authoritative, comprehensive dictionary of the English language. The publication of Johnson's dictionary in 1755 would be a watershed moment for English orthography. The dictionary would single-handedly anchor the spelling and pronunciation of English words; in fact, minimal variation in word spellings has occurred since. Within his dictionary, Johnson laid out a set of rules for spelling.[3] However, as Mark Twain would later recognize, Johnson also attempted to preserve the spelling conventions of *borrowed* words (e.g., Greek, French, Latin), which led to exceptions to his rules. On occasion, he sometimes violated his own rules when selecting a spelling. Still, Johnson's legacy was a system that could—as evidenced by your ability to read this book—be learned, shared, and remain constant. The challenge since Johnson's time has been how to teach this fully evolved alphabetic writing system.

THE CHALLENGE OF TEACHING THE ALPHABETIC CODE

The beauty of the English alphabetic code was that it was designed to be minimalist enough to be learned with some efficiency. There are only 26 letters to be learned and a finite number of spelling patterns that can be used to represent the sounds of English. To achieve this efficiency, though, some cheats were necessary. Expressly, letters and letter combinations in an alphabet represent isolated speech sounds. An *alphabet* is a set of letters or symbols used to represent the basic sounds of a language. Yet speech sounds were not meant to be isolated; we do not speak in single sounds. Instead, we speak in

---

3. The majority of rules Johnson established were adopted by Noah Webster, whose dictionary established the spelling of American English.

strings of syllables (e.g., I am hap•py). Separating sounds is particularly challenging because sounds are co-articulated (Liberman et al., 1974; Melby-Lervåg et al., 2012). The production of one sound is influenced by the sounds that precede or follow it. For example, stretch the /ă/ sound in the word *apple*. Now, stretch the /ă/ sound in the word *can*. The /ă/ sound is not the same. The /ă/ sound changes in the word *can* as the mouth prepares to produce the nasal /n/ sound. As the production of sounds is lightning fast—humans typically produce around four syllables per second (Cruttenden, 2014)—the coordination of muscles demands that the mouth (and brain) prepare for an almost simultaneous production of sounds. This means that separating speech sounds is a difficult and unnatural task, yet speech sounds needed to be separated, identified, and categorized to create an alphabetic code. Those individual sounds are called phonemes. *Phonemes* are the smallest unit of sound in a language that can distinguish one word from another (e.g., the /h/ in *hat* distinguishes *hat* from /băt/).

Another challenge of the alphabetic code stems from the mismatch between the number of phonemes in English and letters in the Latin alphabet. In English, there are 44 phonemes, but only 26 letters available to represent those sounds. In contrast, some languages, referred to as *transparent languages*, have almost a one-to-one correspondence between letters and sounds. Each letter has a precise phonemic translation (i.e., one letter, one sound). As a result, the spelling of words in transparent languages is very consistent. In contrast, languages such as English are considered *opaque languages*. In opaque languages, letters can represent more than one sound (e.g., *a* can represent /ă/ in *cat*, /ā/ in *cake*, /ä/ in *father*, /ô/ in *ball*, /ĕ/ in *many*). In addition, different spelling alternatives can be used to represent one phoneme (e.g., /f/ can be spelled *f, ff, ph, gh*). Letter combinations (e.g., *ch, oo*) are also used to represent sounds.

Therefore, the first thing a teacher needs to understand about teaching reading is that it involves far more than teaching one sound per letter (e.g., /b/ for *b*) or even two sounds per letter (e.g., /ă/ and /ā/ for *a*). Teaching a child to read involves teaching the ABCs but also many other things, such as *th, igh, dge,* the many uses of the letter *e*, and the spelling patterns of *smouched* words.

LACK OF ENGLISH ORTHOGRAPHIC KNOWLEDGE AND READING DIFFICULTY

Unfortunately, many teachers do not receive formal instruction on the structure of English (Joshi et al., 2009; Washburn et al., 2011). As a result, teachers can unintentionally inhibit reading development. In addition, many people do not recall how they learned to read, which adds to the difficulty of figuring out how to teach someone else the process. Most families and preschool and early elementary teachers begin by introducing the alphabet. Specifically, children are taught letter names, letter shapes (most likely capital letters), and some form of letter sounds. Then, a cliff appears, and the road everyone was moving along and feeling pretty good about disappears into thin air. On the other side of the cliff are interesting and entertaining books, but most teachers are unsure of how to get from letters and a rudimentary introduction of sounds to students' ability to accurately and fluently read words.

As has been explored within this chapter on the history of English orthography, understanding what reading is requires that individuals consciously or unconsciously grasp the alphabetic principle. Knowing that letters represent individual speech sounds is key to accurate, efficient decoding. Unfortunately, as obvious as that may seem to skilled readers, many students do not realize that individual letters and letter patterns hold the key to word pronunciation. A reading interventionist once told me about a student she was tutoring. After several weeks of tutoring, the student looked up and exclaimed, "Words have parts!" The fact that this was a revelation to the student is both frightening and enlightening. Over the course of his educational career, the student had learned the alphabet, could match letter names with letter shapes, knew the sounds of the letters [e.g., /buh/ (b); /el/ (l); /errr/ (r)], and had plodded his way through countless picture books often relying on pictures or the repetition of keywords to help him *read* the book, but no one had ever shown him how to break words into parts and map speech sounds to those parts. Because he had incomplete and faulty information about how reading works (i.e., he treated every word he encountered as a logograph), his reading was dysfluent and inaccurate.

Let's break down what was missing for this student. First, as you now know from the history of writing, humans do not produce speech sounds in isolation. The task is unnatural and difficult to do. Sounds are co-articulated and difficult to separate. But, alphabetic languages demand that individuals develop this skill; one of the greatest predictors of reading ability is phonemic awareness (Frijters et al., 2018). *Phonemic awareness* is the ability to identify and manipulate individual sounds in spoken words. The struggling reader probably did not realize that *spoken* words had parts, too. Yet, without an understanding of phonemes, learning an alphabetic system is impossible. Being able to differentiate sounds (e.g., What is the first sound in the word *bat*?) and manipulate them (e.g., "Say /bat/ without the /b/" or "Replace /b/ with /m/") is necessary for mapping sounds to letters and letter combinations, a task required for spelling words. Difficulty with phonemic awareness can be exacerbated by instruction. Specifically, if students are not taught precise sound-spelling correspondences (i.e., letter sounds), this imprecise letter-sound knowledge can make it even more difficult for students to map speech sounds to letters for spelling or letters to sounds for decoding.

Remember the letter sounds the struggling reader knew—/buh/ and /el/? Those letter sounds do not map to speech sounds. The word *bat* is not pronounced /buh-a-t/. The word *log* is not pronounced /el-o-guh/. Yet many students learn that the sound for *b* is /buh/, *l* is /el/, and *g* is /guh/, for example. For some students, the disconnect between learning incorrect letter sounds in isolation and the task of mapping sounds to letters is not a problem. The approximation is close enough for them to make the leap and drop the extra sounds when decoding. For others, though, the gap is wide enough for them never to make a connection. Why? Many early reading programs do not involve explicitly and systematically teaching students how to put those artificially isolated sounds back together for reading.

Have you ever sat next to a child stuck on a word and said, "Sound it out: /m/-/ă/-/t/." Only to have the child look up at you and say, "Table!" How did we get from *mat* to *table*? Teaching students how to blend sounds is often missing in early reading instruction. Stretching sounds /mmmmaaaat/ and continuous blending /mmmmm/ to /mmmmaaaa/ to /mmmmaaaat/ can help students learn how to put speech sounds back together to make words they are familiar with from speech. Like any skill, blending sounds requires practice to learn. A teacher or parent modeling this for students (i.e., "Watch me sound this out.") is insufficient for students to internalize the alphabetic principle. Students require direct teaching and practice blending sounds with different letters and letter combinations to gain reading proficiency.

Unfortunately, widely used practices in early reading instruction further inhibit students' understanding of reading. The first foible is sight-word instruction. On the first day of kindergarten, families receive a list of words for students to learn: *am*, *all*, *at*, *did*, *but*, *do*, *get*, *have*, *he*, *must*, *no*, and so on. There are flashcards, paper or electronic, to help students memorize these words. For many students, this exercise teaches them one thing: Reading is memorizing whole words. Consider how problematic this view of reading is. If an older, experienced reader held this view, novel words such as *obdormition* (the feeling of numbness when a body part falls asleep) could never be decoded. The poor struggling reader mentioned earlier did not know words had parts, because he was never taught to look for parts. Instead he was taught to look at and say the whole word.

This is not the only damage that whole-word approaches inflict. Students also internalize that not only does a whole word need to be recognized as one unit, but the word also needs to be recognized quickly. Did you ever wonder why students rapidly guess their way through words when reading? Like a kid learning to ride a bike, the assumption appears to be: If I could only gain enough momentum, the words will begin to flow, and I will take off reading. These struggling readers are not looking *inside* words for clues; they are looking everywhere else for cues—pictures on the page, the teacher's face, or known words in the sentence—and pedaling as fast as they can to make it sound and feel like fluent reading.

Sadly it gets worse. To practice reading, students may be handed books with predictable patterns. In these books, a phrase is repeated that students can memorize (e.g., "Brown bear, brown bear, what do you see? I see a [color] [animal] looking at me;" Martin, 1967). The brown bear is replaced by a red bird, followed by a yellow duck, and so on. After a few pages, students will not need to look at the words to read the book. They can simply look at the pictures. Although predictable books are delightful and excellent for teaching preschool children concepts of print, colors, and the sounds and richness of language, having early elementary students "read" these books can inadvertently reinforce the notion that readers do not need to look at words to read.

Finally, the fact that reading and spelling are treated as two separate subjects in school further exacerbates the disconnect between letter patterns and reading. In contrast to teaching students that reading and spelling are two sides of the same coin, teachers inadvertently separate the writing system (spelling) from reading (Pan et al., 2021). In many cases, the words and patterns students are asked to read during reading instruction time are entirely different from those they are expected to memorize for spelling tests. In contrast, if reading and spelling are taught in conjunction, we teach students how to unlock the code.

SUMMARY

In this chapter, we traveled from ancient Mesopotamia to contemporary first-grade classrooms to demonstrate how the development of English orthography should inform the teaching of reading. Writing was invented to create a permanent record of language. Early writing systems based on whole-word representations proved too cumbersome to maintain, teach, and use. As writing systems evolved, each system reflected unique characteristics of the representative language. In alphabetic writing systems, letters and letter combinations represent the speech sounds of the language. As languages shifted, expanded, and changed over time, sometimes the spellings of words changed, and sometimes the spelling was retained despite changes in pronunciation. As such, traces of history can be found in current spelling constructions. Given the development of written language, early reading instruction that systematically and sequentially reveals the code can put students on a clear path to accurate and fluent reading.

Despite what is known about how the English alphabetic code was created, different theories about how teachers should teach reading have directly influenced teachers' beliefs and the materials found in contemporary classrooms. In the next chapter, we explore the history of reading instruction in the United States. The history will reveal where some common beliefs about reading instruction originated and why some of the most problematic beliefs persist despite evidence that points to their inefficiency and the conflicting messages they send to individuals about reading.

CODE

A	B	C	D	E	F	G	H	I	J	K	L	M
U	V	W	X	Y	Z	N	O	P	Q	R	S	T

Chapter Three

Reading Instruction in the United States

How individuals are taught to read significantly affects their reading ability. Given this fact, many people assume (a) the best approach for teaching reading is settled science and (b) teachers receive ample preparation on how to teach reading. As you learned in Chapter 2, this is not the case, and many beginning reading instructional practices impede rather than facilitate students' ability to learn the code. Examining the history of reading instruction in the United States offers insights as to why we have arrived at the type of instruction that occurs in many elementary classrooms today.

In this chapter, we explore how the pedagogy of reading instruction has changed over the years. As you will see, *pedagogy*—the methods used to teach a particular skill or subject—is influenced by philosophical and theoretical beliefs about the subject and learner. Beliefs about the elements necessary for learning to read and theories about how individuals acquire the ability to read have shaped and will continue to shape reading instruction in schools.

PRIMERS: SPELLING INSTRUCTION IS READING INSTRUCTION

Throughout the 18th and 19th centuries in England and the United States, primers—small, pocket-size books—were used to teach reading. The term *primer* (pronounced with a short /ĭ/ as in *shimmer*) comes from the Latin word *primus*, meaning "first." The original primers date back to the late 14th century, when *primariums*, Latin prayer books, were used to teach reading (Oxford, 2010). Since then, *primer* has been used to refer to first or introductory texts. The content and organization of the modern (18th- and 19th-century) reading primers were remarkably similar to the Latin primariums. Within the primers, students were first taught letters—vowels and consonants—followed by instruction in reading consonant-vowel (CV) syllables (e.g., *ba, be, bi, bo, bu, by*) and vowel-consonant (VC) syllables (e.g., *ab, eb, ib, ob, ub*; see Figure 3.1). Next, words were presented with syllable division to facilitate correct pronunciation. Finally, students would read sentences and brief passages that frequently retained the moral and religious focus of the early primariums (see Figure 3.2). Although the content of the primers changed

Roman Letters.

a b c d e f g h i j k l m
n o p q r ſ s t u v
w x y z
A B C D E F G H I J
K L M N O P Q R S
T U V W X Y Z.

Italic Letters.

*a b c d e f g h i j k l m n o
p q r ſ t u v w x y z
A B C D E F G H I J K L M N O P Q
R S T U V W X Y Z.*

The Alphabet out of order.

f c p d i e g r a j n l q k o b
ſ m s z w u y t x v h.

Vowels.

a e i o u y

Consonants.

b c d f g h j k l m n p q r ſ s
t v w x z

Figure 3.1. Excerpt from *The American Primer: Or, an Easy Introduction to Spelling and Reading*

From "The American Primer: Or, an easy introduction to spelling and reading," printed and sold by Mathew Carey, 1813, pg. 2-3 (https://library.csun.edu/SCA/Peek-in-the-Stacks/primers).

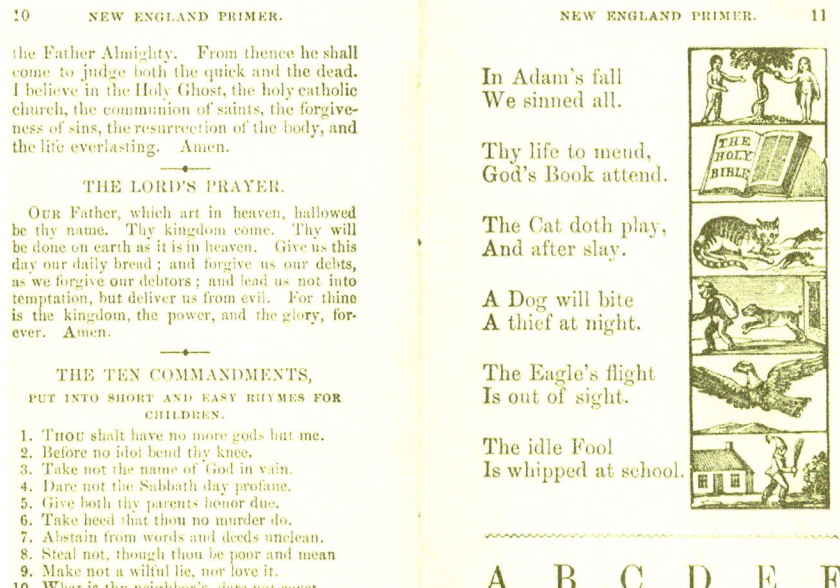

Figure 3.2. Religious content
From "The New England Primer," ca. 1882, pg. 14-15 (https://libwww.freelibrary.org/digital/item/55726).

over the centuries—fairytales and secular content were added—the structure of the books reflected a fairly standardized approach to teaching reading: Students first learned the alphabet, with an emphasis on letter names, and then were systematically taught the spelling patterns of words. Learning to read meant learning the spellings of words. Thus, some primers were referred to as *spellers*.

NOAH WEBSTER'S READING AND SPELLING REFORM

In the late 1700s, though, Noah Webster would challenge the status quo approach of the English primers. His efforts would have a direct effect on spelling and reading instruction in the United States. As the American Revolution was coming to a close, many sought ways to unify and define the new country. Noah Webster was one such nationalist. While saving money for law school, Webster worked as a schoolteacher. Dismayed by the primers of the day and frustrated with how reading was being taught, Webster began work as an instructional designer and spelling reformer. In particular, Webster wanted to move away from focusing on letter names to emphasizing the sounds letters represented (Monaghan, 1983). In 1783,

Webster published the *Grammatical Institute of the English Language*, a three-part series "comprising an easy, concise, and systematic method of education designed for the use of English schools in America." The first part of the series was the speller, commonly referred to as the *Blue-Backed Speller*, owing to its distinct blue cover (see Figure 3.3).

Webster's goal was to teach orthography and pronunciation. The writing system of any language is its orthography. A language's orthography is how the speech sounds of a language are represented by letters (i.e., how words

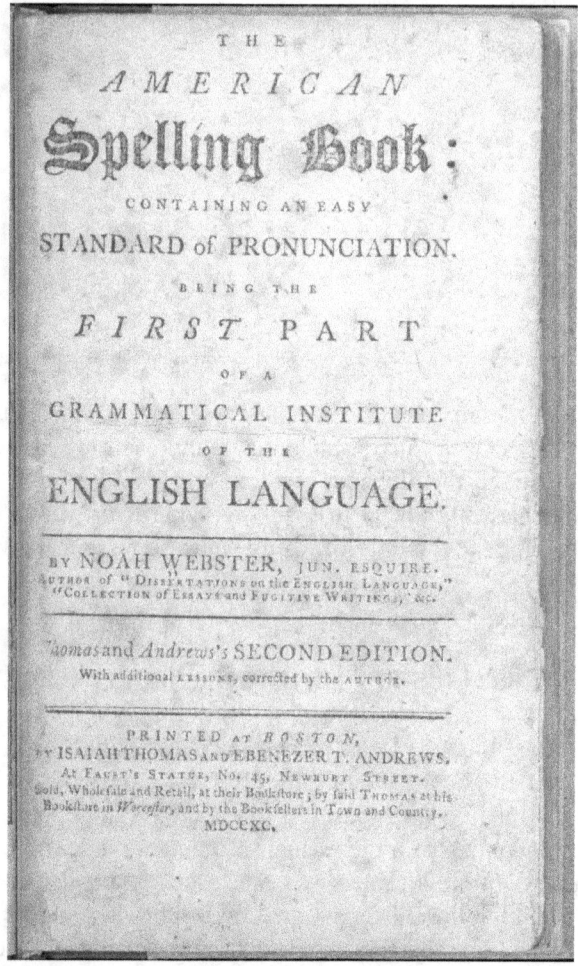

Figure 3.3. Webster's "Blue-Backed Speller"

From "The American spelling book, containing an easy standard of pronunciation : being the first part of a grammatical institute of the English language" by N. Webster, 1790, printed at Boston by Isaiah Thomas and Ebenezer T. Andrews (https://www.loc.gov/item/11012477/).

are spelled). To meet his aim, Webster changed the focus from teaching letter names to the relationship between letters and speech sounds. In addition, Webster included accent marks to aid pronunciation by indicating stressed and unstressed syllables. As Webster pointed out, "In nine-tenths of the words in our language, a correct pronunciation is better taught by a natural division of the syllables and a direction for placing the accent, than by a minute and endless repetition of characters [i.e., letter names]" (Webster, 1822).

Within Webster's introductory materials, teachers were introduced to the differences between consonants and vowels and how they are produced in the mouth (e.g., *labials*, sounds formed by the lips: /b/, /f/, /m/, /p/, /v/; *dentals*, letters formed with the tongue and teeth: /d/, /t/, /th/). Concepts such as diphthongs, "the union of two vowel sounds," and digraphs, "the combination of two letters used to express a single sound (e.g., *ea* in *head* or *th* in *bath*)," were clearly explained. Webster's book also included a Key to Pronunciation to aid teachers and students alike in the correct pronunciation of sounds represented by letters and letter combinations (e.g., *oo* as in *moon*, *oo* as in *foot*). As a result, teachers had a strong grasp of the foundational elements of English orthography and a clear guide for sound pronunciation—critical elements for understanding the alphabetic principle (i.e., words are composed of letters that represent sounds).

Webster would continue his reform efforts as a lexicographer—an author or editor of dictionaries—publishing his first dictionary in 1806, *A Compendious Dictionary of the English Language*. For his uniquely American dictionary, Webster took it upon himself to change some spellings to more accurately reflect their pronunciation. For example, he dropped the *u* in words such as *honour*, *behaviour*, *rumour*, *flavour* and *neighbour*; removed the *k* from the ends of words such as *musick* and *publick*; changed the position of the *e* in words such as *centre* and *theatre*; dropped redundant consonants such as the final *l* in words such as *cancell* and *jeweller*; changed *plough* to *plow*, *draught* to *draft* and *gaol* to *jail*. He also attempted to change some spellings that any first grader would applaud, like *women* to *wimmen* and *island* to *iland* and *soup* to *soop* and *believe* to *beleev*. But, sadly, those did not stick.

MCGUFFEY READERS AND THE INTRODUCTION OF ALTERNATIVE METHODS

Throughout the 1800s, numerous primers and reading programs that reflected a letter-sound approach to reading instruction flourished, including the best-selling *McGuffey's Eclectic Primer* (see Figure 3.4). In the McGuffey primer, new letter-sound relationships were introduced in each lesson, and words were taught that reflected those spellings. The preface of the McGuffey *revised* primer in 1909, though, acknowledged the existence of alternative methods for teaching reading. In the introduction, McGuffey stated: "The plan of the book enables the teacher to pursue the Phonic Method, the Word Method, the Alphabet Methods, or any combination of these methods" (p. iii). As described in *The Eclectic Manual of Methods for the Assistance of Teachers* (Van Antwerp, Bragg, & Co., 1885), written by the publishers of several different primers and readers, those methods were defined as follows:

- [In the Alphabet Method], the child is first taught the letters, then to combine the letters into words, and finally to combine words into sentences. No attention is paid in this method to diacritical marks; and the names of letters are taught, not the sounds.
- The Word Method teaches a child to recognize words as wholes. This method pays no attention to elementary sounds and diacritical marks. After a number of words are taught as wholes, the children are told the names of the letters, and learn to spell.
- By the Phonic Method, the child is first taught the elementary sounds of letters; he is then taught to combine these elementary sounds into words. The sound is first taught, and then the character which represents it; the spoken word is learned, and then its written and printed form. (pp. 36–26)

A final method, the Combined Method, was also described. In this method, students were first taught whole words, then learned to examine component parts that reflect sounds. As defined in the manual, "the Phonic Method is synthetic; the Combined Method is analytic" (p. 44). Within synthetic approaches, students learn to read by blending the sounds in words (i.e., students are taught to "sound words out" part by part). Within analytic approaches, students compare the spelling patterns of whole words to learn to recognize similarities across spelling patterns (e.g., *might, fright, light*).

Elements of each method (alphabet, word, phonic—synthetic and analytic) can be found in contemporary classrooms. For McGuffey, though, his statement was more a reflection of publishing savvy (i.e., no matter which method a teacher or school ascribes, this book can be used) rather than an endorsement of the word, alphabet, or combined methods, as the organization and structure of McGuffey's readers aligned with a synthetic phonic approach (Parker, 2019).

As evidenced by the *Eclectic Manual of Methods*, the close of the 19th century reflected a period of change in reading instruction. Although the phonic method was still widely used in the early 1900s, changing beliefs about who the learner was and the ideal conditions for learning would create a profound

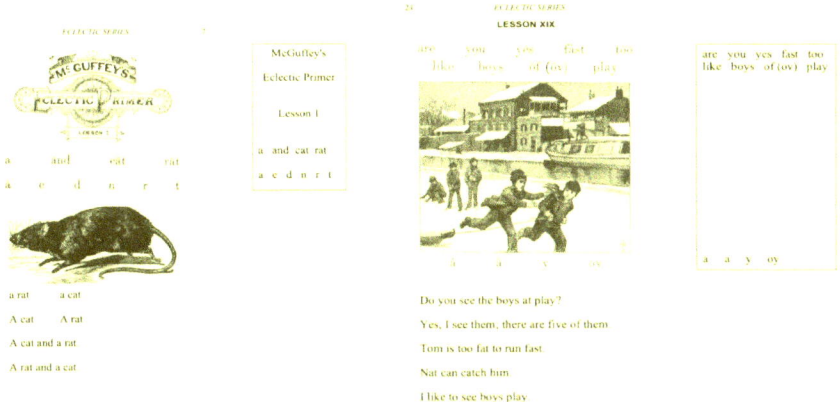

Figure 3.4. Lesson 1 of McGuffey's Eclectic Primer
From "McGuffey Eclectic Primer, Revised Edition" by W. H. McGuffey, 1909, Project Gutenberg (https://www.gutenberg.org/files/14642/14642-pdf.pdf).

shift in reading instruction. Specifically, progressivism would arrive in the United States. Progressive education beliefs about learning were not specific to reading but, when applied to reading, fundamentally changed the definition of "what reading is." As discussed in Chapter 2, reading is the translation of writing (orthography) into spoken language. The English orthography grew out of a complicated history of conquests, nationalism, etymologists who reversed spelling simplifications to capture word origins and lexicographers who attempted to standardize the spelling of every word. Thus, the goal of the phonic method had been to teach students English orthography systematically. With the new wave of progressivism, the focus of reading instruction changed from teaching orthography to teaching reading as a meaning-making process. In the process, they left English orthography behind.

PROGRESSIVE EDUCATION: WHO WERE THE PROGRESSIVES AND WHAT DID THEY BELIEVE?

Progressive education reflects a philosophy of education rooted in the notion that optimal learning occurs when it is self-directed and intrinsically motivated. In other words, learning should stem from an individual's interests and not be imposed upon by others. Humans are naturally curious. As such, the brain will seek information when an individual is ready. When progressive education beliefs are applied to reading instruction, the belief system holds: Just as the child naturally acquires language, so can the child naturally learn to read.

A second tenet of progressive beliefs about reading stemmed from the conflation of the outcome of reading—namely, understanding text—with the processes required to learn to read. Progressive educators hold that if reading is to extract meaning from text and meaning is located within the whole word, then reading instruction should focus on having students map meaning to whole words. As you will recall from Chapter 2, such whole-word approaches ignore the primary utility and purpose of alphabetic writing systems.

Rousseau's Utopian Vision

Where did such beliefs about learning originate? One particularly influential source was Jean-Jacques Rousseau (1712–1778), a French philosopher. In 1762, Rousseau published *Emile, or On Education*, a fictional manifestation of Rousseau's philosophical beliefs about education. In the story, Jean-Jacques serves as Emile's tutor, working with Emile day and night from early childhood through young adulthood. Emile and, by extension, the readers of the story are led to believe Emile only has to do what he wishes. Yet, the tutor, Jean-Jacques, carefully constructs each encounter with Emile to be a learning experience so that Emile will move toward becoming the perfect citizen—independent, uncorrupted by society and a free-thinker (Ashman, 2019). The appeal of the allegory was, in some ways, a reaction against the Calvinist and Puritan depictions of the flawed child who required discipline and structure to learn. Rousseau offered a different perspective: Children are innocent and inherently good, needing only the right environment to awaken their innate desire to learn. What captured the imagination of many American educators was that Emile learned through play and exploration—free from textbooks and a schoolroom full of children doing the same lessons.

Regarding reading, Rousseau believed: "The child who reads does not think—he merely reads; he is not receiving instruction, but is learning words" (1896/2003, p. 137). Rousseau thought education interfered with the development of children's mental capacities; if formal instruction could be withheld until age 12, a child's brain could fully mature and handle abstract ideas (Darling, 1993). Rousseau's ideas would lay the foundation for experiential learning. Or, in Rousseau's words: "Let him know nothing because you have told it to him; he is not to learn science, but to discover it" (1896/2003, p. 137).

Student-Centered, Experiential Learning: Parker & Dewey

In the United States, Francis W. Parker (1837–1902) was inspired by European educational reformers and philosophers, specifically Fröbel, Pestalozzi, and Herbart, who were articulating ways to put Rousseauian ideas into practice

(Kline et al., 1987). As superintendent of schools in Quincy, Massachusetts, Parker developed the Quincy Method, an approach to schooling that reflected the progressive view of child-centered instruction. That is, instruction should follow the child's interests and be directly connected to the child's personal experiences and thoughts. Progressive, child-centered beliefs were rooted in a particular conceptualization of learning—namely, developmentalism (Stone, 1991). Three core beliefs undergird developmentalist perspectives: (a) an individual's natural curiosity is sufficient for learning, (b) interference with natural development is problematic, and (c) learning experiences should reflect the type of learning that happens "naturally" or incidentally through the course of experience or engagement with physical objects (Stone, 1996).

As such, in Colonel Parker's schools, there were no textbooks. Instead, student-led discussions with minimal teacher intervention or re-direction and activity-based projects were the norm (Kline et al., 1987). Parker's approach to reading instruction aligned with the combined method, with whole words being learned first, followed by analytic phonics. As Parker explained, "The word is to be learned consciously as a whole and any attempt to analyze or synthesize it hinders the act of association by absorbing the attention" (Parker & Partridge, 1883, p. 35). Although Parker's observation is accurate, as students are analyzing and synthesizing new words (i.e., decoding them), they have limited cognitive capacity available for comprehension, but his solution was not to make decoding more automatic and thus reduce or eliminate the cognitive congestion. Instead, Parker and other progressives' solution was to skip decoding as the on-ramp to reading. As Parker described, early phonics instruction was replaced by whole-word reading in his schools: "The time given learning to read became time given to study" (Parker, 1902, p. 770). After whole-word instruction in first and second grade, analytic phonics instruction could begin (Kline et al., 1987). Teachers would provide lists of words with common patterns—word families such as *cat, hat, rat* or *hour, flour, scour*—for the students to discover or notice the spelling patterns. This approach is also referred to as *incidental phonics,* as students learn phonics through incidental, repeated, and varied exposure over time.

Following Parker's lead, John Dewey (1859–1952) would take progressivism to schools of education, where it would become firmly entrenched for over a century (Labaree, 2005). After a brief and unsuccessful teaching career (Kellum, 1983), Dewey became a professor. Dewey, not unlike contemporary progressives, thought subject-matter learning was secondary to generic forms of learning such as problem-solving and reflecting (Dewey, 1938/1963). As such, he rejected a focus on traditional school subjects and the accountability of teachers to teach such content (Stone, 1996). Relatedly, Dewey felt that personal interest was the primary source of motivation and, therefore, the content of instruction should be topics relevant to children's immediate environment. "I believe, therefore, that the true centre of correlation of the school subjects is not science, nor literature, nor history, nor geography, but the child's own social activities" (Dewey, 1897, pp. 77–80). Thus, Dewey disparaged the teaching of content knowledge and championed instruction related to students' personal experience—things students could see and experience within their community, not things outside of that realm. "The child's own instincts and powers furnish the material and give the starting point for all education" (Dewey, 1897, p. 77).

Dewey's push away from content or what he considered concepts too abstract for young students to grasp extended to his beliefs about reading. In "The Primary-Education Fetich[1]" (1898), Dewey castigated elementary teachers for their focus on teaching students to read. Teaching students to read was a *fetish* in need of correction. Dewey's fundamental argument was the times had changed, and "to educate on the basis of past surroundings is like adapting an organism to an environment which no longer exists" (p. 19). What had changed? In the past, reading "was practically the sole avenue to knowledge" (p. 19), and "to learn to read and write was an interesting, even exciting, thing: it made such a difference in life" (p. 20). But, Dewey would argue, in modern times, knowledge and information surrounded children and was "no longer amassed in those banks termed books" (p. 21). In a variation of today's argument against fact-learning—"You can just Google it"—Dewey argued that students did not need to learn to read to learn about the world, as students could be equipped with "the scientific methods of observation, experimentation, and testing" (p. 19) to discover knowledge, and modern society immersed students in learning opportunities.

Further, and perhaps more important, learning to read was not developmentally appropriate, Dewey would argue. Primary-grade students were not ready to read, as their minds could not process abstract ideas, their eyes were not fully developed ("oculist tells us that the vision of the child is essentially that of the savage" [p. 24]) and early reading instruction and its mechanical processes lacked relevance to students' interests. Dewey's conclusion on beginning reading instruction was this: "[P]resent physiological knowledge points to the age of about eight years as early enough for anything more than an incidental attention to visual and written language form" (p. 24). And, what was to become of the "intensity and ardor with which our forefathers set themselves to master reading and writing" (p. 19), which Dewey himself described as *interesting* and *exciting* to them? "No one can estimate the benumbing and hardening effect of this continued drill" (p. 28). Disparaging

---

1. Dewey's 1898 spelling of "fetish" was "fetich."

the effort required to master English orthography would become a universal theme of progressive educators.

Dewey's extensive writing and long career would so influence colleges of education that, by the 1940s and 1950s, his ideas were considered conventional wisdom (Cremin, 1964). Despite a lack of empirical evidence demonstrating the efficacy of many of the concepts espoused by Dewey and other progressives, the ideas have had such a stronghold in teacher preparation they are part and parcel of the nomenclature of teachers. Families of struggling readers come face to face with progressive education beliefs when told, "Your child will catch up. All kids develop at a different pace." Or, "If children are surrounded by books that are interesting to them, they will be motivated to learn to read." And finally, resistance to formal, technical instruction in English orthography is articulated as follows: "Learning phonics is boring and will stifle students' desire to read."

Throughout the early 1900s, shifting ideas about how to teach beginning reading were in full force. Along with the movement away from teaching letter sounds, progressive educators were dismissive of the oral reading focus of the previous centuries. Recall Webster's efforts to directly teach and standardize the pronunciation of phonemes. The ability to differentiate individual speech sounds is key to mapping phonemes to letters—a necessary skill for learning alphabetic orthographies. Standardization of the pronunciation further aids reading ability. During *The Great Vowel Shift* in England (1400 to 1700), the pronunciation of Middle English long vowel sounds changed. For example, Chaucer rhymed *food*, *good*, and *blood* with the vowel sound of /ō/. By the time of Shakespeare, the same three words rhymed with the /oo/ sound, as in *food* (Watson, 2006). Now, none of these words rhyme: /food/, /good/, and /bləd/. The shifting pronunciation of sounds makes spelling more difficult, as spellings that previously reflected consistent sound-spelling relationships disappear with novel word pronunciations. A word such as *said* was once pronounced like *paid*. If pronunciation did not change, the spelling of *said* would be more transparent and consistent. Thus, Webster's goal was not to make everyone sound the same but to facilitate learning to read by holding speech sounds constant. This brings us to the error in logic progressive educators employed when pushing against oral reading and advocating for silent reading.

For progressive educators, oral reading reflected mindless word-calling at best and elitist standardization of word pronunciation at worst. For them, it did not matter how a student pronounced the word. What mattered was that a child could recognize and know the meaning of a word. As individuals spend more time reading silently than orally, it only followed that the optimal method of teaching reading would be consistent with how individuals regularly employ the skill. However, it is through oral reading that insight into English orthography is gained. The ability to decipher an alphabetic language depends on an individual's ability to hear and manipulate the individual sounds of speech. The shift from oral to silent reading and a focus on whole words resulted in (a) teachers not teaching letter-sound relationships and (b) the loss of the efficiency of an alphabetic writing system that allows unknown (novel) words to be decoded (sounded out), as novel words cannot be automatically recognized as whole words.

In addition to changing beliefs about *what reading was* (i.e., attaching meaning to whole words rather than learning English orthography) and *who the reader was* (i.e., someone who possessed the innate ability to discover how to read rather than someone who needed direct instruction in the code), other factors would also contribute to changes in reading instruction.

THE BIRTH OF THE LOOK-SAY READERS

The turn of the 20th century would bring more students to the classroom. Between 1900 and 1940, enrollment rates of 5- to 19-year-olds attending school jumped from 51% to 75% (Snyder, 1993). Compulsory attendance requirements, a burgeoning immigrant population, and an increase in Black student enrollment contributed to changes in the overall number of students attending primary school. The increased number of students attending school resulted in larger class sizes (~35 students per teacher), a greater demand for teachers, and the need for efficient, whole-group methods of instruction. These factors culminated in overcrowded, under-resourced classrooms run by teachers with little training who needed to teach a wide range of learners, many of whom were newly arrived immigrants who did not speak English.

William S. Gray and Zerna Sharp provided a novel solution to these educational challenges: Provide teachers with a standardized set of reading materials that reflected an efficient way of teaching reading and could be used with large classes of diverse learners. Gray and Sharp would create the *Dick and Jane* primers, which were based on the look-say approach to reading. Initial instruction consisted of teachers holding up flashcards of whole words to encourage automatic, whole-word recognition (hence, "*Look* at the whole word, then *say* the whole word"). Once a basic corpus of sight words was gained, students would move through leveled readers. Repetition and controlled vocabulary were key elements of instruction. Within each story, only a few words would be presented; those words were repeated frequently to facilitate memorization. The look-say method differed from the child-centered, progressive curricula championed by Parker and Dewey. Rather than being individualized to student interest and perceived development, the look-say readers were standardized and used for whole-class teaching. Thus, the *Dick and Jane* readers allowed teachers to run whole-class instruction without needing specialized training in English orthography. In fact, teachers did not need to know anything about how to teach reading.

Although many look-say authors such as Gray believed phonics instruction was needed after second grade, the phonics they advocated for reflected the analytic or incidental phonics of the early whole-word method (Pearson, 2000). Further, there was little evidence of systematic instruction in phonics taught in conjunction with the look-say method. For example, the author of one study on the efficacy of the look-say method published in the *Journal of Educational Psychology* (Mosher, 1928) pointedly argued against the inclusion of phonics instruction:

> In contrast to the analytical procedure, reading, if it be effective and economical is regarded as perceiving; it is the observation of the printed symbol [i.e., a whole word] and the thinking of the thing for which the symbol stands. . . . [T]here are obvious implications that helping devices, such as the study of the phonetic qualities of vowels and consonants, phonograms, etc., are not employed at any time in the truly 'look-and-say' attack as defined in this article. (p. 185)

Look-say advocates believed teaching students to pay attention to the parts of words, specifically letter-sound correspondences, would instill bad habits—the slow, laborious sounding out of words—and inhibit fluent, silent word reading. As such, teachers emphasized sweeping the eye across the page and discouraged lingering on words. Again, Mosher (1928) explained:

> If teachers wish to accomplish the goal of efficient and economical silent reading, a method which has as its first principle the formation of desirable reading habits, such as rapidly moving the eye across the page, thereby reacting to larger visual units, appeals strongly since it makes for much less waste of time. (p. 186)

Unsurprisingly, Mosher found that students taught using the look-say method recognized more test words in context than in isolation. In other words, when a word was presented in a list with no context, the students could not read the word, but if the word was embedded in a sentence, the students were more likely to identify the word. Mosher noted that this outcome was "hoped for and expected" (p. 192). Without the skills to decode a word, the student must use context to guess the word. As one of the pupils in his study recounted: "If I don't know a word, I look at the next word or the one before. If I can't get it, then, I read the whole sentence skipping it. If I can't get it, then I look at the picture, then I study the word carefully" (p. 193).

For teachers and parents of struggling readers, the performance of students in Mosher's lowest group highlights the limitations of the look-say approach for the most vulnerable learners: "The brighter ones succeeded very well indeed, but the lowest group did little enough."

Champions of the look-say method recognized the speed at which students could learn whole words and, therefore, begin reading books. Whole-word approaches appeared to be a fast track to reading, one that could avoid the drudgery of learning the code. The problem is that kids can memorize words reasonably quickly. First- and second-grade students can memorize the majority of words within their readers with relative ease. This creates an illusion of reading. However, as soon as these students encounter an unfamiliar word and face more complex texts, they are unable to read—specifically, they cannot decode—novel words. Thus, as students move into later grades, the memorization approach plateaus. As such, with whole-word approaches, students cannot keep up with the volume of new words needed to be competent readers.

WHY JOHNNY CAN'T READ: FLESCH IGNITES A FIRE AND CHALL CALLS THE QUESTION

From the mid-1930s to the mid-1960s, look-say approaches with a focus on connecting whole words to meaning became the norm. It is important to note that variations in teaching methods did exist during this time. For example, all look-say curricula were not the same—some provided guidance for direct, analytic phonics early within an instructional sequence, some later, and some offered limited to no advice for word analysis. Likewise, a minority of teachers and scholars continued to advocate for phonics-based instruction (Smith, 1957). Despite this small group of phonics loyalists, a consensus around a set of general principles about reading had become firmly entrenched and widely accepted by the middle of the 20th century. Those principles were constituent elements of a (whole) word-to-reading approach (Chall, 1967; Pearson, 2000). In sum, by this time, whole word was in, and phonics was out.

To return to the opening paragraphs in this chapter, beliefs about what reading was and whom the learner was had shifted dramatically from the days of Webster and McGuffey. Reading was no longer the translation of orthography (i.e., written language) into oral language. Instead, reading was the silent search of words for meaning. Optimal texts were stories directly relevant to students' immediate experiences and personal interests rather than content designed to teach new ideas. Ideally, instruction should begin by building a corpus of sight words followed by analytic approaches that could involve attention to letter sounds and spelling patterns but could also include attention to pictures or context to facilitate the "unlocking" (i.e., recognition) of printed words (Pearson, 2000). In contrast, explicit instruction in letter-sound relationships reflected dull, drill-like instruction, which was harmful to a child's development. And who was the learner in need of instruction? The learner was naturally curious and possessed an internal developmental cycle that needed to be facilitated at appropriate times to awaken the necessary awareness for reading.

Tensions between look-say and phonics groups were thrust into the public arena in 1955 when Rudolf Flesch published a scathing critique of the sight-word method in his now famous book, *Why Johnny Can't Read—and What You Can Do About It*. Flesch was born and raised in Austria. In 1933, Flesch received a law degree from the University of Vienna but was forced to flee to America in 1938 to avoid rising antisemitism and the imminent Nazi invasion of Austria. In the United States, Flesch began studying factors associated with the readability of adult reading material. Flesch championed clear, concise writing and earned a PhD from Columbia University in 1943. His dissertation, *Marks of a Readable Style*, would pave the way for his later work in devising readability formulas (Battistella, 2019). Thus, although Flesch had studied written language, he was an outsider to the reading wars. Moreover, Flesch was unaware of the debate between phonics and whole-word methods; his concerns lay in improving the readability of adult writing (e.g., *The Art of Readable Writing*, 1949). However, that would change when Flesch agreed to tutor Johnny, a 12-year-old boy who could not read.

One of the first words Flesch asked Johnny to read was *kid*. When Johnny guessed the word *kind*, Flesch was flabbergasted. "Nobody born and raised on the continent of Europe can easily grasp the fact that anyone can mistake *kid* for *kind*" (Flesch, 1955, p. 18). Flesch would soon realize that guessing was Johnny's primary strategy for reading, leading Flesch to conclude what many parents of struggling readers observe today: "To my mind, a remedial reading case is someone who has formed the habit of guessing instead of reading" (p. 18). Flesch's experience with Johnny sparked his deep dive into how reading instruction was taught in the United States. Flesch discovered that most leading reading experts were firmly opposed to phonics instruction and felt phonic methods were out of place with modern conceptions of whole-word instruction. But, as Flesch explained to parents, the target audience of his book, phonics is the logical way to teach any alphabetic orthography:

> Imagine, for instance, you are a Hottentot and want to learn how to read and write the Hottentot language. The natural method will be this: First, your teacher will make you aware of the individual sounds you make when you talk Hottentot. Second, he will show you the letter symbols that represent each of those

sounds. Third, he will teach you how to write these symbols and combine them into words—and, at the same time, how to read them. (p. 22)

Flesch discovered that most phonics curricula followed a strikingly similar scope and sequence, moving from simple one-to-one sound-to-spelling correspondences to more complex sound-spelling relationships. As students learned new sound-spelling relationships, they would practice spelling those words. In contrast, Flesch discovered that whole-word approaches separated spelling instruction from reading instruction. Whole-word methods encouraged students to view the "total word picture" or "general word shape" instead of paying attention to individual letters and letter combinations. As such, reading and writing no longer went hand in hand, as students were no longer taught to map speech sounds to print for spelling (/ă/ is spelled with an *a*) or map printed letters to sounds (*s-a-t* maps to the sounds /s/ /ă/ /t/) for reading. "Reading and spelling are two sides of the same thing, and the trouble starts as soon as you separate the two," Flesch lamented (p. 33).

In addition to abandoning attention to the relationship between letter sounds and letters, with whole-word reading approaches, teachers were taught, "If a child substitutes words of his own for some that are on the page, provided that those express the meaning, it is an encouraging sign that the reading has been real" (Dr. Edmund Burke Huey, *The Psychology and Pedagogy of Reading* as cited by Flesch). In other words, if a child reads the word *scared* for the printed word *afraid*, that is fine because, as Dr. Huey explained, "It may even be necessary, to tell it in words that are somewhat variant; for reading is always of the nature of translation and, to be truthful, must be free."

After painstakingly explaining what phonics was and contrasting it with modern reading philosophies taught within schools of education, Flesch took direct aim at *Dick and Jane*. Flesch helped parents understand the rationale for the controlled vocabulary of the look-say readers—students can only memorize so many words at once—and demonstrated how "indirect" phonics instruction that might occur in second grade could do little to break the word-guessing habit of whole-word readers. In the end, Flesch concluded, "Phonics is not 'one of many techniques the child can use to unlock the meaning of words' (you can't possibly imagine how sick I am of all this jargon)—phonics is simply the knowledge of the way spoken English is put on paper" (p. 122). *Why Johnny Can't Read* became an immediate bestseller (*Time*, 1955).

In an attempt to quell the firestorm ignited by Flesch, a group of reading researchers gathered in 1959 to devise a program of research that could, if not lay the question to rest, at least identify a set of reliable, evidence-informed guideposts for the teaching of reading. One of the researchers at the meeting was Jeanne Chall, a professor of reading at Harvard University. Chall was concerned that arguments on both sides of the debate, what she termed as code-emphasis and meaning-emphasis, were driven more by philosophy and emotion than by empiricism. Chall's lofty ambition was to conduct a dispassionate scientific study of beginning reading instruction. Funded by the Carnegie Corporation in 1962, Jeanne Chall began a three-year comprehensive analysis of early reading instruction that involved reviewing existing studies, interviewing leading proponents of particular methods, observing and interviewing teachers, and analyzing existing reading curricula (e.g., readers, workbooks, teacher's guides). Chall published her findings and recommendations in *Learning to Read: The Great Debate* (1967), a five-section book in which she (a) described in detail the prevailing methods of how to teach reading, (b) synthesized findings from existing research, (c) presented the results of her systematic review of current commercial reading programs, (d) reported on her observations of teachers and schools, and (e) detailed her recommendations for practice. In her final analysis, Chall found:

> The research from 1912 to 1965 indicates that a code-emphasis method—i.e., one that views beginning reading as essentially different from mature reading and emphasizes learning of the printed code for the spoken language—produces better results, at least up to the point where sufficient evidence seems to be available, the end of third grade. The results are better, not only in terms of the mechanical aspects of literacy alone, as one supposed, but also in terms of the ultimate goals of reading instruction—comprehension and possibly even speed reading. The long-existing fear that an initial code emphasis produces readers who do not read for meaning or with enjoyment is unfounded. On the contrary, the evidence indicates that better results in terms of reading for meaning are achieved with the programs that emphasize code at the start than with the programs that stress meaning at the beginning. (p. 307)

To add weight to Chall's recommendations, findings from a collection of studies referred to as the *First-Grade Studies* came out in the same year as *Learning to Read*. Funded by the U.S. Office of Education, the studies included over twenty individual quasi-experiments whose findings were published in a new journal called *Reading Research Quarterly*. The main finding of the *First-Grade Studies* was that any code-based program, whether it was synthetic phonics, a linguistic approach (grouping words by pattern), or the use of a special alphabet (e.g., the Initial Teaching Alphabet), outperformed the business-as-usual, look-say-based basal reading programs (Pearson, 2000). In addition to Chall's recommendation for early, systematic instruction in the code, she also recommended improving the quality of reading material. As a by-product of the look-say approach, the reading material provided to students included repeated exposure to a limited number of words (Hoffman et al.,

2002). Chall recommended providing students with something more interesting to read. Like Flesch, Chall recognized the importance of student engagement with high-quality materials for developing language comprehension.

Although these events would herald the end of *Dick and Jane*, the next three decades would move the field of beginning reading instruction into even murkier territory—further entrenching the definition of reading as a meaning-making endeavor and raising more questions about the role of the learner in the process.

Whole Language Emerges to Side-Step the Question

Although Chall's publication and the *First-Grade Studies* presented a compelling rationale for embracing a code-emphasis approach to beginning reading instruction, other disciplines began to weigh in, providing alternative theories about learning to read. In particular, ideas from psycholinguists challenged the notion that reading was a skill requiring direct teaching. Instead, psycholinguists held that children's ability to read would unfold through a process of exploration. Students did not make *errors*, per se, in their reading and writing; instead, "miscues" were signs of students' underdeveloped thinking that were part of their process of "working out" written language. Miscues would naturally resolve themselves in the same manner that children's errors in verbal syntax (e.g., "Me want ball.") resolved themselves as children aged. The idea that children could develop reading and writing abilities in the same way they developed oral language skills—naturally and motivated by a desire to communicate—was not unlike the ideas of early progressive educators. In the 1960s, though, the ideas were boosted by theories from linguistics, such as Chomsky's nativist view of language development and a shifting emphasis on reading comprehension by cognitive psychologists.

Two prominent psycholinguists, Kenneth Goodman and Frank Smith, would be particularly influential in defining and shaping the next wave of reading reform. In 1967, Goodman published "Reading: A Psycholinguistic Guessing Game," which would lay the foundation for a new approach to beginning reading instruction: whole language. Goodman's premise was that reading was *not* "a precise process . . . [involving] exact, detailed, sequential perception and identification of letters, words, spelling patterns, and large language units" (p. 126). Reading was "a psycholinguistic guessing game" in which students make "partial use of available minimal language cues selected from perceptual input on the basis of the reader's expectation" (p. 127). In other words, readers *anticipate* what a word will be before seeing the word and then confirm or reject their guess using minimal language cues such as context, syntax, and graphic representations. Goodman explained how all "deviations" (e.g., reading *the* when the word was *your*) should not be treated as errors. As both *the* and *your* are noun markers that serve the same grammatical purpose, their substitution will have minimal to no effect on comprehension and should not be corrected. Similarly, Goodman provided an example where a student read, "Might as well study what it means" when the actual text was, "Might as well study word meanings first." In this case, Goodman applauded the reader for transforming the grammar and vocabulary of the statement into something that made sense to the reader. Finally, Goodman found no issue with a girl who substituted the word *toy* for *train*. When the phrase "toy train" appeared later in the text and the reader was stumped, Goodman explained: "There appears to be a problem for many first graders when nouns are used as adjectives." Ah! The first grader was not *developmentally ready* for attributive nouns. The girl's inability to read the phrase was not reflective of a problem with instruction; as the girl aged, she would grow out of this and read correctly. In sum, a student's inability to accurately translate print into speech was not a problem for Goodman. If a student produced a meaningful sentence, that was the goal; the exact translation of print was not the goal.

Ultimately, the premise of whole language was that children naturally pick up the skill of reading. Immersion in books that were interesting and relevant to their lives facilitated reading development. Smith and Goodman would explain (1971):

> The child learning to read, like the child learning to speak, seems to need the opportunity to examine a large sample of language, to generate hypotheses about the regularities underlying it, and to test and modify these hypotheses on the basis of feedback that is appropriate to the unspoken rules that he happens to be testing. None of this can, to our mind, be formalized in a prescribed sequence of behaviorally stated objectives embalmed in a set of instructional materials, programmed or otherwise. (p. 180)

Whole language differed from the whole-word, look-say approach to reading. Like Flesch, who had a problem with the insipid language ("look, look") of the *Dick and Jane* readers, whole language proponents recommended that students be presented with *authentic* texts. In contrast to the look-say readers with highly controlled vocabulary and paltry plots, authentic texts were any reading material that had been written for an authentic purpose, such as entertaining (e.g., children's literature), informing (e.g., articles in a newspaper), explaining, and so on. Yet, the difference between what Flesch suggested as the solution—systematic instruction in phonics *in parallel* with adult-child/teacher-student reading of interesting books—and what whole-language supporters wanted—phonics-free instruction and students using pictures and context to guess words or sample bits of text and generate their own sentences—would serve to further banish the direct teaching of orthography out of beginning reading instruction.

Frank Smith (1994) would famously remark, "[M]y own recommendation for how reading and writing should be taught is perhaps radical; they should not be taught at all" (p. 299). Goodman and Smith found a receptive audience of academics who were more than willing to reject behavioristic notions that individuals could be controlled by their environment. Smith and Goodman's philosophy would be widely embraced by faculty in colleges of education, textbook publishers, and professional organizations (Moats, 2000).

The whole-language movement, as it would be described by its proponents (Y. Goodman, 1989), would change the question from "What is the best way to teach students to read?" to "What does it mean to be a literate person?" For whole-language advocates, the key to being a skilled reader lies in emulating the reading behaviors of highly literate individuals. Advocates argued against a phonics-based, bottom-up approach to reading. Teaching students parts of words (i.e., phonemes and letters) detracted from students' ability to extract meaning from words. In contrast to a bottom-up approach, whole-language supporters promoted a top-down, holistic approach. Within a top-down approach, the characteristics of an expert are identified, and students are taught to mimic those behaviors.

To understand how changing the terms of the question would change teacher practices, let's explore how a top-down focus would change instruction or preparation in another area: cooking. With a top-down approach, if you wanted to be an excellent chef, you would observe how master chefs behave in the kitchen, interview them to learn about their decision-making, and create a cross-referenced list of similarities. Unfailingly, you would notice that master chefs chop quickly and efficiently, have multiple things cooking at one time, and constantly taste and make adjustments based on their knowledge of the properties of the various ingredients. A novice attempting to emulate these practices would meet with disaster. Volumes of research demonstrate the quantitative and qualitative differences between novices and experts (e.g., experts know more and think differently due to their extensive background knowledge). These differences hold whether the expertise is a skill like playing soccer or mastery of a cognitive domain such as calculus (Ericsson, 2005).

The whole-language movement shifted the question from "What are the skills necessary to read the words on a page?" to "What do expert readers do, and how can kids emulate those behaviors?" Given this change in focus, it is easy to see how the behaviors of silent, fast reading for meaning were transformed into a pedagogy. Teachers embraced the changing pedagogy and were happy to replace *Dick and Jane* with interesting and entertaining children's literature. However, the pedagogical weakness of the approach lay in its assumptions about the reader: Students only needed motivation and authentic purpose to unlock their reading ability.

The heart of the problem was that reading comprehension became conflated with decoding (i.e., the accurate reading of print). As a result, whole-language enthusiasts focused entirely on meaning-making, bypassing the skills required to recognize words accurately. To further confuse the issue, Goodman attempted to co-opt the term *decoding* and redefine decoding as an interpretation of print rather than a strict translation of print (K. S. Goodman, 1967). To make matters worse, Goodman's "decoding" reflected an elevated level of knowledge, whereas literal decoding was simply a parlor trick, a low-level task with limited functionality or purpose.

DRIVERS OF INSTRUCTION: BASAL READING PROGRAMS

The intermediary between scholarly ideas and what happens in classrooms often resides within the curricular materials provided to teachers. Although the practice of providing teachers with sets of grade-level readers can be traced back to the 1800s (e.g., The McGuffey Readers), by the 1930s, the addition of teacher's guides and student workbooks would expand the scope of the materials provided by publishers. These comprehensive sets of materials are referred to as *basal reading programs* (Austin & Morrison, 1961).

The basal reading programs published in the 1970s and early 1980s reflected an enigmatic collection of materials whose intent appeared to appease various philosophical positions rather than provide a cohesive, comprehensive approach to reading instruction. For example, rather than offering materials that provided early and systematic instruction in the code and reflected high-quality texts as recommended by Chall in *The Great Debate*, by and large, publishers retained the look-say method while adding a handful of disconnected, supplemental phonics activities. As for the content, the stilted, unidimensional *Dick and Jane* stories were replaced with adaptations of more diverse children's literature, but those adaptations aligned with the controlled-vocabulary approach of the earlier look-say readers.

At this point, it is important to differentiate between controlled vocabulary texts and the type of reading material used within code-emphasis approaches called *decodable texts*. Controlled vocabulary texts contain a limited number of words that are used repeatedly. For example, in the Scott-Foresman basal program of the 1970s, upon completion of fourth grade, students would have only been exposed to 1,554 words within their readers (Flesch, 1981).

In contrast, within code-emphasis approaches, students are provided with reading material that contains the phonics patterns that have been previously taught, along with high-frequency words that do not follow regular sound-spelling patterns (e.g., *come, was, of, were*). Whereas the intent of controlled vocabulary is to prompt the guessing of words using minimal language cues such as context or first letter recognition, the purpose of decodable texts is to provide practice in using knowledge of letter-sound relationships to decode an increasing number of words, including novel words (words never seen before) that make use of previously taught sound-spelling relationships. By fourth grade, students who complete a phonics series will be able to read any words within the full complement of their listening and speaking vocabulary (~40,000; Flesch, 1981).

Thus, in the 1970s, children's literature began to appear in basal reading programs, but the stories had been adapted to minimize the variety of words, which changed the flow and richness of the stories. In parallel to providing controlled-vocabulary readers, the basal programs also offered separate, skills-focused materials (Popp, 1975). The skills lessons were detached from the readers, which allowed basal publishers to appear to meet the public demand for phonics instruction, but the phonics lessons were often disconnected from the reading students engaged in. For example, the first pre-primer story in one basal series was titled "Look and Listen," but phonics instruction on the sound of *oo* was not provided until third grade, and silent *t* was never taught (Flesch, 1981). Skills lessons were not limited to phonics either. Lessons on every possible reading-related skill were provided (e.g., find the main idea, circle the median consonant; Popp, 1975).

In his 1981 review of the basal reading landscape, Flesch identified only 5 basal series that reflected a true, synthetic phonics approach to teaching reading. In contrast, he identified 12 mainstream basal series, which he called the Dismal Dozen, that firmly retained the look-say approach to teaching reading. The Houghton Mifflin series, which spanned kindergarten to eighth grade, even cautioned junior high teachers: "Some students have not yet learned how to decode easily and quickly the printed form of the language into the oral form which they are thoroughly familiar. . . . They are probably not sufficiently aware that any specific reading passage consists of letter symbols in a sort of secret code" (as cited in Flesch, 1981, p. 8). In contrast, when Flesch visited P.S. 251 in Brooklyn, which used the phonics-based Open Court basal series, most first- and second-graders he encountered could read his test words—*flamingo, curlicue, delicacy, inert, stoic,* and *squabble*. Sadly, schools were more likely to be using the Dismal Dozen than a phonics-based program.

By the late 1980s and early 1990s, the whole-language movement's push for a literature-based approach to reading would begin to influence basal reading programs. Policy initiatives would also significantly impact the content of basal reading programs. For example, California's English-Language Arts Framework of 1987 took a direct anti-phonics stance, as was made clear in the introductory paragraph: "When the study of language ceases to help us understand ourselves and our world, and when language is fragmented or treated only in its disconnected forms, learning is lost to boredom, except perhaps to linguists or grammarians" (p. 16). Throughout the Framework, calls for a literature-rich, meaning-focused approach to reading instruction were made:

- Although students in the early grades must be taught to identify individual words by sounding them out and using context clues, the most effective teaching techniques help students get to sense quickly, often leaving the more difficult task of learning individual words until after students have experienced the delight of understanding meaning in sentences. (p. 20)
- For students in kindergarten through grade three, the understanding of meaning is the first and most important reason for learning language and the primary focus of all language activities. Learning to read means learning to understand meaning from the first efforts to read. (p. 38)

Consequently, the content of basals did change. Basals began to include commercially published children's literature, and stories were no longer "adapted" to meet stringent vocabulary control features. However, a new text feature would gain prominence during this time: predictability. Predictability was typically achieved through syntax. For example, Eric Carle's *The Very Hungry Caterpillar* (1969) contains a predictable pattern: "On [day of the week], he ate [number] [food]. But he was still hungry." Highly predictable texts facilitate students' ability to use text features such as pictures, context, and syntax to "read" words. Thus, predictability was regarded as a valuable text feature (Hoffman et al., 1994). However, as noted by Hoffman et al. (2002) in their summary of the early 1990s basals: "[L]ost in the enthusiasm for authentic literature was any systematic attention to the decoding demands of the texts. In fact, decoding demands increased dramatically with the new programs and vocabulary control all but disappeared." In other words, not only did the basals fail to provide synthetic phonics instruction with corresponding decodable texts for practice, but there was no systematic attention to the words provided, which rendered the reading material inaccessible for independent reading by elementary students.

In addition, by this time, the basal programs had become large and unwieldy. Schools adopting a program would receive multiple boxes stuffed with colorful, richly illustrated literature; small books for children's independent reading; big books for teacher reading; and a wide array of supplemental materials. Code-emphasis advocates criticized the programs for their lack of phonics content. At the same time, whole-language enthusiasts continued to resist the idea of a standardized curriculum of any form, even if it was literature focused, because someone other than the teacher selected the literature. This anti-basal sentiment provided fertile ground for the growth of two basal-free approaches to reading: Reading Workshop and guided reading.

Reading Workshop is a framework for teaching wherein teachers provide brief (fewer than 10 minutes) lessons followed by long periods of independent reading (35 to 45 minutes). Although the method's roots can be traced back to Donald Graves (1983) and his writing research, his student, Lucy Calkins, would expand the approach to reading and bring it to notice and widespread use. During the mini-lesson component of Reading Workshop, teachers provide a prompt such as "think about what the author was trying to communicate in the story" or "compare and contrast the characters in the story." Although these are laudable literary concepts, there was little to no direct teaching of how to *read* the words. In other words, the mini-lessons were not phonics lessons. Following the mini-lesson, students would have 35 to 45 minutes of silent, independent reading time. Then the teacher would move around the classroom conducting individual conferences with the students to follow up on the mini-lesson topic. Small-group or partner work may be conducted during this time, but the focus was on reinforcing the mini-lesson's meaning-focused topic of the day. Finally, the lesson would conclude with 3 to 5 minutes of students sharing what they learned (Serafini, 2001). Shortly after the turn of the 21st century, Lucy Calkins would become synonymous with the approach.

The second basal-free approach, guided reading, grew out of a whole-language-based reading intervention program designed in New Zealand by Marie Clay called *Reading Recovery* (DeFord et al., 1991). In the United States, the approach would be transformed from a one-on-one intervention to small-group instruction for use in general education classrooms. Two key elements of guided reading were then and are now: (a) the matching of students to books at their *instructional reading level* and (b) the use of specific reading strategies to promote reading development (Fawson & Reutzel, 2000). In contrast to the leveled readers of the early phonics programs (e.g., McGuffey Readers) or the controlled vocabulary of the look-say readers (e.g., *Dick and Jane*), a unique formula was devised to determine the reading level of children's books (Fountas & Pinnell, 1996). The criteria for leveling included many of the meaning-focused constructs of whole language, such as text structure (narrative texts have a familiar structure that facilitates readability; predictability facilitates guessing); content (familiar topics facilitate word recognition); sentence complexity (shorter sentences are easier to read); vocabulary (texts that contain many of the same words are easier to read); and illustrations (more pictures make the "reading" easier). You will note that decodability or alignment with a phonics scope and sequence was and is not a part of determining the reading level of books. Using the leveling criteria, a squishy science at best, kindergarten through third-grade books were classified on a scale from A to R. If a student could read a book with approximately 90 percent accuracy, that book was considered a "just right" reading level book for the student. During small-group instruction, teachers helped "students develop strategies for orchestrating multiple cueing systems into fluent, silent, independent reading" (Fawson & Reutzel, 2000, p. 86). Voila! Whole language was now reinvented into *strategic instruction* wherein students did not *naturally* use the cues of syntax, meaning, and grapho-phonics (i.e., the sampling of letters to confirm or support a guess) to read words but were explicitly taught to rely on pictures, meaning, and initial letters to guess words. Similar to what Calkins would do with Reading and Writing Workshop, two faculty members from The Ohio State University, Irene Fountas and Gay Su Pinnell, would transform guided reading into a curriculum that would become a ubiquitous part of elementary classrooms in the first two decades of the 21st century.

A WOLF IN SHEEP'S CLOTHING: BALANCED LITERACY

Ironically, just as Reading and Writing Workshop and guided reading were gaining a foothold in classrooms, Congress was moved once again to determine why so many students failed to attain reading proficiency in the United States. In 1997, Congress requested the National Institute of Child Health and Human Development to convene a 14-member panel of administrators, teachers, and scientists to examine existing research on reading and provide recommendations for practice, training, and future research. The panel reviewed over 100,000 studies that had been published between 1970 and 2000. In 2000, the panel released its findings in *A Report of the National Reading Panel: Teaching Children to Read.*

The panel found overwhelming evidence for phonics-based approaches to support beginning reading. Under the umbrella term *phonics*, the panel differentiated between incidental approaches, wherein teachers do not follow a planned scope and sequence but provide phonics instruction opportunistically in the course of student reading, called incidental phonics, and explicit approaches, wherein teachers directly and systematically teach letter-sound or sound-spelling relationships. Throughout their report, the superiority of systematic phonics over non-phonics approaches was made clear:

- [V]arious types of systematic phonics approaches are significantly more effective than non-phonics approaches in promoting substantial growth in reading. (2-93)
- The conclusion drawn from these findings is that systematic phonics instruction is significantly more effective than non-phonics instruction in helping to prevent reading difficulties among at-risk students and in helping to remediate reading difficulties in disabled readers. (2-94)
- The type of nonsystematic or non-phonics instruction given to control groups to evaluate the effectiveness of systematic phonics instruction varied across studies and included the following types: [non-phonics] basal programs, regular curriculum, whole language approaches, whole word programs, and miscellaneous programs. The question of whether systematic phonics instruction produced better reading growth than each type of control group was answered affirmatively in each case. (2-95)

By this point, the evidence was overwhelming that the ability to read words accurately and fluently would not develop naturally and, contrary to what whole-language purists believed, did require direct teaching. In fact, for the most vulnerable learners, students from low-income families or students with learning disabilities, systematic phonics instruction was crucial and particularly helpful when received early. However, rather than abandoning the meaning-first, motivation-centered philosophy that undergirded whole language, the approach was reinvented as *balanced literacy*. Advocates would argue that students could experience the best of both worlds. The rebranding was so effective that *balanced literacy* can be found in the majority of elementary schools in the United States today.

And, what were the poster curricula for balanced literacy? Calkins's Reading Workshop curriculum titled *Units of Study* (2015) and Fountas and Pinnell's *Leveled Literacy Intervention* (*LLI*, 2017). Within these curricula, teachers instruct students first to use context to guess words. In *Units of Study*, teachers helped students explore "essential questions" such as: How can the pictures help us learn to read words on a page? What are some things readers can try to do when we come across a word we do not know? (Unit 2, Super Powers, Kindergarten). In *LLI*, teachers taught students to use the *Eagle Eye* strategy, which was to look at the picture, and *Tryin' Lion*, which meant to try a word students thought would make sense. Sadly, there was also the *Skippy Frog* strategy, which encouraged students to simply skip words they did not know. All the strategies were grounded in the whole-language, three-cueing philosophy. Students were directly taught that learning to read was a process of guessing words and then checking to see if the words: (a) made sense, (b) sounded right, and (c) looked right. Although balanced literacy supporters frequently rebuffed characterizations of the approach as being anti-phonics, phonics was a strategy of last resort. In addition, within balanced literacy, students were not provided with a comprehensive, systematic program of phonics as recommended by the National Reading Panel. Instead, students were taught to sample letters (e.g., use *Lips the Fish* to say the beginning sound [then guess the word], use *Chunky Monkey* to look for a chunk of the word that is familiar [i.e., analogy phonics]) and use phonics for confirmation rather than generation.

Balance cannot be achieved when one method directly undermines the other. Balanced literacy approaches emphasize word guessing and deemphasize the systematic sounding out of words. The message young children internalize from their very first encounter with learning to read is: Words should be recognized automatically as a whole unit; if I do not know a word, I should look for clues outside of the word to guess. This is why frustrated parents of struggling readers will complain that when they sit down to read with their children, their kids won't look at the words on the page, will skip words or make up words, and will often confuse similarly spelled words, because they are not paying attention to specific spelling patterns.

Therefore, despite the evidence, very little would change regarding what happened in elementary school classrooms during the first part of the 21st century. Just as Flesch lamented in 1981 about the "window-dressing" treatment of phonics in the last century, the emphasis in too many kindergarten and first-grade classrooms today is on building a corpus of sight words, using cues to guess words, and providing incidental or disconnected phonics that does not offer instruction in the full scope of skills needed to decode words.

THE LEGACY OF PROGRESSIVE EDUCATION: ACTIVE, STUDENT-CENTERED, CREATIVE INSTRUCTION

Part of what perpetuates the use of reading methods that counter what has been found by research as effective is the romantic picture of the education ideal created by progressive educators. Future teachers are taught dualities. Education is child-centered or teacher-centered, active or passive, experiential or rote, natural or artificial (imposed), developmental or formalist. The connotations are clear, and teachers internalize a fear that they may be doing harm by employing the *wrong* approach. Unfortunately, many of these dualities are not based on science, but their grip on teachers is firm, which can lead teachers to embrace questionable practices.

Learning requires two things: attention and thinking (Dehaene, 2020). Yet, progressive educators have convinced generations of teachers that students have two states: active and passive. If a teacher is telling students something, students are passive. If students are busy with their hands or mouths, they are active. In the sense of physical movement, this is true. In one situation, students are sitting (hopefully quietly during the receptive part of instruction), and in the other, the students are moving their bodies. In terms of what is happening mentally, though, the concept makes no sense. Is a child passive or active when reading a book? To be passive mentally means the brain is not paying attention. One can be passive when listening, reading, or even driving a car. Teachers have internalized the belief that moving and talking students are learning students. The question that rarely gets asked is: What are the students learning? One can be a very busy bee, yet the result can be a misconception, not learning the target concept, or even not learning anything. For reading instruction, a student could have selected a high-interest book and be sitting in a cozy corner to read, but without the skills to read, the best the student may be able to do is look at the pictures and guess the words. In this case, the student is not active or passive; the student's instructional time is simply being wasted.

Let's return to the brain. All learning requires active mental engagement. There is no such thing as passive learning. If you are not paying attention, you are not learning. This leads us to a second firmly held belief of progressive educators: Student-centered instruction is superior to teacher-centered instruction. The difference between teacher-centered and student-centered work stems from who determines what work will be done. For teacher-centered instruction, the teacher—who holds deep knowledge and expertise on the subject—carefully selects and sequences instructional activities designed to promote student learning. (Note: If you replace the word *teacher* with *coach*, the enterprise holds more mass appeal.) The teacher will assess if students are learning and adjust teaching accordingly. In contrast, in student-centered approaches, students select the learning material or activity that interests them most. The rhetoric of the belief system shapes teacher behavior and leads to misinterpretations of observed outcomes. If a teacher firmly believes "child-centered instruction is good" and "teacher-centered instruction is bad," it will be difficult for the teacher to engage in or consider practices that do not appear to be aligned with a child-centered philosophy. To make matters worse, lack of learning will not be attributed to specific teaching methods but individual child characteristics (e.g., poverty, laziness, distractibility, lack of motivation, disability). Thus, many teachers end up blaming the child for lack of progress rather than evaluating the methods used for teaching: "Of course, my methods are good; they reflect active, student-centered instruction!"

Returning to the task of teaching a child to read, most parents and prospective teachers make the assumptions presented at the beginning of this chapter:

How to teach a child to read is known, and teachers receive training in how to do it. Most prospective teachers enter colleges of education assuming they will learn how to teach students to read. What they receive is a tremendous amount of progressive education theory. Teachers leave their credentialing programs believing the myth that teaching students to read is primarily based on a teacher's ability to instill a love of reading within their students. And, although they don't know too much about phonics, teaching it would be deconstructivist (bad) and probably involve some drudgery.[2]

A final legacy of progressive education beliefs is the notion that the act of teaching is, at its foundation, a creative enterprise. The most dismaying reason for the failure of teachers and teacher educators to embrace phonics approaches lies in resistance to the curricular materials themselves. Simply put, teachers did not want to be told what to do. Synthetic phonics programs are designed to have teachers begin by teaching the most straightforward letter-sound relationships (e.g., m = /m/, a = /ă/, t = /t/) and systematically move through more complex ones (e.g., ch = /ch/, a_e = /ā/, $-tion$ = /shən/). The materials provided to teachers are very explicit: Teach this first and do it this way, then have students read this material. For teachers who firmly believe interest and motivation are the keys to unlocking students' reading ability and teacher creativity is the primary vehicle for instructional delivery, the thought of following a "boxed" curriculum or set of instructional guidelines is anathema.

A foundational tenet of the progressive education philosophy is that teachers are experts, they know best, and their judgment should be trusted. The problem was that they were never trained in the knowledge required to make informed decisions about reading instruction. The low-hanging fruit of this argument is medicine. Doctors acquire a vast amount of knowledge during their medical training, including training in *standardized protocols* for diagnosis and intervention. After mastery of this knowledge has been obtained, doctors begin to accrue clinical knowledge. Clinical knowledge allows for flexibility and creativity in assessing and delivering treatment. Unfortunately, the majority of teachers, through no fault of their own, have not been provided the foundational training in reading required for the application of flexible and creative clinical practice.

---

2. It always struck me as odd that the drudgery of school has historically been framed as bad, not helpful, most likely harmful, and something to be avoided, yet the drudgery associated with any other great accomplishment (e.g., those of scientists, athletes, writers, performers, inventors) is notable, exceptional, worthy of high esteem, and inspirational. Can the roots of inequity be tied to the characterization of educational drudgery as bad? The hidden message to students is: I worked very hard, laboring over the details of my craft, but I will not model, support, or teach you to master the foundational skills of learning; for you, learning should be natural and fun.

SUMMARY

This chapter began with Noah Webster's call for teaching beginning readers the relationship between speech sounds and letters. Understanding the alphabetic principle requires individuals to recognize words are composed of letters that represent speech sounds. Over the decades, however, directly teaching students how alphabetic orthographies work fell out of favor. The idea that reading ability should be "caught" rather than "taught" captured the imagination of many scholars and teachers. For them, the number of students who did learn to read in the absence of direct teaching of the alphabetic code was sufficient evidence that reading, like language, could be developed naturally through exposure to rich and varied texts.

The fly in the ointment of this belief is the counterfactual: Many students in the United States do not learn to read or read well and efficiently. Data collected by the National Assessment of Educational Progress (NAEP) from 1992 to 2022 have consistently demonstrated that many students are not learning to read or learning to read well. In 2019, a dismaying 65 percent of fourth graders failed to meet or exceed proficiency; of that 65 percent, an alarming 34 percent did not meet NAEP's minimum basic level (NAEP, 2022). And perhaps those students who appeared to learn to read were not reading as well as they could, as only 9 percent of fourth graders demonstrated advanced proficiency in reading. Claims of the inadequacies of standardized assessments for measuring reading ability ("Reading is more than what can be captured on a standardized test!") are of little consolation for the struggling reader or parent of the struggling reader.

Perhaps change is on the horizon. Recent syntheses of research findings from cognitive science, neurobiology, and linguistics (e.g., Dehaene, 2009; Seidenberg, 2017; Snowling et al., 2022) have provided additional support for code-emphasis approaches. In addition, new forms of public pressure to change reading instruction are beginning to converge (Gearin et al., 2020). For the first time, support for balanced literacy is starting to wane (Goldstein, 2022). Parents, teachers, and school administrators are beginning to realize that balanced literacy did not fulfill its promise to deliver the best of both worlds—immersion in rich literature and teaching the code. Instead, it taught students to guess words and use their fragmented understanding of phonics to figure out unknown words.

Thus, to move away from the seemingly neutral but misleading characterization of reading instruction as balanced, reading scholars have begun to use a new term, *structured literacy*. In the next chapter, we will examine the latest in reading science and how that science can inform the delivery of more efficacious reading instruction.

Chapter Four

Reading Science and Individual Differences in Reading

Now that we have (a) put to rest the notion that guessing is equivalent to reading and (b) established that methods promoting guessing move students away from the one thing learners should be paying attention to (i.e., the letters within words), we can turn our attention to what current research suggests about the mechanisms at play when individuals read. Understanding these mechanisms can illuminate why some students experience difficulty in learning to read. In doing so, we will move from a singular focus on *decoding* to the broader concept of *word recognition*. Within the concept of word recognition, meaning will be brought to bear. In addition, we examine theoretical models of reading and explore how these models inform and align with current research findings about typical and atypical reading development. In particular, we will explore the factors that influence the expression of dyslexia.

FROM BIG PICTURE TO NUANCED DETAIL: UNDERSTANDING WORD-LEVEL READING

Reading is a multi-dimensional, complex behavior. Not unlike the elephant in the parable of the blind men and an elephant,[1] the act of reading has been examined by researchers using different lenses, angles, and tools. This varied research has expanded our understanding of typical and atypical reading development as well as shed light on the practices that support or inhibit the growth of reading ability. But viewing reading from a multitude of lenses can obscure the gestalt of reading. Sometimes, a global conceptualization can

---

1. When an elephant is brought to town, a group of blind men inspect it by touching it. Each man comes to a different conclusion about the properties of an elephant depending on what part of the elephant he touched (i.e., trunk = snake; ear = fan; leg = tree trunk; side = wall; tusk = spear).

capture the essence of a complex concept and provide an organizing framework upon which nuance and complexity can be added.

In 1986, Gough and Tunmer proposed such a framework, The Simple View of Reading. In their framework, the two suggested that reading comprehension (R) was the product of decoding (D) and language comprehension (C) expressed as the formula: $R = D \times C$. At the time it was proposed (i.e., amid the whole-language vs. phonics debate), the framework was particularly useful in demonstrating that decoding, the ability to decipher a word, was necessary but not sufficient for reading. To wit, recognition of the printed word cannot be overlooked or downplayed, but word recognition, in and of itself, is not all that is required for reading. Language comprehension, the ability to bring meaning to words, is needed for understanding and making sense of print. Thus, in Gough and Tunmer's elegant but simple model, reading was the product of a person's ability to lift words off the page and bring meaning to those words. In the 30-plus years since the Simple View of Reading was first proposed, research has yielded a more detailed understanding of these constructs and their interactions. However, the Simple View of Reading continues to serve as a useful organizing heuristic for understanding the broad landscape of reading, in general, and the topic of dyslexia, in particular (Kirby & Savage, 2008).

The Simple View of Reading

One of the advantages of the Simple View of Reading was that it could situate the role of decoding within a larger framework of reading ability. On the one hand, a student who can decode ($D = 1$) but does know what the words mean ($C = 0$) will not achieve reading comprehension ($1[D] \times 0[C] = 0[R]$). Conversely, a student who is unable to decode words ($0[D]$) will never be able to bring meaning to those words ($0[R]$) even if the student's language comprehension is excellent ($0[D] \times 1[C] = 0[R]$). Thus, the Simple View of Reading made it clear that decoding was not "one of many ways to read words"; it was an essential component of the reading formula. Students who did not possess the skill would not achieve reading competence.

Gough and Tunmer thought a particular utility of the Simple View of Reading was its ability to capture the topography—the surface features—of categories of reading difficulty. For dyslexia, the unique, negative correlation between decoding and language comprehension was a particular hallmark of the disorder. For students with dyslexia, research had demonstrated that *unlike* most of the population, where a strong, positive correlation between decoding and language comprehension was found (strength in one area was associated with strength in the other), this was not the case.

> We take no position on whether there is one or more ultimate causes of dyslexia. But we suggest that there is a common denominator in every case of dyslexia, a deficit which could well stand as the *proximal* cause of the disorder. This is an inability to decode. (Gough & Tunmer, 1986, p. 8; emphasis in the original text)

In the decades that followed the introduction of the Simple View of Reading, many research studies confirmed its basic premises: (a) Some students can have good decoding skills but experience poor language comprehension, while some students can have poor decoding but intact language comprehension, and (b) the basic formula is predictive of future reading performance during the first four years of reading acquisition (Kirby & Savage, 2008). In addition, some clarifying adjustments were made in terms of terminology. Specifically, although Gough and Tunmer's use of the term *decoding* was inclusive of phonetic decoding (i.e., sounding words out using knowledge of grapheme-phoneme correspondence) and orthographic decoding (i.e., automatic recognition of words that had been previously learned), the term *word recognition* was determined to be a better fit (Hoover & Tunmer 2020).

What Is Word Recognition?

Word recognition is the ability to identify words accurately. Word recognition occurs when a person either immediately and accurately recognizes a whole word or when a novel word is decoded (e.g., the first time the word *nocturnal* is encountered, it would need to be decoded). Decoding can occur part by part (e.g., /noc/-/tərn/-/əl/) or phoneme by phoneme (e.g., /n/-/o/-/k/-/t/-/ər/-/n/-/əl/). Advocates of whole-word methods believed that automatic, whole-word recognition occurred due to students memorizing the whole word's shape (Adams, 1990; Smith, 1973). In addition, they believed that readers did not pay attention to the individual letters within words. Instead, the letters in words were sampled only enough to gain the gist of the words (e.g., attention to the first or final letters of a word was sufficient for word recognition). However, research has consistently demonstrated that letter sampling leads to errors, while attention to letters and letter patterns is essential for accurate word reading (Castles et al., 2018; Samuels et al., 2011). For example, recall Flesch's astonishment when he asked Johnny to read the word *kid,* and Johnny said *kind*.

A unifying characteristic of dyslexia is difficulty with word recognition (automatic or decoded). The question for researchers has been *why*. To answer this question, researchers have proposed theories as to how word-level reading skills are acquired and tested these theories using behavioral research (i.e., studying students' behavior as they are learning to read) and neurological research (i.e., studying the brain as it is reading or before and after reading instruction). These theories are particularly instructive for understanding how word-level reading skills are acquired and how differences in the underlying reading processes can result in dyslexia.

Orthographic Mapping: The Importance of Phonological Recoding for Word Recognition

The work of two researchers, Linnea Ehri and David Share, has been particularly robust in framing the processing involved during word reading. In 1978, Ehri proposed that visual word recognition, pronunciation, and meaning became amalgamated (i.e., united) during the reading process. The result was a reader's ability to automatically call to mind a word's pronunciation and meaning upon sight of the word. Ehri and others have conducted numerous studies spanning several decades, which have provided empirical support for the theory (Ehri, 2020). As a result, the process, now referred to as *orthographic mapping*, is widely accepted. But how does the amalgamation happen? What does the reader need to do to facilitate robust mapping? And, what accounts for the rapid growth of readers' amalgamations (i.e., acquisition of sight words) once they develop basic reading skills?

Orthographic mapping occurs when readers convert letters to sounds through a process called *phonological recoding* (Share, 1995). The result is a single lexical unit, bonding the spelling and pronunciation of the word. For many readers, a word needs to be decoded (sounded out) or encoded (spelled out) only a handful of times before this bonding is cemented (Shahar & Share, 2008; Share, 2008). After that point, the word can be instantly recognized, bypassing the need for sounding out the word, which is necessary for rapid, autonomous visual word recognition.

Orthographic mapping can occur with *phonetically regular words*, words in which letters and letter patterns represent their most common sounds (e.g., *cat* – c = /k/, a = /ă/, t = /t/; *ship* – sh = /sh/, i = /ĭ/, p = /p/), and in *phonetically irregular words*, words that do not follow the most common phonics patterns (e.g., *was* – w = /w/, u = /u/, s = /z/; *said* – s = /s/, ai = /ĕ/, d = /d/). Share described this process of phonological recoding as the *sine qua non,* an essential component, of reading (Share, 1995). Without phonological recoding, reading cannot happen.

The power of orthographic mapping appears to lie in the specific attention paid to letters and letter patterns within words and the mapping of phonemes to those letter patterns (Ehri, 2014; Ehri, 2020). This type of mapping can occur only if learners possess working knowledge of the alphabetic system. The mapping of orthographic parts (i.e., individual letters, chunks of words) to phonemes is the glue that secures the word in memory rather than arbitrary letter-string association. Research has demonstrated, in contrast to wholeword memorization, once a word has been bonded via orthographic mapping to its pronunciation and meaning, the word can be automatically accessed (Nation et al., 2007). In addition, the word can be accessed regardless of font, capitalization, or other differences in word formatting (e.g., sHiP, ship, *ship*).

Orthographic mapping results in an orthographic memory—a memory of the spelling, pronunciation, and meaning of the word fused together. Once a word is mapped, it becomes a *sight word*. *Sight words* are words that are recognized automatically, upon sight.[2] Orthographic memories are stored within a student's mental lexicon, a mental dictionary that houses words' spellings, meanings, and pronunciations. Thus, a student's *sight word* vocabulary is created through the process of creating orthographic memories.

If orthographic mapping explains how fluent, accurate word reading is acquired, why might students experience difficulty with this process? First, orthographic mapping depends on grapheme-phoneme conversion, converting letters and letter patterns to speech sounds. Grapheme-phoneme conversion requires students to grasp the alphabetic principle (i.e., words are composed of letters representing sounds). If students are primarily taught via whole-word instruction, they will not realize that words have parts that can be decoded. Further, incidental, haphazard, or indirect phonics instruction can be insufficient for developing students' awareness of the alphabetic principle; without sufficient alphabetic awareness, students will continue to guess words using inefficient letter sampling techniques. Thus, internalization of the alphabetic principle is a critical first step for orthographic mapping, but this awareness can be fostered only through instruction that teaches students to attend to letters and letter patterns within words.

Second, orthographic mapping requires phonemic awareness. If students are unaware of individual speech sounds or have difficulty processing individual phonemes, they will not be able to map sounds to letters. Phonemic awareness enables students to blend individual sounds when decoding (e.g., transforming the printed word *train* to blended sounds for the pronunciation of /t/-/r/-/ā/-/n/) and segment sounds for spelling (e.g., segmenting the phonemes /ch/-/o/-/p/ to spell *chop*). Orthographic mapping is strengthened when students engage in decoding or encoding (spelling), but difficulty with phonemic awareness can inhibit the mapping process. Research has demonstrated that many students with dyslexia often experience difficulty with phonemic awareness (Snowling, 2000; Wagner & Lonigan, 2022).

---

2. Unfortunately, within schools, a practice called "sight-word instruction" refers to the practice of teaching students to memorize whole words, not orthographic mapping. More information about that practice can be found in Chapter 5.

Finally, knowledge of phonics is necessary for orthographic mapping. Although understanding that words have parts (i.e., the alphabetic principle) is a critical first step to unlocking the code, students need to be explicitly taught enough letter-sound correspondences to read words independently. Therefore, instruction must go beyond teaching the 26 letters of the alphabet.[3] As researchers have consistently demonstrated, systematic instruction beginning with the basics, followed by the introduction of more complex letter patterns, facilitates students' mastery of phonics (Castles et al., 2018; Rose, 2006). As students gain more insight into the various ways speech sounds are represented in print (e.g., /f/ can be spelled *f*, *ff*, *ph*, *gh*), they can be increasingly flexible in their attempts to decode novel words.

Students can encounter difficulty mastering phonics due to insufficient instruction or difficulties often associated with dyslexia, such as limitations in verbal short-term memory, oral language development, and processing speed (Peterson & Pennington, 2012). However, despite the difficulties students may encounter when learning phonics, research has also demonstrated that early, systematic phonics instruction is a protective factor and can improve reading outcomes for students with dyslexia (Torgesen, 2005). Therefore, although progress may be slower and require more intensity (e.g., time, repetition, examples), students with dyslexia require direct teaching of the code to facilitate the orthographic mapping required for fluent word reading.

Only after students have acquired sufficient phonics knowledge can they expand their sight-word vocabulary and develop the fluent word-reading skills necessary for independent reading and reading comprehension. It is estimated that skilled readers can efficiently recognize more than 40,000 words (Anderson & Nagy, 1993; Brysbaert et al., 2016). Share's *self-teaching hypothesis* holds that when readers encounter a novel word and apply their knowledge of grapheme-phoneme correspondence to sound out the word, this phonological recoding (i.e., transforming graphemes into sound units) is the process necessary for adding new words to their sight-word lexicon (Share, 1995). For students to independently add new words to their sight-word lexicon, they need to (a) possess explicit or implicit knowledge of grapheme-phoneme correspondence, (b) attend to and hold the pattern of the grapheme-phoneme correspondence in working memory, and (c) have the phonological capacity to blend the sounds to create a unit.

The self-teaching hypothesis helps account for the rapid expansion of students' sight-word lexicon. Students do not need to be directly taught every word; if a student knows how sounds are represented by letters, they can

---

3. Surprisingly, top-selling reading curricula do not include systematic instruction in letter-sound correspondences (Kurtz et al., 2020), and many elementary education teachers are not trained within their teacher preparation programs to teach phonics (Binks-Cantrell et al., 2012; Graham & Walsh, 2020).

apply that knowledge when encountering new words. Share's self-teaching hypothesis does not mean that a first grader who encounters the novel word *reign* will be able to recode that word phonologically, but the first grader who has knowledge of the most common letter-sound correspondences of single consonants and vowels, as well as knowledge of consonant digraphs (i.e., a single speech sound represented by two consonants), could read novel and nonwords such as *zed, tad, neg, chug, with,* and *such.* The concept of self-teaching is primarily applied during independent reading. As students independently read texts and encounter novel words, they can use their phoneme-grapheme correspondence knowledge to phonologically recode the word. The context of the reading may also impart meaning, which results in an orthographic memory or amalgam, to use Ehri's term, which can be added to students' mental lexicon. As stated earlier, many students require only a few instances of phonological recoding to map a word. After that point, the word can be automatically recognized on sight without the need for phonological recoding. The rate and level of skilled word reading depends on learner and environmental (e.g., instructional) conditions.

The Acquisition of Word-Reading Skills

Word-reading skills change over time due to changes in student learning (Ehri, 2020). Pre-readers, who are either unaware or have limited awareness of the alphabet, recognize words as pictures, drawing upon familiar colors or shapes or the environmental location of the word (e.g., familiar logos, their names on cubbies or lunch boxes) to facilitate word recognition. At this point, their ability to identify a word is *pre-alphabetic,* as they are not using letter knowledge for word recognition.

As young children are introduced to letter names and sounds, they begin to apply letter knowledge for (a) reading (e.g., applying limited letter name or sound knowledge to guess printed words) and (b) spelling (e.g., using limited letter knowledge to write words; *have = hv, big = bg*), but they have difficulty decoding words, because they have yet to be taught a full array of letter-sound correspondences or how to blend sounds to read words. Words read or spelled at this level reflect *partial alphabetic* understanding. As students acquire decoding skills, they can apply these skills for reading and move into what Ehri termed *the alphabetic phase* of reading. Alphabetic word recognition occurs when students can apply their phonics knowledge for reading and spelling.

Note that movement from across phases is directly linked to instruction; students must learn how sounds are represented by letters and letter patterns to apply that knowledge in practice. In addition, movement from phase to phase is specific to taught or learned patterns; understanding that *-igh* represents /ī/ does not generalize to the recognition that *-ough* represents /ŭf/ in words like *rough* and *tough*. As a result, a student's reading or spelling of one word may reflect partial alphabetic understanding. In contrast, the reading or spelling of another word may reflect a more advanced alphabetic knowledge. The final phase of word reading is the *consolidated alphabetic* stage, wherein students apply their knowledge of morphemes (e.g., suffixes, prefixes) and syllables (i.e., students' ability to analyze syllabic units) for fluent, accurate word recognition (Bhattacharya & Ehri, 2004).

Beyond Decoding: The Role of Context and Oral Vocabulary for Word Recognition

Researchers have firmly established that context-independent word reading is foundational for skilled reading: Students must learn the code to be proficient readers (Perfetti, 2007; Castles et al., 2018). At times, though, decoding, the process of sounding out a word through the application of grapheme-phoneme conversion, alone is insufficient for *word recognition*. In particular, when words are ambiguous[4] (e.g., *live/live, read/read*) or have variant (i.e., irregular) spelling patterns (e.g., *aisle, island, listen*), context and a student's existing vocabulary knowledge facilitate accurate word recognition.

Set for variability is a term used when readers self-correct the mispronunciation of a word through the use of a partial decoding strategy along with context and prior word knowledge (Steacy et al., 2019; Tunmer & Chapman, 2012; Venezky, 1999). All readers, from novice to skilled, have had the experience of reading a word silently and retrieving an incorrect pronunciation (e.g., pronouncing *hyperbole* as "hyper-bowl" rather than /hī/-/per/-/bō/-/lē/ or comptroller as "comp-troller" rather than /con/-/trōll/-/er/; my daughter when independently reading Harry Potter thought it was the /trĭ/-/wĭz/-/ard/ tournament not /trī/-/wĭz/-/ard/). However, if the word is already a part of the reader's oral vocabulary (i.e., the reader is familiar with both the oral pronunciation of the word and its definition), then he or she can self-correct the mismatch between the initial decoding attempt and an accurate pronunciation of the word. This self-correction process is referred to as a reader's *set for variability*, which is dependent on the reader having a "set of words" in his or her mental lexicon of which he or she knows the meaning and pronunciation (Dyson et al., 2017; Nation & Cocksey, 2009). For example, a novice reader may initially decode *smile* as "smill" and then self-correct to /smīl/, as *smill* is not a familiar word and *smile* fits the context of the sentence. Set for

---

4. In heteronyms, the meaning of a word is changed due to differences in how the vowel is pronounced (e.g., *read, live, wind, wound, tear, close, excuse*) or where the stress is placed (e.g., *address, affect, compress, conduct, contest, digest*).

variability is particularly useful for irregular words. For example, if sounding out the irregular word *what* results in "wat," the reader can self-correct to the known pronunciation of /wŭt/.

Researchers have found that students who experience difficulty with reading have less lexical flexibility (Elbro et al., 2012; Tunmer & Chapman, 2012; Steacy et al., 2019). But direct teaching can increase students' set for variability and use of flexible decoding strategies (Dyson et al., 2017; Savage et al., 2018). For example, Dyson and colleagues taught one group of 5- to 7-year-olds a strategy for reading irregular words as well as word definitions and rhyming words. After the training, the children were given a battery of tests, including a mispronunciation correction task in which the researchers used a puppet to prompt the children: "My puppet is going to say some sentences, but he's going to say the word at the end wrong. Can you help him and tell him the correct word?" After the puppet task, students were given a list of words used in the puppet task and asked to read and define them. Students who received the training had more success reading the taught irregular words and matched untaught words. The findings demonstrated that in addition to knowing the correct pronunciation (i.e., phonology) of a word, knowing the meaning of the word aided correct pronunciation (i.e., semantics).

Morphology: Another Key for Unlocking Word Recognition

Morphemes are the smallest units of words that contain meaning. A morpheme can be an affix such as a prefix (e.g., *un-* meaning "not" as in *unhappy* or not happy; *re-* meaning "again" as in *redo* or to do again) or a suffix (e.g., *-er* meaning "one who" as in *worker* or one who works; *-less* meaning "without" as in *fearless* or without fear). Morphemes can also be *bases* or *roots*. Bases can stand alone in English (e.g., *cycle, civil*), but affixes can be added to change the meaning of the word (e.g., *bicycle, uncivilized*). In contrast, root words are derived from Greek or Latin. They cannot stand alone as words in English (e.g., "aud" meaning something related to hearing, as in *audiology, auditorium,* and *audience*).

As students gain experience with printed words, they become attuned to the meaning provided by morphemes. For example, the *-ed* at the end of the word indicates past tense. If my daughter was familiar with the prefix *tri-*, meaning *three*, she could have applied that knowledge to aid in correctly pronouncing the Triwizard Tournament. Researchers have found that students with dyslexia are less attuned to morphology, and limitations in morphological awareness can affect their reading and spelling (Bourassa et al., 2006). There is evidence to suggest, however, that direct teaching of morphemes can aid students' word-level reading (Galuschka et al., 2020; Goodwin & Ahn, 2010). Although morphological instruction can begin in early elementary[5], researchers have found a particular boost when older students are provided with morphological instruction (Galuschka et al., 2020) and when instruction in morphemes is combined with other components of literacy (e.g., spelling and phonology; Morris et al., 2012).

Word Recognition: Summary

The ability to recognize words develops over time in conjunction with a learner's understanding of the alphabetic principle, capacity to apply knowledge of grapheme-phoneme correspondence to recode words phonologically, use of flexible decoding strategies informed by context or prior knowledge of the spoken word (i.e., set for variability), and morphological awareness. Thus, word recognition is informed by context-independent factors (grapheme-phoneme conversion) and context-dependent factors (meaning-facilitated pronunciation). To explore how these factors interact, word-level reading models can be instructive.

WORD-LEVEL READING MODELS

What are the processing mechanisms in the brain that allow for accurate word recognition? Understanding these processes can help researchers pinpoint areas that contribute to reading difficulty and, perhaps, shed light on ways to remediate such difficulties. Reading researchers generate scientific hypotheses, which allow them to test their theories empirically. Researchers have transformed several theories of reading into computational models. These models attempt to account for various cognitive variables involved in reading words aloud (i.e., moving from printed words to spoken words) and can be used by researchers to empirically examine hypotheses about the processes involved during reading (Castles et al., 2018; Perry et al., 2007). Mathematical computational models allow researchers to create simulations of impaired and accurate word-level reading by manipulating various aspects of the reading process. Although the models differ in terms of the precise timing and specific relations across variables, they converge on a unifying conceptualization: There are two routes to word recognition—one that involves the translation of spelling to sound (i.e., through the phonological recoding of graphemes meaning can be accessed) and one that reflects

---

5. Information on what early and later morphological instruction looks like can be found in Chapter 5.

a direct route from spelling to meaning (i.e., immediate access to meaning upon sight of the word). The decoding route is necessary for processing new and unfamiliar words but taxes cognition and creates an intermediary step between visual recognition and meaning. In contrast, automatic word recognition provides a direct path from visual recognition to meaning and is a more efficient route (Share, 2008).

Dual-Route Cascaded Model of Word Reading

Dual-route models reflect static models of skilled word reading and highlight specific processes involved within two processing streams used for word recognition: lexical and non- or sublexical (see Figure 4.1). Within a dual-route model, words are processed simultaneously along these two processing streams (Church et al., 2021). The lexical route (far right side of Figure 4.1) reflects the route taken when processing whole words, such as those with irregular spellings (e.g., *was*, *yacht*) or regular words that have been previously orthographically mapped. In contrast, the sublexical route[6] (i.e., the left-side path) reflects the phonological processing stream used when grapheme-phoneme conversion is used for word recognition. The sublexical route is necessary for reading (decoding) nonwords and novel words. Thus, the lexical route reflects an assigned phonological route—connecting a whole word with its pronunciation—whereas the sublexical route reflects an assembled phonological route—blending sounds for word pronunciation (Brysbaert, 2022).

The dual-route cascaded model is a reading-aloud model wherein the reader moves from a print stimulus (top of the model) through the processing streams for speech production (Coltheart et al., 2001). Word reading is the result of the combined activity of the sublexical and lexical routes, with the familiarity of the word determining if the reader reads the word as a whole (assigned phonology) or assembles the sounds of the word during the reading process. Beginning or less skilled readers, for whom a direct lexical route has not been established, rely on the sublexical route. The lexical route, which allows for more rapid processing, is the dominant route for skilled word reading.

The dual-route model aligns with what has been observed in children learning to read languages of different orthographic depths. Specifically, children take longer to learn more opaque languages (Caravolas, 2022). The orthographic depth of a language refers to the extent to which there is a one-to-one

---

6. Coltheart and colleagues more frequently refer to this route as *nonlexical*, but I prefer the term *sublexical*, as it semantically captures the "below the whole-word level" of processing that occurs when sounding out words.

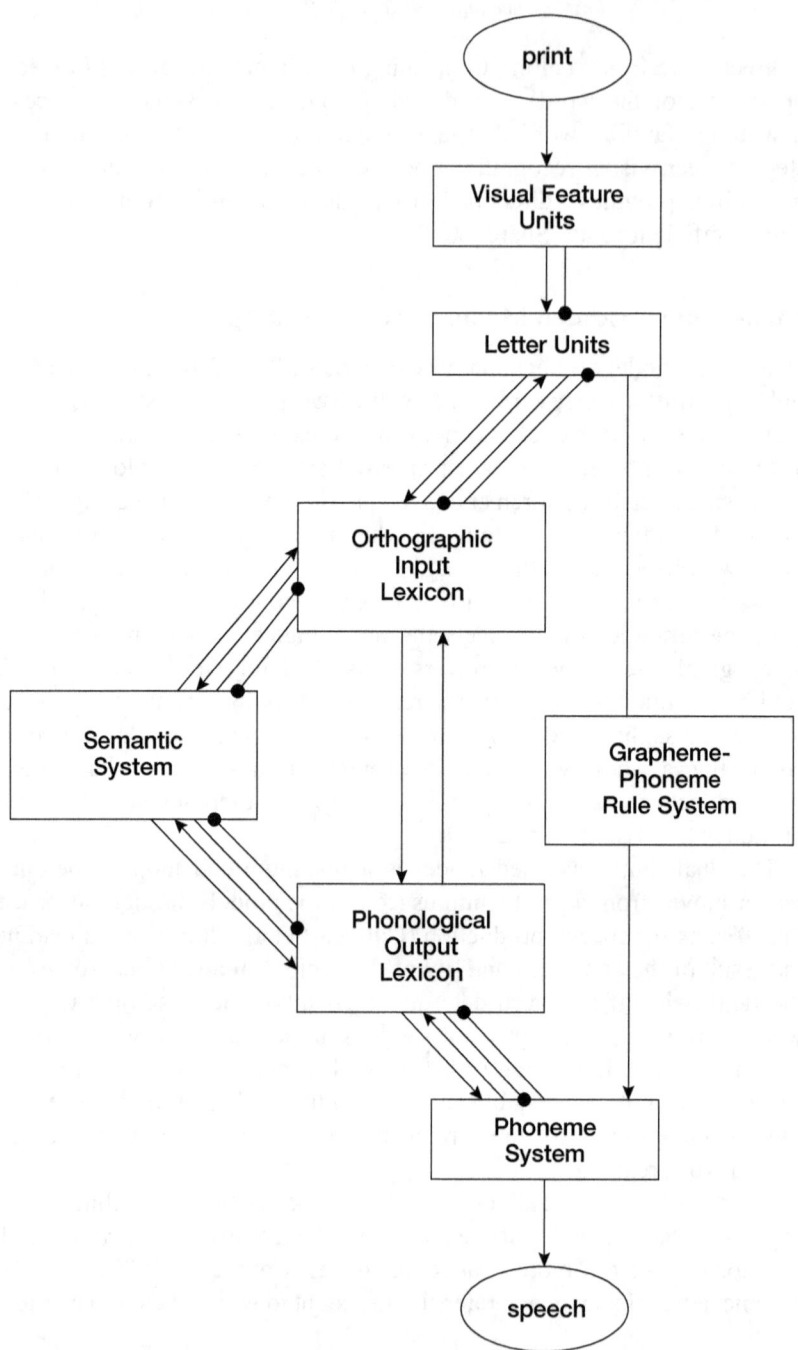

Figure 4.1. Dual-route cascaded (DRC) model.
From "DRC: A dual-route cascaded model of visual word recognition and reading aloud" by Coltheart et al., 2001. Copyright © 2001 by the American Psychological Association. Reprinted with permission.

correspondence between letters and speech sounds. In highly transparent languages (e.g., Spanish, Italian, Finnish), most letter and letter combinations reflect only one speech sound. In contrast, English is considered an opaque language, because the pronunciation of letters and letter combinations differs between words. For example, the *a* is pronounced differently in *cat*, *water*, *about*, *bake*, and *fall*. Given the opacity of English, it is not surprising that it takes several years for students to strengthen the lexical route for reading.

Triangle Model of Word Reading

The triangle model of reading accounts for the types of processing that contribute to word reading:[7] orthography, phonology, and semantics (see Figure 4.2). Recall the factors that contribute to accurate word recognition: (a) attention to the specific letters in the word (i.e., the orthography); (b) facility with sounds of speech (i.e., phonology); and (c) the application of meaning to words (i.e., semantics). A triangle model, also referred to as a connectionist or parallel distributed processing model, was first proposed by Seidenberg and McClelland (1989). In this model, all three domains are inter*connected* (hence the descriptor *connectionist* model) and modified by learning. The

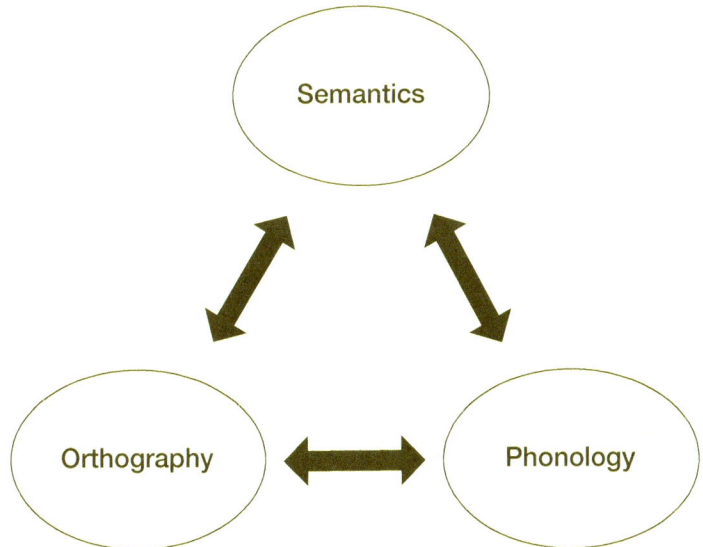

Figure 4.2. The triangle model
Adapted from Harm & Seidenberg, 2004 and Seidenberg & McClelland, 1989.

---

7. It is important to note that the dual-route cascaded and triangle models are models of single-word reading, not models of reading comprehension.

model captures both the process of learning to read and a picture of proficient reading. Within early reading, more resources are used to develop the connections between orthography and phonology, whereas as reading proficiency grows, the semantic pathway assumes a more prominent role in word-level reading. Yet, all domains are interconnected and interdependent. As orthographic, phonological, and semantic weights for each word are strengthened, reading becomes more automatic (Taylor et al., 2013).

Connectionist models can be helpful for conceptualizing reading difficulties. Specifically, difficulty with word-level reading could be attributed to any of the domains or in establishing connections across domains. In other words, students could have diminished capacity of a domain (e.g., difficulty with phonemic awareness), or a student could have difficulty with learning the connection between phonemes and graphemes (e.g., perhaps due to memory limitations). The bulk of research on dyslexia has focused on difficulties with phonology and the capacity of individuals to make connections with orthography. For example, researchers have found that students with dyslexia experience particular difficulty reading nonwords (e.g., *yete, blost, zegger, rampedant*), which requires the capacity to map phonemes to letter patterns and *blend* the sounds to pronounce a word. Such nonword reading requires phonological recoding (sounding out via application of phonetic principles), as nonwords cannot be retrieved automatically based solely upon orthography (spelling).

The Utility of Computational Models of Word Reading

Computational models allow researchers to test hypotheses about the reading process and move beyond intuitions about the processes involved in reading based solely on observing the reading behaviors of individuals. Notably, the models reflect what is known about word-level reading: Although novice and skilled readers use phonological recoding (decoding) when reading novel words, this system is bypassed for automatic word reading. Automatic word reading reflects a direct path from the printed word to meaning (Castles et al., 2018). Further, the two pathways of word recognition, lexical and sublexical, have been demonstrated in neuroimaging studies (Taylor et al., 2013).

NEUROIMAGING AND DYSLEXIA

Over the past few decades, tremendous gains have been made in neuroimaging research in understanding the specific circuitry involved during reading. This imaging has confirmed and expanded theoretical (verbal) explanations and computational (mathematical) models of skilled reading and dyslexia. In particular, functional magnetic resonance imaging (fMRI) has been used to explore how functions of the brain relate to observed reading behaviors. fMRI technology allows researchers to explore activation patterns in adult and child populations and those with and without reading difficulty. For example, during an fMRI scan, researchers can track the flow of oxygenated blood within the brain as participants engage in reading tasks. The flow of blood indicates areas of activation.

Neuroimaging research on dyslexia has demonstrated that activation during reading occurs primarily in the left hemisphere of the brain. This is the same region of the brain that is activated when we listen to spoken language, which makes intuitive sense, as listening requires the processing of phonology and semantics, as does reading. Thus, we can think of the left hemisphere of the brain as the language center wherein spoken and written language is processed.

Activation during reading occurs within three primary regions in the left hemisphere: the occipitotemporal cortex, the parietal-temporal region, and the inferior frontal gyrus (see Figure 4.3; Church et al., 2021; Taylor, 2013). Early fMRI research demonstrated distinct differences in activation patterns across these three areas in the brain functions of individuals with and without dyslexia (Shaywitz et al., 2002). Specifically, researchers consistently found underactivation of these critical reading-related areas in individuals with dyslexia (Habib, 2021; Paulesu et al., 2001; Richlan et al., 2011). For

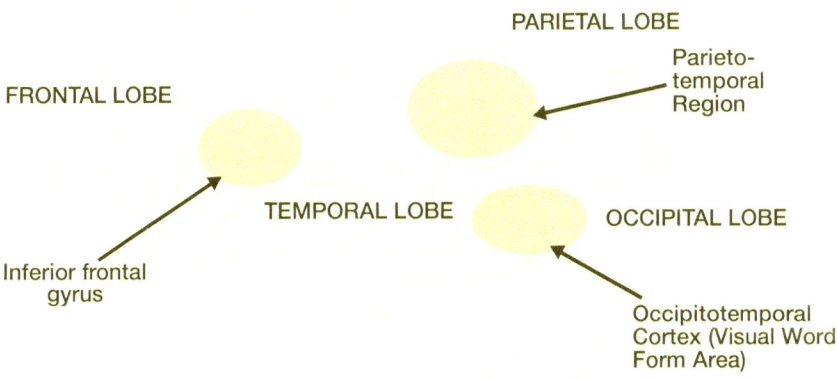

Figure 4.3. The brain reading network

phonological tasks such as identifying rhyming words, underactivation can be seen in the inferior frontal gyrus, which includes Broca's area (an area associated with speech production) and the parietal-temporal region. However, what is seen most clearly is less activation in the visual word form area (VWFA), which overlaps with the occipital lobe (vision center) and the temporal lobe. The VWFA is where letters are recognized and processed. Underactivation in this area is consistent with behavioral observations of students with dyslexia who demonstrate difficulty decoding written words.

More recent neuroimaging research has focused on how the brain responds to different types of reading tasks and changes over time in relation to reading instruction. In alignment with theoretical and computational models of reading, neuroimaging research has demonstrated two processing routes for word reading (Brysbaert, 2022; Church et al., 2021; Taylor et al., 2013). Effortful, sublexical processing required for assembled phonology occurs along the dorsal pathway. The dorsal pathway moves up through the middle temporal and inferior parietal regions to connect the phonology-related areas of the brain. This dorsal route reflects a less efficient route to accessing meaning, but one that is required for processing novel words (see Figure 4.4).

In contrast, more efficient, rapid lexical processing occurs along the ventral route. The ventral pathway, the lower system, makes use of the VWFA. The VWFA, also referred to as the brain's *letterbox*, is where letters and

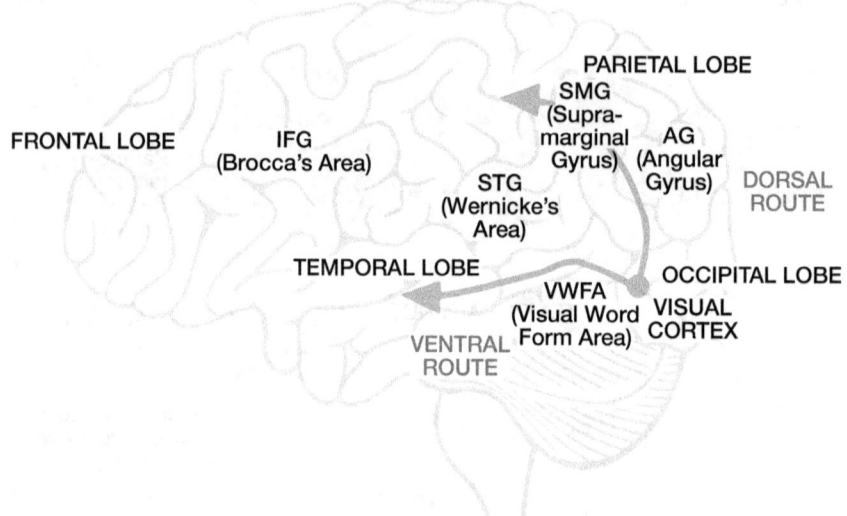

Figure 4.4. Dorsal and ventral routes of word reading
Note. IFG: Inferior frontal gyrus; STG: Superior temporal gyrus.

words are processed. Specifically, researchers have found increased activation in the VWFA in response to words, particularly by age nine (after several years of reading instruction) but as early as age six for early readers (Dehaene et al., 2015).

Finally, for teachers, families of struggling readers, and struggling readers, the power of neuroimaging research lies in its ability to shed light on human *neuroplasticity*. A brain's functioning is not static; with appropriate instruction, the brain can be rewired (i.e., the brain can form and reorganize neural connections), which results in more accurate and efficient word reading (Dehaene, 2011). In other words, results from neuroimaging studies offer hope. Poor readers do not need to remain poor readers. The brain is changed by learning to read. In fact, findings from neuroimaging studies demonstrate changes in activation as a result of reading intervention (Fletcher et al., 2019). As reading skills improve, greater activation of key reading-related areas increase. Even in previously illiterate adults, researchers have observed the development of the same neural networks (dorsal and ventral) as the adults learn to read that emerge in children during the acquisition of reading skills (Dehaene et al., 2015). In adults, dorsal activation begins with the onset of literacy skills. Ventral route activation is slower to develop, but gains have also been demonstrated here. Thus, learning to read results in brain reorganization across age groups.

MULTIFACTORIAL CAUSAL MODELS OF DYSLEXIA

Finally, genetic research has yielded insights into the role of genetics and heritability on the manifestation of dyslexia. Specifically, certain heritable gene combinations place individuals at risk for reading difficulty (Church et al., 2021). As a result, these individuals have a greater likelihood of experiencing difficulty learning to read than the typical population. However, having a particular genetic profile does not mean an individual will grow up to have dyslexia. Thus, in contrast to historical conceptualizations of dyslexia as a fixed or predetermined condition resulting from a person's genetic makeup, contemporary conceptualizations demonstrate that dyslexia results from the interaction between biological factors and the environment. Therefore, although a child may be predisposed to dyslexia due to the inheritance of a specific genetic profile, other internal and external factors can serve as a buffer in the severity of the expression of the condition. As a result of the interactive relationship between biology and environment, most causal models of dyslexia take into account a variety of factors that interact over time to produce different degrees of reading skill (Pennington,

2006). Thus, these interactional models account for the interplay between genetic and environmental risk factors. But what are the factors at play, and how do they interact?

In 2006, Bruce Pennington proposed a *multiple deficit model* for conceptualizing the etiology (i.e., the cause or set of causes) of developmental disorders (see Figure 4.5). *Developmental disorders* are conditions that begin during initial development (i.e., initiating in childhood) and are typically present throughout the lifespan. Developmental disorders include autism spectrum disorders, attention deficit/hyperactivity, intellectual disability, and learning disorders. Indeed, it is widely accepted that these disorders are not caused by a single cognitive deficit associated with a single gene. Research on commonly co-occurring disorders (e.g., dyslexia and ADHD) has been particularly instructive for understanding the relationship between genes and the manifestation of complex behavioral disorders. For example, researchers have found that the same gene can influence different traits (e.g., phonology and attention; a construct called *pleiotropy*), yet the expression of a particular trait may occur only in relation to the presence of other factors. Thus, there is evidence of genetic overlap in developmental disorders. Similarly, there is

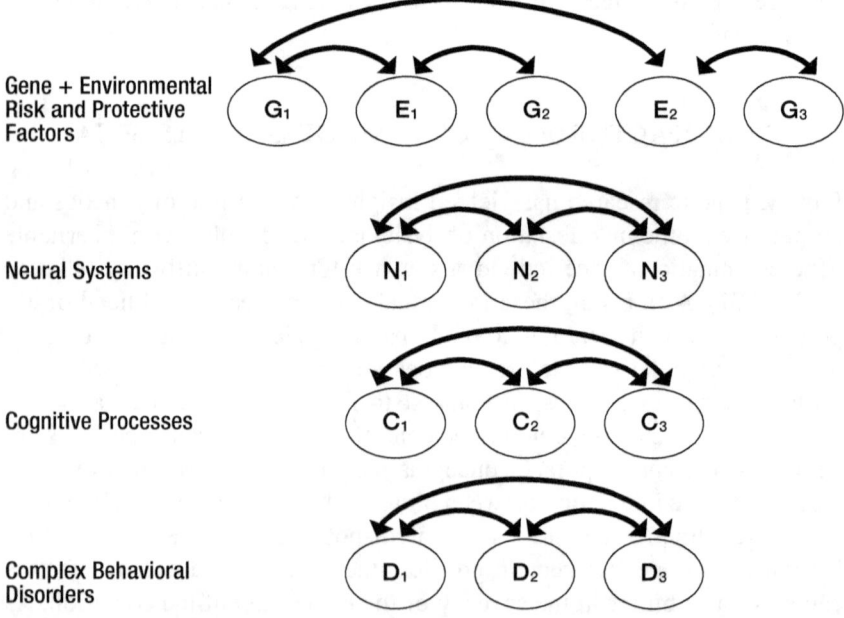

Figure 4.5. Multiple deficit model

Note. G = genetic risk or protective factor, E = environmental risk or protective factor, N = neural system, C = cognitive process, D = disorder. Adapted from "From single to multiple deficit models of developmental disorders," by B. F. Pennington, 2006, *Cognition, 101,* 385 – 413. Copyright 2006 by Elsevier. Adapted with permission.

evidence of cognitive overlap; multiple cognitive factors likely contribute to the expression of a complex behavioral condition like difficulty learning to read (Wilcutt et al., 2005). Finally, genetics, the environment, and behaviors affect neural systems. For example, difficulty with reading will result in less exposure to words, which limits the type of neural systems development discussed in the previous section on neuroimaging.

Thus, Pennington's *multiple deficit model* represents the interaction between (a) genes and the environment (Level 1); (b) highly plastic neural systems (Level 2); (c) measurable cognitive traits (e.g., phonological awareness, inhibition, processing speed; Level 3); and (d) complex, observable behavior disorders (Level 4). In addition, interactions between levels (not represented on the diagram) further contribute to the manifestation of the disorder(s). Finally, and of particular importance, these factors change over time, such that difficulty in phonology at a young age may not result in a reading disability later.

Researchers have identified several internal and external factors that influence the expression of dyslexia. Understanding these factors further contributes to a deeper understanding of dyslexia and points to possible approaches for addressing reading difficulties.

Internal Factors

Dyslexia is both familial and hereditary. *Familial* means that dyslexia runs in families. A child of a parent with dyslexia has a 40 percent to 60 percent risk of developing dyslexia (Schumacher et al., 2007). Additional evidence of genetic influence comes from twin studies. Monozygotic twins have a concordance rate of about 60 percent (i.e., a 60 percent likelihood of exhibiting dyslexia) in contrast to dizygotic twins, who have a concordance rate of around 30 percent (Paracchini, 2022). These findings demonstrate a clear genetic basis for dyslexia (Bishop, 2009). However, remember that while a particular genetic profile can increase the likelihood of dyslexia, other genes can serve as protective or mitigating influences.

Further, even for conditions with a clear genetic marker, there is often not a one-to-one correspondence between the genotype (i.e., the existence of a specific gene) and the phenotype (i.e., expression of the predicted condition). Therefore, although genes can influence the presentation of dyslexia, other factors play a role in the degree of reading difficulty a person will experience. Current findings from genetic research indicate that, given the complexity of reading behavior, it is likely that multiple genes contribute to dyslexia; in other words, reading disability is not likely caused by a few select genes (Paracchini, 2022). These findings align with Pennington's (2006) multiple deficit model.

Second, several linguistic factors have been identified as potential contributors to dyslexia. As is well-addressed within models of word reading and demonstrated in behavioral research, difficulty with phonology is often considered a primary risk factor associated with dyslexia. Researchers have consistently demonstrated that difficulty in processing the sounds of language contributes to difficulty in learning to read (Peterson & Pennington, 2015). However, not all students with dyslexia demonstrate difficulty with phonological awareness (Pennington et al., 2012). These findings suggest that other factors can contribute, independently or in conjunction with phonological deficits, in the manifestation of reading difficulty.

Specifically, difficulty with rapid automatized naming (RAN; also called *naming speed*) and oral language deficits have been identified as additional linguistic risk factors (Georgiou & Parrila, 2013). RAN refers to the ability to quickly name a series of items. For example, a RAN assessment will test the speed by which a person can connect visually presented information (e.g., a series of letters, numbers, colors, or objects) to the linguistic processes needed to state the name of the items (Kirby et al., 2010). Considerable research has demonstrated that slow naming speed is characteristic of students with dyslexia, and naming speed makes a unique contribution outside of phonology to reading ability (Kirby et al., 2010; Vander Stappen & Van Reybroeck, 2018). Similarly, specific language impairments also are considered contributing linguistic risk factors. Oral language problems are among the earliest predictors of dyslexia (Snowling & Melby-Lervåg, 2016). Specific aspects of oral language other than phonology, which has been previously addressed, include semantics (e.g., vocabulary knowledge, morphological awareness) and syntax (e.g., the capacity to produce grammatically correct sentences). As accounted for in the triangle model of reading, semantics makes a unique but interconnected contribution to reading ability.

External Factors

As reflected in the multiple deficit model, internal conditions interact with external environmental conditions, which can serve as additive risk factors or protective agents. One external source is the writing system itself. Learning to read in more orthographically transparent languages is easier, as evidenced by the speed of reading acquisition and the fewer people identified with dyslexia (Ziegler & Goswami, 2005). Poverty is another external environmental factor associated with increased risk. Low socioeconomic status correlates with many conditions, including reduced language and literacy exposure, low maternal education, stress, and poor nutrition, all of which can increase risk (Dilnot et al., 2017). Although poverty-related factors can contribute to risk, other external factors can serve as protective factors. For example, considerable evidence has demonstrated that a robust home literacy environment can serve as a protective factor (Torppa et al., 2022). Similarly, preschool and school literacy instruction can also serve as a protective agent. Specifically, researchers have found that early intervention can reduce the severity of reading difficulty (Gabrieli, 2009; Lovett et al., 2017).

SUMMARY

Reading science sheds light on the underlying cognitive processes involved in reading and provides frameworks and tools for exploring the manifestation of dyslexia. Despite the complexity of reading development, individual lines of research add depth of understanding of component parts, and interactive frameworks help us to understand the interdependency of these factors over time. Thus, we leave this chapter wiser than the blind men with the elephant.

Reading science is inherently hopeful, as it demonstrates the malleability of reading performance. Although genetics and environment may contribute to difficulty with reading, brain plasticity reflects the potential of instruction for changing reading outcomes. Specifically, neuroscience underscores the importance of early intervention and the power of intervention at any age to improve the reading circuitry of the brain. Although observations from behavioral research have demonstrated the importance and efficacy of teaching sound-symbol relationships (i.e., phonics) within initial reading instruction, neuroscience confirms the foundational role phonological instruction plays in the development of the dorsal system and its relationship to the development of ventral pathways. In addition, individuals require ample exposure to print to facilitate fluent word-reading skills and growth in semantics, which are necessary for reading comprehension and developing a robust sight-word vocabulary.

Thus, one important conclusion that can be drawn from a deeper understanding of the reading brain and where difficulty in learning to read may reside is that students with dyslexia will likely benefit from multicomponent reading interventions that address key cognitive functions associated with fluent, accurate reading performance. Practices subsumed under the umbrella term *structured literacy* align with this recommendation.

Chapter Five

Structured Literacy: Word Recognition

Structured means "arranged . . . according to a plan so as to elicit a desired response or outcome. Also more loosely: formal, organized, not haphazard" (OED Online, 2022). Thus, *structured literacy* is an approach to teaching students to read and write that follows a plan to unfold the knowledge and skills necessary for accessing and producing written text. The approach is not haphazard but carefully sequenced. The concept of a structured approach to reading instruction runs contrary to romantic notions of natural, incidental learning. Rousseau painted a beautiful picture of Emile, a child who came to books when he wanted knowledge, and having a purpose for reading was all he needed to unlock the mysteries of written language.

Of course, we all know that motivation alone does not enable any skill. Instruction and practice are required for skill acquisition. A child surrounded by books will not learn to read, just as a child who watches a parent play the piano every day will not magically learn to read music or play the piano. Many parents feel guilty when their child struggles with reading: Perhaps I did not read enough to my child? Many teachers may also harbor similar assumptions: If only the literacy home environment were better, these children would read better. But the key to learning to read does not lie in motivation or prior exposure to text. The key to learning to read lies in a child's ability to understand the alphabetic principle that is the basis of all written alphabetic languages—words are composed of letters representing speech sounds. Decades of research on reading confirm that direct teaching of the code enables reading acquisition (Castles et al., 2018; Ehri, 2020; NICHD, 2000; Rose, 2006). It is the absence of *structured* teaching that leaves students grasping to make sense of the printed word.

Although the term *structured literacy* was officially coined by the International Dyslexia Association (IDA, 2019), the roots of the term can be traced back to the instructional methods of Webster, Orton, and other advocates of systematic methods for teaching English orthography. Such structured approaches contrast with progressive education beliefs that learning should be natural, unstructured, and internally motivated. For progressive educators, student difficulty with learning to read has often been attributed to a lack of readiness or motivation or emotional and social issues. In other words, difficulty with reading lay primarily within the reader. As these ideas took hold in the early part of the 1900s, it was scholars such as Orton who suggested that *the methods* used to teach reading may be at the heart of reading difficulty (Chall, 1997).

Advocates for structured approaches to teaching reading have noted that despite differences in students—whether limited exposure to early literacy experiences or internal conditions such as dyslexia—a key differentiator between students who learned to read and those who did not was their exposure to methods that directly taught them how written language works (Castles et al., 2018). Thus, although the term *structured literacy* is relatively new, the principles that undergird the concept have been integral to effective reading instruction for centuries.

Notably, the concept of structured literacy is *descriptive* rather than *prescriptive*. That is, structured literacy guidelines do not provide explicit recommendations on what materials must be used (e.g., magnetic letters, sound boxes, morphology matrices) or endorse a particular pace or scope and sequence (e.g., introduce three letter-sound correspondences per week, teach continuous sounds [/mmmm/, /ssss/] before stop sounds [/b/, /g/], teach students to write the letter *c* before the letter *w*). Instead, practices captured under the construct of *structured literacy* align with basic principles extracted from many different research studies. For example, numerous studies have confirmed the value of teaching phonics. As *phonics instruction* is a method for teaching reading that involves directly teaching sound-symbol correspondence, it is not surprising that teaching a person to read an alphabetic writing system requires direct teaching of the code. Research has confirmed, though, that various methods for directly teaching the code are effective (Chall, 1996; Ehri et al., 2001; Torgesen, 2002). In addition, these different methods are more effective than non–code-based approaches (Ehri et al., 2001). Therefore, the broad recommendation to "directly teach the code" is a fundamental principle of structured literacy.

Despite the apparent need to teach students sound-symbol correspondence, phonics instruction is only one part of a comprehensive approach to literacy subsumed under the umbrella concept of structured literacy. As we explored in Chapter 4, understanding word meaning (semantics) and language structure (oral and written) also plays a part in word recognition and comprehension. To boost students' knowledge and skills in these areas, research has demonstrated the power of planned and sequenced (i.e., structured) instruction, particularly for struggling readers, in vocabulary (Elleman et al., 2009; NICHD, 2000), morphology (Galuschka et al., 2020), and comprehension (Filderman et al., 2022). Similarly, as literacy involves not only reading text but also producing written language, writing is an integral aspect of a comprehensive approach to literacy instruction (Graham et al., 2018).

Given all these things, what is a *structured literacy* approach? Structured literacy refers to instruction that reflects features and content associated with gains in reading development. Instructional features refer to *how* teachers provide instruction. Structured approaches are direct, systematic, and cumulative. The content of structured literacy involves *what* teachers teach. The content elements of structured literacy include the knowledge and skills that underlie proficient reading and writing, namely phonemic awareness, phonics, orthography (specifically, an understanding of spelling patterns), morphology, syntax, and semantics (IDA, 2019; Spear-Swerling, 2022). Given the broad framework of structured literacy, many commercially available programs align with a structured literacy approach. Similarly, teacher-designed instruction and intervention can align with a structured literacy approach.

This chapter will focus on one aspect of structured literacy—word recognition. To do so, we will revisit Gough and Tunmer's the Simple View of Reading (see Figure 5.1). Their theory can help us organize our thinking about the interrelated aspects of literacy instruction, namely those aspects associated with unlocking word recognition skills and those associated with bringing meaning to reading and writing (i.e., language comprehension). Under the umbrella construct of *word recognition*, we will explore areas of instruction aimed at teaching students to quickly and accurately identify words as well as write and spell words accurately. In the next chapter (Chapter 6), techniques for building language comprehension will be explored, focusing on knowledge building and discourse writing.

WORD RECOGNITION

In Chapter 2, we traced the history of English orthography. English is an alphabetic language, meaning letters and letter combinations represent speech sounds. Therefore, teaching students to read begins by teaching them how the alphabet works. Specifically, students need to learn which speech sounds are represented by the letters and letter combinations they find within words. Thus, a structured approach to reading instruction will begin with grapheme-phoneme correspondence instruction (i.e., basic phonics instruction). Once

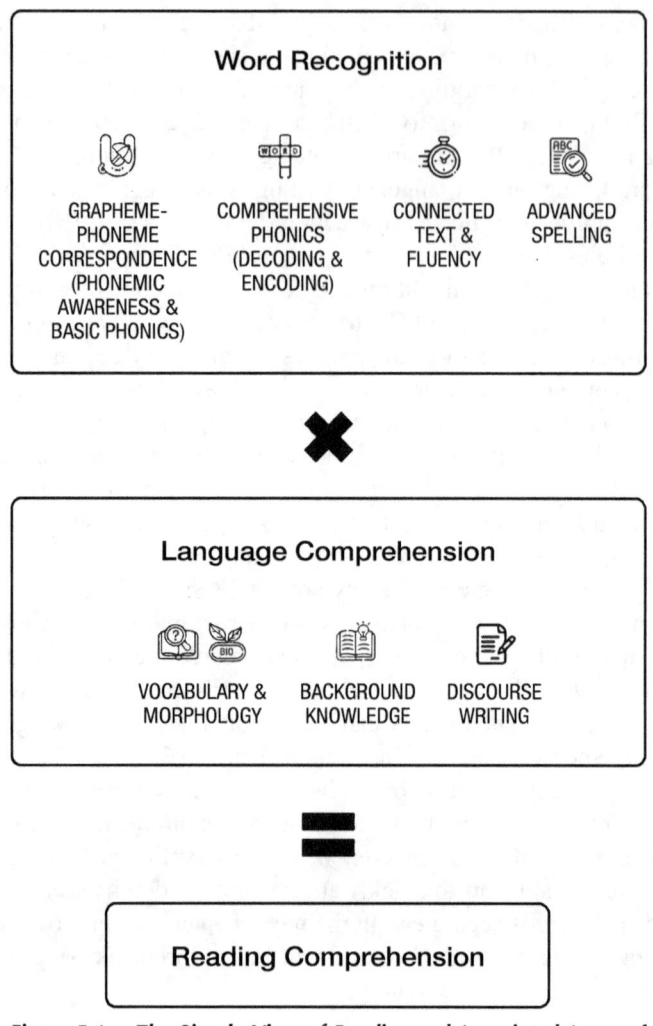

Figure 5.1. *The Simple View of Reading* and Associated Areas of Instruction

foundational grapheme-phoneme correspondence is established, teachers can introduce more complex spelling patterns and multisyllabic words (i.e., comprehensive phonics instruction). As students learn these concepts, they practice applying those skills by reading words, sentences, and longer passages (i.e., reading connected text). Each stage of this process is further supported by making a reading-writing connection (i.e., encoding/spelling instruction; Graham et al., 2018; Shanahan & Lomax, 1986). As students hear sounds, they will spell the sounds. As students hear words, they will spell the words.

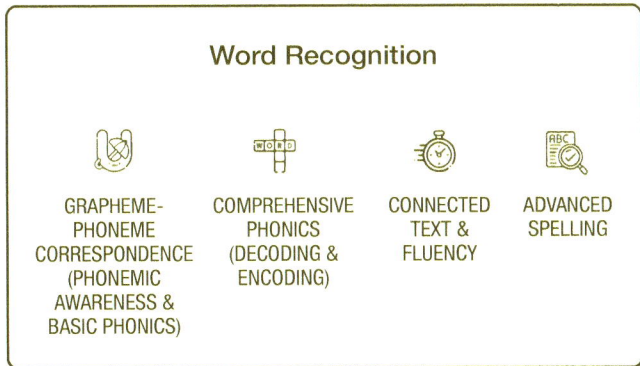

Figure 5.2. Elements of Instruction that Contribute to Word Recognition

As students hear sentences, they will write the sentences. Finally, advanced spelling instruction that includes the teaching of morphology will enhance students' word recognition skills. As such, each of these elements of instruction contributes to the word recognition aspect of the Simple View of Reading equation (see Figure 5.2).

Grapheme-Phoneme Correspondence

Grapheme-phoneme correspondence involves attention to phonology (speech sounds) and orthography (letters and letter patterns). Mastery of an alphabetic language allows students to move from print to speech (seeing a written word and being able to decode it) and from speech to print (translating a spoken word into written form). The print-to-speech translation is called *reading*, whereas speech-to-print translation occurs during *spelling*. Integrating reading and spelling during grapheme-phoneme correspondence instruction strengthens students' awareness and understanding of the alphabetic principle (Bazis et al., 2022).

Phonemic Awareness and Phonics

Mapping speech sounds to letters involves isolating phonemes within words. Separating phonemes is difficult, as most phonemes are co-articulated. For example, students can struggle to identify individual sounds within words when presented with tasks such as "What is the first sound in the word *mat*? or "What is the last sound in the word *fish*?" Ample research has demonstrated that although it is difficult for young children and some struggling readers to separate phonemes within words, with appropriate instruction, students can learn to unglue the sounds of spoken language (Rice et al., 2022). Tools such as tokens, blocks, or felt pieces can be used as a concrete representation of moving, separating, or replacing speech sounds. Research has also demonstrated that using letters, such as magnetic letters, letter cards, or digital letters, during phonemic awareness instruction is a particularly efficient and effective way to build students' understanding of the alphabetic principle (NICHD, 2000; Rehfeld et al., 2022).

Thus, a reciprocal relationship exists between phonemic awareness and phonics. As students learn letter-sound correspondences, their awareness of individual speech sounds increases. Similarly, as students' ability to separate speech sounds develops, their ability to map speech sounds to letters and letter patterns improves. In other words, phonemic awareness is integral to learning to read and spell. For teachers, modeling clear, accurate phoneme production can facilitate students' reading and spelling development.

Phonemic awareness is the ability to identify and manipulate individual sounds in spoken language. Surprisingly, many teachers are unable to accurately and fluently model phoneme production (Sayeski et al., 2017). Yet, the ability to hear, produce, and manipulate phonemes lies at the heart of reading and spelling. Therefore, a critical first step for planning for reading is understanding the elements of effective alphabet instruction.

Thankfully, researchers have identified teaching practices that facilitate learning letter-sound relationships and those that hinder or slow the learning process. For example, teaching a letter a week in alphabetical order is an inefficient and ineffective practice (Jones & Reutzel, 2012; Justice et al., 2006; Sunde et al., 2020). Although it may seem logical to start with the letter *a* and move systematically through all the letters of the alphabet, this practice is problematic for several reasons. First, students begin school with varying knowledge of letters. For students who enter school knowing quite a few letters, the slow pace of teaching is not an effective use of their instructional time.

In contrast, for students with limited familiarity with letters, the letter-of-the-week pace of instruction will be far too slow for these students to acquire the knowledge needed to move from letter-sound correspondence to reading words in a timely manner (Piasta & Wagner, 2010b). In other words, the faster students are introduced to letters, the faster they can apply that letter knowledge to the tasks of reading and spelling. A second problem with the letter-per-week approach is that the approach limits the amount of practice with letters by means of reading and spelling in which students can engage. Specifically, researchers have found that earlier access to letters facilitates earlier reading and spelling performance (Ehri, 2004; Jones et al., 2013). The sooner students can read and spell basic words, the more practice they get, which promotes automaticity. A third reason for not teaching a letter per week is that some letters and letter patterns occur more frequently within beginning reading texts. For example, the letters *v*, *j*, and *q* appear less often in the single-syllable words commonly contained within early readers. By teaching letters in order from more commonly occurring to less commonly occurring, teachers can get students to practice reading and spelling with a greater volume of words sooner within an academic year (Solity & Vousden, 2009).

A more efficient way for students to learn the code is to teach letters at a faster pace (Jones & Reutzel, 2012). Contrary to what may be assumed, a quicker pace of instruction has been demonstrated to be particularly beneficial to students who start school with minimal alphabet knowledge (Sunde et al., 2020; Vadasy & Sanders, 2021). Changing the sequence of instruction to reflect highly occurring letter-sound correspondences facilitates a faster transition from letter learning in isolation to word reading and spelling, moving students who enter school behind in their skills on a faster track for learning (Carnine et al., 1997). For example, if the first letter-sound correspondences a student learns are the most common sounds for the letters *a*, *m*, *t*, *s*, and *p*, the student can *blend* those sounds to read *mat*, *Sam*, *at*, *am*, *pat*, *Pam*, *tap*, and *map*. Conversely, students can *segment* the sounds in words for spelling. The sooner students see the connection between learning their letters and reading and spelling words, the sooner they will internalize the alphabetic principle.

Finally, debate exists regarding the importance of directly teaching students letter names. Some reading researchers have argued that learning letter names facilitates letter-sound learning (Adams, 1990; Ehri, 1998). For many letters, the letter name provides an auditory cue of its sound, either at the beginning or end of its name. For example, the name of the letter *b* begins with the /b/ sound, /bē/, and the name of the letter *f* ends with its sound, /ĕf/. In contrast, other scholars advocate directly teaching sounds and only teaching letter names after students have learned letter sounds (McGuinness, 2004). In a sounds-first approach, the letter *m* would be referred to as /m/. Within a sounds-first approach, teachers (and parents) would remark, "Write /m/," or "Find the /m/ in the word." Sounds-first advocates point out that letter name knowledge is not necessary for decoding words; students only need to be able to blend sounds to decode words. The same is true for spelling; knowledge of the letter name is not necessary to spell a word. In addition, although many letter names reflect letter sounds, some letters do not, which can cause confusion. For example, the letter name for *y* begins with the /w/ sound, and the letter name for *w* begins with the /d/ sound.

Interestingly, a somewhat natural comparison of approaches to alphabet learning was conducted by comparing the learning outcomes of students in the United States with students in England (Treiman et al., 2013). Instruction in the United States focuses on teaching letter names first. This cultural practice begins in the home with families and continues within early childhood classrooms (Ellefson et al., 2009). Within England, however, families and schools adopt a sounds-first approach. In addition to this difference in how letters are addressed, formal instruction in England begins during *reception year*, when students are around four years of age, rather than at five years of age, when U.S. students start kindergarten.

For the study, researchers compared the spelling performance of students at the end of their first year or years of schooling (United States, ~ age 6 after kindergarten; England, ~ age 5 after reception year; England, ~age 6 after Year 1) of schooling. Findings from the study demonstrated that all students performed better when asked to spell words with short vowel sounds (e.g., *bag, mud, dock*) than when asked to spell words with long vowel sounds (e.g., *gate, bike*). However, Year 1 students in England produced more correctly spelled short vowel words than U.S. kindergarteners. In addition, for long vowel sounds, students in the United States were more likely to use a single letter (e.g., spelling the word *game* as *gam*). This error is likely attributed to students using the letter name, /ā/, to spell the word rather than its sound /ă/. When students in England made such an error, which was less prevalent, they were more likely to use an uppercase letter (e.g., gAm). In England, letter names are typically taught using capital letters *after* letter sounds have been taught. Thus, students in England were more likely to associate a lowercase *a* with the short vowel sound /ă/ and the letter name /ā/ with an uppercase letter *A*. Correspondingly, students in England were less likely to select an uppercase form of a letter when asked to identify a letter by its sound (e.g., "Point to /ă/") than were students in the United States. When asked to spell nonwords (e.g., *pum, gop*), though, reception year students performed significantly worse than U.S. kindergartners on spelling (5-year-olds vs. 6-year-olds). However, the additional year of schooling did not provide a notable difference in spelling between the Year 1 students in England and the U.S. kindergartners (6-year-olds vs. 6-year-olds). Thus, although cultural differences, as expressed by informal and formal instruction, do appear to affect the spelling patterns of students, a significant advantage was not demonstrated by a sounds-first emphasis.

Other research reviews on alphabet learning bear similar findings (Piasta & Wagner, 2010a; Roberts, 2021). Findings from these research syntheses demonstrate that although there may be a slight benefit from a sounds-first approach, no harm is done by teaching letter names, and for some children, a slight advantage may be found in teaching them. Further, teaching names and sounds simultaneously appears more beneficial than a names-only or sounds-only approach (Roberts, 2021). However, the most potent effects for alphabet learning seem to occur when alphabet instruction is part of a multicomponent instructional approach.

Specifically, differences in *how* letters are taught can result in meaningful differences in learning outcomes. For example, embedding mnemonics within letter instruction (e.g., making the letter *a* look like an apple or using letter characters such as "Dippy the Duck" for the letter *d*), adding a fluency component (i.e., having students practice recalling letter names or sounds quickly), and connecting multiple modalities (e.g., seeing letters and saying sounds, hearing sounds and writing letters, attending to mouth movements when producing sounds) all contribute to more robust alphabet learning (Roberts, 2021).

In summary, researchers have found that effective alphabet learning can occur within either a sounds-first or letter-names-first approach. More important is the manner in which instruction occurs. Efficient instruction will move students rapidly from individual letter-sound work to reading words (i.e., decoding). Instruction will integrate hearing sounds and spelling those sounds (/ă/ = *a*), seeing letters and making the sounds those letters represent (*m* = /m/), and applying letter-sound knowledge for decoding (reading) and encoding (spelling). These practices rely on teacher knowledge of correct phoneme production.

Phoneme Pronunciation

There are approximately 44 distinct phonemes in English.[1] Some phonemes are relatively easy to pronounce in isolation, such as /m/ and /s/, whereas others present more of a challenge. For example, consider /b/, /r/, and /ng/. Those sounds are definitely more tricky to produce! Within this section, we will explore why some sounds are more difficult to isolate and the techniques for teaching them, but we will start with unpacking the features of phonemes that make them unique. Teachers who know the differences and similarities across phonemes can help students who may be confusing sounds, have difficulty producing sounds, or are unable to hear or separate individual phonemes in words. Knowledgeable and skilled teachers will say things such as: "Watch my mouth as I produce this sound" or "That sound is similar to this sound. Except for when we make this sound, our voice is turned on, and for the other it is not. Let's practice" or "Place your tongue behind the top of your teeth and try to make that sound again."

Phonemes are divided into two classes: consonants and vowels. Although most teachers associate consonants and vowels with specific letters (i.e., vowels are the letters *a, e, i, o, u,* and sometimes *y,* and consonants are the rest), the terms *consonants* and *vowels* refer to the speech sounds those letters

---

1. Separating speech sounds is difficult, which is why even linguists disagree on the exact number of distinct phonemes. Of course, dialect and regional differences in pronunciation also contribute to the differences.

represent (Moats, 2020a). Consider the word *cow*. The phonemes in *cow* are /k/ and /aʊ/. The symbol /aʊ/ is the International Phonetic Alphabet (IPA)[2] symbol for the sound spelled with the letters *o* and *w* in words like *how*, *brown*, and *crown*. Knowing that consonants and vowels are sounds can be helpful for teachers when they need to explain spelling variations to students as they introduce more advanced phonics concepts. So, if consonants and vowels are sounds, what should teachers know about these sounds?

Consonants. First, consonants are a class of sounds produced via obstruction of air by the lips, teeth, tongue, or a combination of those parts of the mouth. The phonemes /b/ and /p/, for example, are produced by pressing the lips together. In contrast, the phonemes /t/ and /d/ are produced by pressing the tongue to the back of the teeth. The consonants /f/ and /v/ are produced by placing the top teeth on the bottom lip. Phonemes can also be *voiced* (i.e., produced as a result of vocal cord vibration) or *unvoiced* (i.e., produced without vocal cord engagement). Place your hand on your throat. Now say the phoneme pairs that were just introduced, /b/ and /p/, /t/ and /d/, and /f/ and /v/. Did you feel the vibration when you produced the /b/, /d/, and /v/ phonemes? Those phonemes are voiced. Phonemes are also classified as *continuants* or *stops*. Continuant phonemes can be produced uninterrupted for the duration of a breath (e.g., /mmmm/, /ŏŏŏŏ/, /ssss/). In contrast, stop phonemes are produced by stopping airflow (e.g., /k/, /g/, /h/). These sounds cannot be stretched. Teachers and parents often add a vowel to the end of these phonemes when teaching them (e.g., k is "kuh," g is "guh"). Adding a vowel to the consonant can make blending and segmenting phonemes more difficult. For example, a student blending the sounds in the word *bat* may say /buh/-/ă/-/tuh/ and struggle to blend those sounds to produce a recognizable word (e.g., "Buatuh?"). Similarly, students segmenting sounds for spelling can encounter similar difficulties, leading them to use incorrect or unnecessary vowels when spelling words. Teachers who know where and how sounds are produced are more likely to model clear, crisp phonemes for their students.

Recall the research that demonstrated *how* grapheme-phoneme correspondence is taught significantly impacts student learning (Roberts, 2021). One technique that can enhance mastery of phonemes is teaching students articulatory gestures (i.e., the movements of the mouth required for phoneme production). Researchers have found that students with dyslexia or at risk for reading difficulty benefit from being taught articulatory gestures (Boyer & Ehri, 2011; Fälth et al., 2017; Galazka et al., 2021). To teach students articu-

---

2. Within the International Phonetic Alphabet (IPA), each speech sound is represented by one symbol, which allows for a precise representation of phonemes. However, as most teachers and families are not familiar with IPA, those symbols are used only sparingly throughout this book.

latory gestures, teachers need to know which articulators (e.g., lips, tongue, teeth) and by what manner of articulation (e.g., short burst of air, vibrating vocal cords) the sound is produced.

Table 5.1 lists consonants grouped by their place and manner of articulation. Teachers can use information from this chart to inform their production of a precise phoneme model and understand the difficulty students may experience in differentiating sounds produced in similar ways but with subtle differences.

There are six categories of consonants: stops, nasals, fricatives, affricatives, glides, and liquids. As discussed earlier, *stops* are produced when air is constricted by an articulator (lips, teeth, tongue, or a combination) and then explodes in a burst of air. There are three pairs of stops: (a) /p/ and /b/, which are produced by bringing the lips together; (b) /t/ and /d/, which are produced by placing the tongue behind the teeth; and (c) /k/ and /g/, which are produced by raising the tongue against the soft palate in the back of the mouth. The only difference between the pairs is voicing.

As the goal of phoneme instruction is for students to map speech sounds to graphemes, Table 5.1 also includes spelling variations for each phoneme. Although the number of spelling variations may seem overwhelming, remember that a structured approach to reading instruction begins with the most common sound-spelling pairings and systematically introduces new spelling patterns as students gain familiarity with the most common associations (i.e., the bolded spellings).

Table 5.1. Consonant Labels and Spelling Variations

Stops						Nasals		
/p/	/b/*	/t/	/d/*	/k/	/g/*	/m/*	/n/*	/ng/*
p	**b**	**t**, -ed, -bt, -pt	**d**, -ed	**c, k,** -**ck,** ch	**g**, gh	**m**, mb	**n**, -gn, kn	**-ng**

Fricatives								
/f/	/v/*	/th/	/th/*	/s/	/z/	/sh/	/zh/*	/h/
f, -ff, ph, -gh	**v**	**th**	**th**	**s, c,** -ss, sc, ps	**z, s,** -zz	**sh,** ch, ti, si, ci, xi	si, s	**h**

Liquids		Affricates		Glides			Two Sounds	
/l/*	/r/*	/ch/	/j/*	/hw/	/w/*	/y/*	/kw/	/ks/
l, -ll	**r**, wr	**ch,** -tch	**j, g,** -dge	**wh**	**w,** wh	**y**	**qu**	**x**

*Indicates that the sound is voiced.

Nasals are produced by allowing air to flow through the nasal cavity. Say /mmmm/. Now hold your nose while saying /mmmm/. Most consonants are produced in the oral cavity, but nasals are not. The position of the mouth to produce /m/ is the same as it is at the beginning of /b/ and /p/ (i.e., lips together). Similarly, the mouth position for /n/ is the same as for /t/ and /d/, with the tongue behind the teeth. Finally, the /ng/ is produced in the same manner as /k/ and /g/, with the tongue raised in the back of the mouth.

Fricatives are produced as a result of friction caused by the partial obstruction of airflow—a steady but restricted flow of air results when these sounds are produced. Fricatives, similar to stops, can be grouped into voiced and unvoiced pairs: (a) /f/ and /v/, which are produced by placing the teeth on the bottom lip; (b) /th/ and /th/, which are produced by placing the tongue between the teeth; (c) /s/ and /z/, which are produced by placing the tongue behind the teeth; and (d) /sh/ and /zh/, which are produced by pulling the tongue to the back in the mouth. The only fricative without a partner is /h/, which is produced via restricted airflow through the throat.

Affricates are a combination of a stop and fricative. There is one pair of affricates in English, /ch/ and /j/. The phonemes combine the stops /t/ and /d/ with the fricatives /sh/ and /zh/, respectively[3] (e.g., /t+sh/ = unvoiced affricate; /d+zh/ = voiced affricate). The spelling variations of these sounds reflect these combinations. For example, the /ch/ sound can be spelled *-tch* in words like *patch* and *twitch,* whereas the /j/ sound is spelled with *-dge* in words like *judge* and *badge*.

Liquids are among the most challenging phonemes to produce. Liquids are produced when the tongue creates a partial closure in the mouth, resulting in a resonant, vowel-like sound. There are two liquids, /l/ and /r/. To produce the /l/ phoneme, the tongue is lifted behind the teeth on the hard part (rounded bump) of the top of the mouth called the alveolar ridge. The /r/ sound is produced by pulling the tongue behind that ridge while the tongue is floating, not touching the roof or bottom of the mouth.

Glides are continuant sounds that precede vowels; in other words, the sound *glides* into a vowel. There are three glides, /hw/ as in *white* and *which*, /w/ as in *water* and *well*, and /y/ as in *yes* and *yarn*. Although the /hw/ phoneme is the voiceless partner of the voiced /w/, many Americans no longer make that distinction in their speech. As a result, teachers tend to teach the same pronunciation for *wh* and *w*.

Finally, the phonemes chart includes two letters of the alphabet that reflect two sounds. As discussed in the next section, many teachers begin by teaching the most common sound of single letters of the alphabet. For a sounds-spelling chart to be complete, those pairings are included. The letter *q* is

---

3. Using IPA notation, /ch/ is expressed as /tʃ/, and /j/ is written as /dʒ/.

produced by combining the phonemes /k/ and /w/. The letter *x* is produced by combining /k/ and /s/. Further, as *u* always follow the letter *q* in English spellings,[4] the spelling of the /kw/ phoneme is *qu*.

Vowels. The second class of phonemes consists of vowels. Vowels are unobstructed speech sounds produced with an open mouth. There are fifteen vowels in English, with an additional three created when an /r/ is added (i.e., /er/, /ar/, /or/). All vowels are continuants and voiced. The position of the lips, tongue, and vocal cavity determines the distinguishing features of the sound. The majority of vowels are typically presented in a U shape referred to as the *Vowel Valley* (see Figure 5.3). The U is a visual representation that indicates the position and height of the tongue as it moves from the front of the mouth, where the tongue is high and front, and the mouth is smiling (e.g., /ē/ and /ĭ/), down to the bottom of the mouth where the tongue is low and the mouth is wide open (e.g., /ŏ/), and, finally, to the back of the mouth where the tongue is high and back and the mouth becomes small and rounded (e.g., /ū/).

Word Recognition

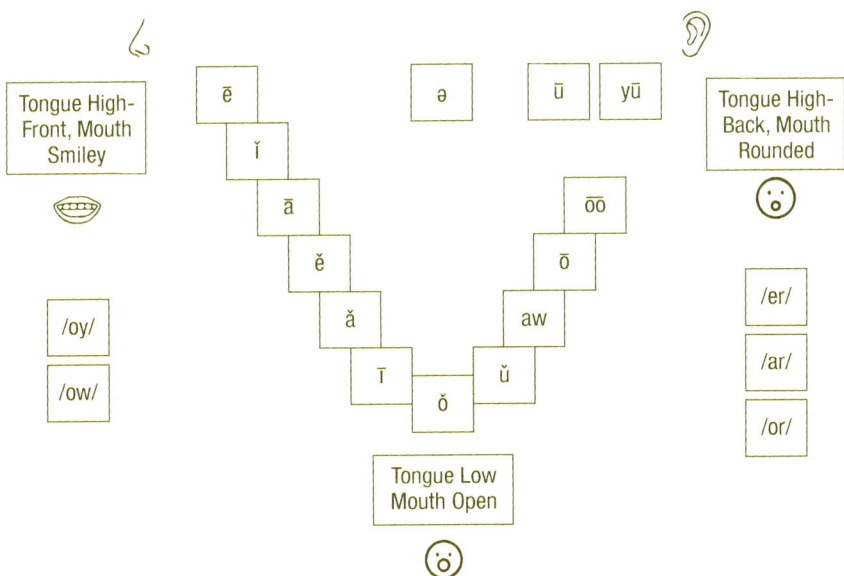

Figure 5.3. Vowel Valley

---

4. There are some words used in English in which the *q* is not followed by a *u* but these words are often of Arabic, Chinese, or Hebrew origin (e.g., burqa, cinq).

The chin will drop as the phonemes on the left side of Figure 5.3 are pronounced and then slowly close when moving up the right side of the chart. In addition, the lips will change from smiling (down the left side of the chart) to rounded (up the right side of the chart).

Phonemes not included in the Vowel Valley are two *diphthongs*, the *r-controlled vowels*, and the *schwa* [ə]. *Diphthongs* are vowels that glide from one sound to another. The two diphthongs not included in the Vowel Valley are /oy/ and /ou/. These are represented in IPA with two symbols that denote the sounds contained within the phoneme, /ɔɪ/ and /aʊ/. *R-controlled vowels* occur when an *r* immediately follows the letters *a, e, i, o*, or *u*. The presence of the *r* influences the pronunciation of the vowel to create a unique sound (i.e., /er/, /or/, /ar/). The schwa is an unstressed sound that primarily occurs in multisyllabic words. Teachers often refer to the schwa as a lazy vowel, a vowel too tired to say its regular sounds. The underlined letters in the following words represents the schwa: *about, family, banana, item, pencil*, and *carrot*. Teachers need to be aware of the schwa, as it can influence students' spelling.

Finally, vowels are commonly referred to as *short* and *long*. These terms differentiate between the /ă/ in *mat* (short) and the /ā/ in *mate* (long). Although the duration of long vowel pronunciation is variable and determined by the features of the consonant that follows the vowel (i.e., vowels are shorter before voiceless consonants; consider *mate* vs. *made*). Vowels are also categorized by the amount of tension used to produce a sound. *Tense vowels* are produced with more tension in the tongue. In contrast, *lax vowels* are produced with less tension. Feel the difference in your jaw as you switch from saying /ā/ (tense) to /ă/ (lax) or from /ō/ (tense) to /ŏ/ (lax). Lax vowels typically occur in one-syllable words ending in a consonant, such as *put, bat, mob*, and *clutch*.

Knowing the similarities and differences across sounds can help teachers pinpoint pronunciation and spelling challenges their students may experience when learning to read. As a final note, dialect will influence teachers' and students' pronunciation of sounds. Noting students' natural variations helps teachers guide students in matching students' phoneme pronunciation to letters for reading and writing.

Comprehensive Phonics Instruction: From Basic to Advanced

Recall from Chapter 3 Rudolf Flesch's three-step process for teaching a person to read the fictional language of Hottentot.

> The natural method will be this: First, your teacher will make you aware of the individual sounds you make when you talk Hottentot. Second, he will show you

the letter symbols that represent each of those sounds. Third, he will teach you how to write these symbols and combine them into words—and, at the same time, how to read them. (Flesch, 1955, p. 22)

At this point, you will be heartened to know that learning the sounds of English is the hardest part of teaching reading. Teachers with a firm grasp of the sounds of English and their subtle yet important variations will have a much easier time with the second part of the process—showing students which letter and letter patterns represent which sounds. Thus, it is a worthwhile endeavor for a teacher to practice hearing, producing, and manipulating the sounds of language. Knowing what they are, how they are produced, and why they differ from each other will make the process of teaching reading feel less daunting. Indeed, confidence in English phonemes will facilitate explaining and demonstrating sound-spelling mappings to students. Once a comprehensive understanding of those mappings is established, English will feel less haphazard and full of exceptions, and the logic that underlies English will be revealed (Eide, 2012).

Most teachers know that teaching the alphabet is part of reading instruction but do not know how to teach the alphabet (as described previously with the one-letter-per-week approach) or what to do when instruction goes beyond single-letter-sound correspondences (i.e., after alphabet instruction). Researchers have continually demonstrated that teachers have a weak grasp of the structure of English orthography. This, of course, is through no fault of their own; teachers simply are not being taught how English works within their preparation programs (Binks-Cantrell et al., 2012; Moats, 2014). Yet, knowledge of language structure is necessary for teachers to guide students in breaking words into their parts. Recall the epiphany of the struggling reader referred to in Chapter 1, who exclaimed: "Words have parts!" Indeed, words have parts. It is the teacher's job to show students how to break written words into those parts for decoding and to break spoken words into their parts for spelling.

Given the importance of phonics instruction, the negative connotations associated with phonics may be surprising to the general public and alarming to families of struggling readers. One reason for the resistance to phonics instruction is that many people possess an incomplete understanding of what phonics is. For many, phonics is simply learning the sound or sounds associated with each letter of the alphabet. Their phonetic knowledge may be limited to "The letter *m* makes the /m/ sound, the letter *a* makes the /ă/ sound, and the letter *t* makes the /t/ sound, etc." Further, those letters can be combined to make the word *mat* or *at* or *Tam*. This basic understanding works for many simple three- and even four-letter words, but readers will quickly encounter what appears to be an *exception*. For example, if the letter *s* is taught as representing the /s/ sound, beginning readers can change /mat/ to /sat/ but will experience confusion when presented with words like *is*, *his*, and *as* and plurals such as *birds*, *cars*, and *planes*. Strong phonics instruction goes beyond teaching single letters of the alphabet and a handful of rules (e.g., add the letter *e* to the end of a word to make a vowel say its name; mat → mate, hid → hide). Unfortunately, many elementary teachers are not taught how to go beyond the alphabet and rarely get information about how to teach the multiple sounds represented by a single letter or letter combination (e.g., *s* = /s/ and /z/; *a* = /ă/, /ā/, /ä/, /ô/; *ch* = /ch/, /k/, /sh/), and they receive almost no instruction on how to teach the more complex letter combinations (e.g., *-eigh*, *-gh*, *-dge*) or multisyllabic words (e.g., How do we get students from *mat* and *cat* to *purple*, *buttons*, and *water*?).

In addition to a lack of knowledge about English orthography, persistent myths about phonics hamper teachers' understanding of the value of phonics instruction within a comprehensive approach to reading (Castles et al., 2018). Table 5.2 presents a handful of commonly expressed myths about phonics. These falsely held beliefs reinforce the public perception that learning phonics is a dull and mindless endeavor that hinders students' ability to experience the joy and wonder stories and learning can bring. Of course, nothing could be further from the truth. Mastering the code is the onramp to reading independence.

Despite the prevalence of these persistent phonics myths, researchers have found that approximately 80% of single-syllable words can be pronounced by learning only a few patterns, and the other 20% typically only have one variation in grapheme pronunciation (e.g., the *pint* example presented in Table 5.2; Castles et al., 2018). Phonics instruction will facilitate students' attention to and capacity for adapting to these variations. For phonics instruction to be effective, though, instruction must be direct and explicit. A hangover of progressive education beliefs is the notion that natural, authentic, and embedded engagement is superior to artificial, decontextualized instruction. In other words, according to the "authentic and contextualized" viewpoint, exposing students to print through books would be superior to sound-spelling learning in isolation. An abundance of research has demonstrated that this is not the case.

Researchers have found that direct attention to letter-sound relationships during initial reading instruction is essential. Specifically, researchers have demonstrated that young children will not incidentally notice letter-sound relationships and generalize these connections to new words. Byrne and colleagues conducted a series of experiments to test whether students could induce (i.e., figure out on their own without direct instruction) letter-sound mappings (Byrne, 2005). Within the studies, for example, preschool students

Table 5.2. Phonics Myths

Myths	Facts
Phonics will destroy students' love of reading.	Students who are skilled readers enjoy reading (van Bergen et al., 2021). In other words, skills influence reading enjoyment. Conversely, being unable to read or being an inefficient reader is the most significant impediment to students' love of reading. Further, solving the mystery of reading is exciting and provides reading options students would not have otherwise.
Phonics is boring and tedious.	Students are naturally curious and can enjoy learning to decode words. In addition, the positive effects of initial success with decoding boost motivation, increase the likelihood of more reading, and can result in higher self-esteem (Castles et al., 2018; McArthur & Castles, 2017).
Phonics interferes with comprehension.	Ehri et al. (2001) conducted a meta-analysis that demonstrated phonics instruction facilitated comprehension. Specifically, automaticity in word-level reading frees mental processing capacity. Thus, phonics is necessary but not sufficient for comprehension. Content familiarity is also needed for meaning making.
English is too irregular for phonics instruction to be beneficial.	Partial decoding can lead to correct pronunciation. Partial decoding occurs when a student sounds out a word applying an incorrect letter-sound association but corrects the pronunciation by mapping the decoded word to a known word from oral vocabulary; for example, reading *pint* as /p//ĭ//n//t/ and then self-correcting to /p//ī//n//t/ (Share, 1995). In addition, comprehensive phonics instruction ensures that students will learn most sound-spelling relationships.
Phonics is developmentally inappropriate for young children; kindergarten is too early for phonics.	"Although conventional wisdom has suggested that kindergarten students might not be ready for phonics instruction, this assumption was not supported by data. The effects of systematic early phonics instruction were significant and substantial in kindergarten and the 1st grade, indicating that systematic phonics programs should be implemented at those age and grade levels." (NICHD, 2000, para. 22)

were shown the words *fat* and *hat* and told, "This word is *fat*. This word is *hat*." The children were then shown *fun* and *bun* and asked to determine which word was *fun*. "In the experimental series, . . . in which over 80 preschool children participated, there were virtually no individual instances of a child succeeding at the transfer task" (Byrne, 2005, p. 114). In contrast, much research has demonstrated that with explicit instruction, kindergartners and first graders can quickly learn sound-spelling mappings, including multi-letter spellings (Vadasy & Sanders, 2021).

Phonics Concepts for Beginning Reading Instruction

A simple-to-complex sequence of phonics instruction is presented in Table 5.3. Teachers will unfold this knowledge by systematically engaging students with words that reflect these concepts. As students practice with these patterns, they acquire the skills necessary to decode a wide range of words they will encounter in beginning reading texts.

CVC and VC words. As discussed in the section on alphabet learning, an efficient way to introduce letter sounds to students is to begin with a handful of high-frequency letters and teach students the most common sounds the letters represent. For example, if a teacher spends the first two weeks of reading instruction teaching the letters *m*, *s*, *a*, *t*, *p*, *i*, and *f*, at the end of those two weeks, decoding instruction using consonant-vowel-consonant (CVC) and vowel-consonant (VC) could begin. Therefore, after only two weeks of reading instruction, students could read real words such as *mat, sat, map, sit, sip, it, at, fit, fat, Sam,* and *am* and nonwords such as *fip* and *pim*. CVC and VC instruction does not simply involve teaching letter sounds; teaching students to read means teaching students how to blend sounds to make words.

Table 5.3. Simple-to-Complex Sequence of Phonics Instruction

Phonics Concept	Vowel	Examples
CVC and VC* words	short	mat, hid, sip at, in
Digraphs and Blends	short	ship, chat, path flip, stop, fist
Long Vowels (VCe words; vowel teams; CV and V words)	long	hide, made, rode, cute meet, play, eat, grow I, go, be, my
R-controlled vowels and diphthongs	r-controlled glide	bird, car, for foil, boy, mouth pair, fear
Affixes (prefixes and suffixes)	varies	replay, preview, unlock, painted, treats
Complex multisyllabic words	varies	handle, purple
Advanced phonics patterns (e.g., low-frequency spellings, advanced affixes)	varies	weigh, gnome, judge, potion, nature, dancer, enjoyment, comfortable

*CVC and VC are shorthand for consonant-vowel-consonant and vowel-consonant words.

A critical, overlooked aspect of decoding is *blending*. As mentioned earlier in the chapter, most teachers do not receive instruction on phonics. As a result, many teachers may assume that knowledge of letter-sound correspondence is sufficient for decoding words; if a student knows the sounds for *m*, *a*, and *t*, reading the word *mat* should be no problem. Yet, surprisingly, blending sounds for decoding can be very challenging for some students, particularly students with dyslexia (Schatschneider & Torgesen, 2004). Therefore, teaching students how to blend sounds can circumvent potential challenges students may experience when first learning to decode words.

Continuous blending is a method of decoding wherein words are sounded out without stopping between the sounds. When initially teaching students to blend sounds for decoding, teachers can use their consonant knowledge to scaffold instruction. Specifically, continuant consonants are easier to blend than stops. Therefore, using words that begin with a continuant, such as /m/, /s/, and /f/ (e.g., *mad*, *sip*, *fog*), will be easier than using words that begin with stops (e.g., *cat*, *got*, *dip*). In contrast to continuous blending, some teachers may stop between the sounds, "Say /mmm/. [Pause.] Say /ăăă/. [Pause.] Say /t/. What is the word?" The small break between sounds can add a layer of difficulty, causing some students to use the last sound presented to guess the word (e.g., "Tap!") rather than connecting all the sounds to produce the word *mat* correctly. Continuous blending facilitates efficient decoding.

Finally, continuous blending can be used with stops at the beginning of the word, but students will need to be directed to say the first two sounds together. For example, for the word *bat*, students will say the /b/ and /ă/ together for /băăă/ and then add the /t/. Therefore, continuous blending can be used even with a stop phoneme at the beginning of a word. To return to the teacher who taught *m*, *s*, *a*, *t*, *p*, *i*, and *f* within the first couple of weeks of instruction, once students were doing well with their blending of continuants in the initial position, words such as *pat*, *tap*, and *Tim* would be added to the decoding and encoding (spelling) practice.

Digraphs and Blends. As students gain familiarity with single-letter graphemes, multi-letter graphemes and blends can be introduced. A *consonant digraph* is when two letters represent one consonant (e.g., *ch*, *sh*, *th*, *ck*, *wh*, *ph*). Consonant digraphs occur in many single-syllable words that appear in beginning reading texts. Introducing students to consonant digraphs early in their reading instruction will expand their word-reading repertoire (e.g., *ship*, *this*, *chip*, *with*, *when*, *luck*, *sick*). Digraph instruction can also include teaching students the *protector* or *FLSZ* concept, which is that the letters *f*, *l*, *s*, and *z* will double at the end of one-syllable, short vowel words (e.g., *puff*, *staff*, *hill*, *bell*, *miss*, *less*, *buzz*). Recent research has demonstrated that students as young as kindergarten can readily learn two-letter spellings for single phonemes (Vadasy & Sanders, 2021).

Consonant blends are groups of two or three consonants that retain their distinct sounds with no intervening vowel. The sounds in consonant blends are produced quickly, making it difficult for students to hear individual sounds (e.g., *bl-, br-, cl-, cr-, gl-, str-, spl-, -mp, -st*). The technical term for a blend is *consonant cluster*. Consonant clusters can occur at the beginning or end of words (e.g., *stop, must, trip, lamp*). In English, one third of single-syllable words begin with a consonant cluster (McLeod et al., 2001). Yet many students experience difficulty with consonant clusters. Consider the difficulty in blending the sounds in the single-syllable word *strength*. Students' challenges with consonant clusters can be seen in their earlier spelling (Treiman, 1993). For example, students may spell *hand* as *had* and *stay* as *say*. Therefore, explicit instruction in consonant clusters can help students hear the sounds and spell words containing consonant clusters correctly.

As with other decoding skills, consonant digraph instruction begins with simpler words (i.e., words with fewer graphemes) and moves to more complex words as students gain proficiency with the concepts. The most commonly occurring digraphs are introduced first (i.e., *ch, sh, th, wh*). After students are directly taught (i.e., "The letters *ch* spell the /ch/ sound"), repeated practice with the sound spelling will reinforce the concept and facilitate automaticity. Students can practice reading (sounding out; decoding) and spelling words to gain proficiency. In addition, students can achieve fluency with the concepts through instructional activities such as word sorts (e.g., say and sort words by the target digraph) and games such as Go Fish (e.g., "Do you have any words with the /ch/ sound? Yes? I can make a pair.").

Given the challenge students can experience with blends, consonant cluster instruction is usually reserved after single graphemes and the most commonly occurring digraphs have been taught. Consonant cluster instruction typically begins with consonant blends in the initial position within four-phoneme words (CCVC words; e.g., *stop, frog, swim*). Next, final consonant blends would be introduced (CVCC words; e.g., *held, elf, lamp*). Eventually, more complex patterns are added (CCVCC words; e.g., *shelf, drank, slump, print*). Practice that includes print-to-speech (decoding) and speech-to-print (spelling) will strengthen students' attention to the sound-spelling relationships within words that contain consonant clusters.

New Topics and the Role of Continuous Review. Note that at this point in an instructional sequence, students have only been working with words that contain short vowels (CVC, VC, CCVC, CVCC, CCVCC); it is time to introduce students to long vowels. As new concepts are introduced, teachers should be aware of critical features of instruction that facilitate student learning. Specifically, students move through various stages of learning as they acquire a new skill (Haring et al., 1978). The first stage of learning is acquisition. At this stage, the learner is beginning to gain competence in a skill but is not yet proficient (100% accurate) or fluent (automatic). The question that arises is: Should students have mastered a concept before introducing a new one? Researchers have found that 100% mastery in the initial stage of instruction is not necessary or efficient for learning (Sun et al., 2022). Learners should have a firm enough grasp of a concept not to be randomly guessing, but if students are accurately making sound-spelling maps more often than they are making errors, teachers can introduce new concepts. Optimal learning occurs when students are provided with *continuous review* interspersed with the presentation of new material (Chen et al., 2021).

Two concepts undergird continuous review: spaced practice and interleaving. *Spaced practice* means that a lapse of time occurs between practice sessions. Spacing can be distributed across days or weeks (e.g., daily, every other day, or weekly practice). The power of spaced practice lies in the forgetting that occurs during the rest period (i.e., during the period in which the learner does not attempt to retrieve or think about the material). When the brain tries to retrieve the material after a period of rest, the effort required for retrieval strengthens the memory (see Cepeda et al., 2006).

In contrast to spaced practice, which refers to the timing of practice, *interleaving* reflects the content included within a practice session. When content is interleaved, exemplars of different concepts are interspersed. For example, students who have been working on reading CVC words are introduced to the *ch* digraph. During their practice session, words that contain the *ch* digraph will be interleaved with CVC words (e.g., *cat, sip, chat, fin, chip, cod*). In contrast to interleaving, some teachers and curricula provide massed or blocked practice. Within blocked practice, students would only practice the new skill or concept, such as words with the *ch* digraph (e.g., *chop, chip, chat, much*). Robust research has demonstrated the superiority of interleaving over blocked practice (Firth et al., 2021). Thus, continuous review means that teachers will provide regular practice sessions distributed over time, and review and new concepts will be interspersed within each practice session.

Finally, it is important to note that spaced practice and interleaving are not at odds with the concept of mastery learning (Bloom, 1971; Ericsson, 2008). Mastery learning does not occur in a single or a handful of sessions. Instead, mastery learning happens over time due to planned and structured practice that includes direct feedback from the teacher. Within a mastery learning context, teachers are explicit about the knowledge and skills they want students to master. Thus, structured literacy is based on mastery learning, as the heart of structured literacy is the clear delineation of the knowledge and skills students need to learn. Frequent, formative assessment of these skills guides instruction and allows teachers to monitor students' progression toward mastery

(Guskey, 2010). If teachers notice that students experience difficulty during regular progress monitoring, reteaching will occur.

Therefore, within effective reading instruction, concepts will be revisited on an iterative basis over the course of instruction. Over the course of instruction, some concepts may take a little more time (repetitions) for students to initially grasp, while other concepts may be more readily grasped. Teachers can move quickly to the next skill, knowing that continuous review will help solidify students' application of the concept during reading and spelling practice.

Long Vowels. Within single-syllable words, there are two primary patterns for long vowels: the VCe pattern (e.g., b<u>i</u>k<u>e</u>, m<u>a</u>d<u>e</u>, st<u>o</u>n<u>e</u>) and the vowel team or vowel digraph pattern (e.g., m<u>ee</u>t, st<u>ay</u>, gr<u>ow</u>, p<u>ie</u>). Like a consonant digraph, a *vowel digraph* is a group of two letters representing a single sound (/ē/ = *ee, ea, ei, ie, ey*). Vowel digraphs most commonly represent long vowels; the *ea* in *head* is an example of a vowel digraph representing a short vowel. There are also a handful of long vowel spelling patterns that can be taught as special cases. These include CV and V words (e.g., *go, me, my, I*) and "kind, old, wild, ghost" words (i.e., *-ind, -ild, -old,* and *-ost*).

In the United States, many curricula will introduce the concept of long vowels with the VCe pattern, commonly referred to as the *Silent, Magic,* or even *Bossy E* pattern. The pattern goes like this: "When *e* is added to the end of a three-letter word like *hid* or *fad*, the letter says its name to become *hide* and *fade*." The pattern is more commonly referred to as a *split digraph* in the UK and other English-speaking countries. For example, vowel digraphs (e.g., *ae, ee, ie, oe, ue)* can be split by a consonant to make words like *made, Pete, time, poke,* and *flute*.

Given these differences, the instructional sequence will differ depending on how a teacher or program introduces long vowels. Again, it is common in the United States for teachers to move from teaching students the blending of CVC and CCVC words to the VCe pattern (i.e., adding an *e* changes the vowel pronunciation from short to long). Learning activities may include teaching students a story about the power of *e* to make a vowel say its name and ample practice changing words from short to long vowel spellings (e.g., *tap* to *tape, fin* to *fine, plan* to *plane, cap* to *cape, rip* to *ripe*).

In contrast, if the long vowel VCe pattern is taught as a split digraph, the sequence of instruction may begin with teaching spelling variations of different long vowels. For example, instruction may begin by teaching students the concept of a vowel digraph and introducing students to vowel digraph spelling variations for long o (/ō/), such as *oa, ow, oe,* and *o_e*. Practice would include blending (decoding), sorting, and spelling words that follow these patterns (e.g., *boat, road, toad; row, glow, snow; toe, foe, hoe*). To reinforce the concept of the split digraph, teachers would have students change *oe* words to *o_e* words by inserting a consonant (e.g., change *toe* to *tote*, *hoe* to *hope*). In addition, nonword words can be used to reinforce concepts. For example, the nonword *boe* can be changed to the real word *bone*.

R-Controlled Vowels and Diphthongs. The next phonics concepts that are typically introduced are r-controlled vowels and diphthongs. Recall that *r-controlled vowels* occur when the letter *r* follows the letters *a*, *e*, *i*, *o*, or *u*. The presence of the *r* influences the pronunciation of the vowel (i.e., /er/, /or/, /ar/). The most common pattern is the sound spelling /ar/ = *ar*. Instruction would begin by having students learn the sound spelling map and then practice applying the concept for decoding and spelling (e.g., read and spell words such as *car*, *mat*, *fat*, *far*, and *bark*). Teachers can also have students practice substituting sounds, such as replacing the /ă/ in *had* with /ar/ to make the word *hard*. Again, students would practice saying, spelling, and reading the words. As students gain familiarity with /ar/, other *r*-controlled sounds would be introduced. These sounds will have several spelling variations. For example, the /er/ sound is spelled with *er* (*term*), *ir* (*bird*), and *ur* (*fur*). Lower frequency spelling variations for /ur/, such as *or* (*word*, *worm*, *worth*), *ear* (*earth*, *early*, *learn*), and *ure* (*treasure*, *measure*), would be introduced separately.

Diphthongs are vowels that glide from one sound to another (e.g., /oy/, /ou/). When introducing diphthongs, teachers may begin by teaching the spelling variations for the /oy/ diphthong—*oi* (e.g., *boil*, *foil*) and *oy* (*joy*, *boy*, *toy*)—and then move on to /ou/ spellings—*ou* (e.g., *cloud*, *loud*, *ouch*) and *ow* (e.g., *cow*, *now*, *brown*, *howl*). The long vowels /ī/ as in *cry* and *crime*; /ā/ as in *say*, *braid*, *make*, and *break*; and /ō/ as in *slow*, *groan*, and *dough* are also diphthongs, but those sounds are taught when first introducing long vowel sounds.

Finally, there are three diphthong and *r*-controlled combinations: /ear/, /air/, and /yur/. The spelling variations for /ear/ as in *steer* and *hear* would be taught separately before teaching /air/ variations (i.e., *air* as in *fair*, *pair*, *chair*; *are* as in *care*, *dare*, *share*; *ear* as in *bear*, *pear*, *wear*) and /yur/ as in *pure* and *cure*. These variations are typically introduced during advanced phonics instruction (i.e., second grade).

As with all structured literacy instruction, *r*-controlled vowels and diphthong instruction will be interleaved, allowing students to compare and contrast sound spellings and further solidify associations between spelling patterns and pronunciations for decoding and the segmenting of sounds for spelling.

Affixes. English is a morphophonemic language. This means that the spelling of English words reflects *phonology*, the sound system of language (e.g., the /b/ sound is spelled with the letter *b*), and *morphology*, the grammatical structure of words (e.g., adding an *s* to the end of words to indicate more than one; adding *re-* at the beginning of a word to indicate the meaning "to do again"). Thus far, we have been exploring phonological relationships—the relationships between the speech sounds in words and their spelling variations.

To learn to read and spell English, students also need to know about morphemes. *Morphemes* are the smallest units of words that contain meaning (e.g., prefixes, suffixes, roots, or bases). Information about how to teach the meaning of affixes will be addressed in the next chapter. However, within the context of word-level reading, teachers benefit from understanding that sometimes letters and letter combinations are added to words to add meaning to the words rather than as a phonological tool. For example, the letter *s* simply represents the /s/ sound in the word *sit*, but the letter *s* represents a morphological unit indicating "more than one" in words like *bats* and *cars*. Adding a morpheme to a word allows meaning to be communicated (e.g., *-ed* to indicate past tense), but the base element will influence the pronunciation of the morpheme. For example, the suffix *-ed* will sound like /t/ in words that end with an unvoiced phoneme (e.g., *walked, biked*); /d/ in words that end with a voiced phoneme (e.g., *smiled, saved*); and /ĕd/ in words that end with a /t/ or /d/ sound (e.g., *painted, acted*). Similarly, the suffix *s* will sound like /s/ when it follows a voiceless sound (e.g., *cats*) or /z/ when it follows a voiced sound (e.g., *birds*). Some reading programs will direct teachers to teach students the reasons for the variation in pronunciation explicitly. In contrast, other programs reinforce the concept through sequenced, planned, and repeated practice with the variations without direct teaching of the rules regarding pronunciation. Both options reflect structured (i.e., planned and sequenced) instruction; one just includes fewer cognitive explanations or rules to be learned.

Complex Multisyllabic Words. At this point, students have learned the many variations found in single-syllable words and have been introduced to basic multisyllabic words to which foundational affixes (e.g., *s, -ed, re-, un-*) have been added. Teaching students to read complex multisyllabic words, though, requires teaching a new spelling pattern, consonant-le (C-le). The C-le pattern is also referred to as the final stable syllable, as it only occurs at the end of words. Words that end with *-le* used to be spelled *-el*, making the syllable's pronunciation easier to understand (/consonant/ + /əl/). Consider the following words: *ta•ble, twin•kle, pad•dle, gig•gle, tur•tle,* and *pur•ple*. Once students are introduced to the concept and sound-spelling correspondence, they can begin practicing blending and segmenting sounds by syllable for decoding and spelling. For example, if the word is *turtle*, the student would start by saying the first syllable or sound chunk, /tur/, and then the second syllable, /təl/. If students struggle with the *r*-controlled vowel *ur*, teachers can scaffold the pronunciation by pointing out the *ur* letter combination and have the student practice blending the /t/ and /er/ sounds for /ter/. The second syllable combines the /t/ and /əl/ phonemes, which ends with the schwa or *lazy e* plus the consonant *l*. The students would engage in the reverse process for spelling—segmenting the sounds and writing the spelling patterns.

Teachers can use several ways to support students in separating words into syllables or chunks. *Syllables* are a unit of speech consisting of at least one vowel, with or without consonants (e.g., a•ble, sat•ur•day, rock•et, ze•bra). Recall the Vowel Valley. Vowels are produced by opening the mouth, which causes the chin to drop. Therefore, one way for students to identify syllables within words is to place their hands under their chins as they pronounce words. Every time their chins hit their hands, that is one syllable. For example, say the following words while holding your hand below your chin: *apple*, *happy*, and *popcorn*. Having students talk like a robot or whale will also result in syllable separation, as the vowels are the vocalized units within words. Finally, some programs will have students pound the syllables by making a fist with one hand and creating a flat surface with the other. The students pound their fists on their flat hands as they pronounce syllables.

Reading programs embrace different approaches for teaching students to divide words into their parts. *Syllabification*, or syllabication, is the separation of words into spoken or written syllables. Some structured literacy reading programs include formal instruction in syllabification. Within these programs, students may be taught rules for how to divide syllables (e.g., divide syllables between consonants; rab•bit, let•ter, hap•py) and steps to follow to break words into syllables (e.g., label the vowels, mark the consonants, and divide the syllables). Within such programs, students also learn that digraphs and consonant blends can't be divided (e.g., *th*, *ch*, *str-*, *-ck*). Practice will involve marking words, blending sounds for decoding, and segmenting words for spelling.

Other programs are less formal in their approach. Within these programs, teachers prompt students to break words into manageable parts for decoding and spelling, even if those parts do not reflect formal dictionary syllabification (e.g., comm•on, fi•nish, perf•orm; Bhattacharya & Ehri, 2004). Within these programs, students may learn a generic strategy, such as identifying the vowels, joining the vowel teams, counting the parts [syllable exemplars], and blending the sounds to pronounce the word (Kearns & Whaley, 2019). Rather than teaching students the names of different syllable types (e.g., open, closed) or specific rules associated with those syllable types (e.g., closed syllables typically have a short vowel, open syllables usually have a long vowel), students learn the patterns through repeated practice with breaking words into parts.

As vowel pronunciation provides the most significant challenge to multisyllabic word reading, the focus of any syllabification strategy—generic or dictionary based—is to help students identify the correct vowel pronunciation. Within multisyllabic words, vowels can be long (a•ble), short (af•ter), or schwa (a•bout). Therefore, students may be taught the generic strategy to "flex" the vowel. That is, students are taught to try several vowel pronunciations, which will help them map their pronunciations with words in their oral vocabularies (i.e., "Let me try ē•lĕ•fĕnt. Oh! That word is ĕl•ə•fənt!"). In contrast, within rule-based programs, students apply their rule-based knowledge (i.e., "That is a closed syllable with a short vowel sound").

While there is evidence that teaching students formal syllabification strategies can be helpful (Diliberto et al., 2009), there is also evidence that simplified methods, such as chunking (i.e., breaking words into parts), peeling off (i.e., identifying affixes first), or flexing vowels (i.e., trying different vowel pronunciations), can also be effective (O'Connor et al., 2015; Toste et al., 2019; Vadasy et al., 2006). The key to teaching multisyllabic words is for students to recognize that (a) words have parts, (b) breaking words into chunks helps with decoding and spelling, and (c) flexing the vowel can help match a decoded word to a word that is within their oral vocabulary. Students with dyslexia or who struggle with reading experience the greatest difficulty with dividing words into parts, but through direct instruction in segmentation strategies, these students can learn how to segment for decoding and spelling multisyllabic words (Bhattacharya & Ehri, 2004).

Advanced Phonics Patterns. Finally, advanced phonics patterns include low-frequency spellings and advanced affix instruction. Keep in mind that many of these patterns typically are not taught until second grade (Blevins, 2017). Students at this level are more attuned to identifying patterns in words. Lower frequency spellings, including the less common long vowel spelling variations (*-ild, -old, -ind*); the range of spelling variations for /ā/ (e.g., *ei, ey, ea, eigh,* and *aigh*), /ī/ (e.g., *ie*), /ō/ (e.g., *oe*), and /ē/ (e.g., *y, ey, ie, ei*); soft *c* and *g* sounds; inflectional endings with spelling changes; and affixes such as *-sion, -tion,* and *-ture,* will be introduced or reinforced during advanced phonics instruction.

At this point, it is abundantly clear that teaching phonics involves much more than teaching the most common sounds of the letters of the alphabet. Yet, when students are introduced to the concepts systematically, moving from simple to complex, they become attuned to the patterns of English. Notably, a teacher's awareness of the structure of English orthography can be transformative for instruction. Rather than feeling overwhelmed when helping a student read or spell a word, the knowledgeable teacher can say, "That is a new spelling pattern. Let's look at the parts."

Irregular Word Instruction

As students learn phonics, they will encounter words that do not follow the most common sound-spelling patterns or new patterns that have not been taught. These words are commonly referred to as *irregular* words. Some reading programs categorize words as *permanently irregular* and *temporarily irregular*. *Permanently irregular* words have spelling patterns that apply to so few words that the pattern is taught as an exception (e.g., *was, once*). With *temporarily irregular* words, the spelling pattern is one that students have not yet been taught (e.g., r-controlled vowels, digraphs), but the word needs to be known for the novice reader to access beginning reading texts or write sentences.

How should irregular words be taught within a structured literacy approach? To address that question, we begin by addressing a firmly entrenched early reading practice: *sight-word instruction*. Remember the *Dick and Jane* readers? That widely disproven approach to teaching reading was abandoned in the 1960s, but the legacy of "see a word, say a word" is ubiquitous in kindergarten and first-grade classrooms. Within the first few weeks of school, parents are provided with a list of "sight words" their child is expected to memorize. For many students, their first introduction to formal reading instruction is via a flashcard—see the word, say the word. The whole-word approach to reading instruction undermines students' ability to grasp the alphabetic principle and is not how students should be introduced to reading.

Beyond the problematic whole-word approach, the terminology is also incorrect. *Sight words* are words that are recognized accurately and quickly. Skilled readers will read the vast majority of words on this page by sight. There is no need to decode the words *skilled* or *readers*. You did not need to "peel off" the affixes or pay particular attention to the vowel digraph to read the words *skilled* and *readers*. Recall from Chapter 4 the two routes to word reading—lexical (whole word) and sublexical (phonological). Once a word has been repeatedly assembled via the phonological route, the word can be automatically recognized. Further, processing via the sublexical route facilitates orthographic mapping. Irregular word instruction can tap into sublexical processing by teaching students to pay attention to letters in words and how they map to sounds. In other words, teaching irregular words within a structured literacy approach looks remarkably similar to phonics instruction.

Another source of confusion when it comes to the misnomered "sight-word" instruction stems from the source of the words. In the 1930s, Edward Dolch identified English's most frequently occurring words (Dolch, 1936). In the 1950s, Edward Fry expanded on Dolch's list and identified the 1,000 most commonly used words (Fry & Kress, 2006). It is estimated that a student who knows all of the Dolch and Fry words can read about 90% of elementary-level books. Thus, if students can memorize these high-frequency words, they will "be able to read" almost everything; such was the lure of *Dick and Jane* and other whole-word methods. Unfortunately, while such memorization appears to be a fast track to reading, students' reading ability will plateau, bad habits of whole-word guessing will become entrenched, and students will generate their own rules about letter-sound correspondences, which can lead them astray when it comes to decoding new words.

High frequency means "highly occurring." *High frequency* does not mean irregular. The majority of words found on the Dolch list are *regular* (Farrell et al., 2019); students can decode these words by applying the most common grapheme-phoneme correspondence patterns (e.g., *at, but, am, in, if, him, had, did, that, big, six, fast, ask, its*). Thus, there is no reason why these words should be taught as whole words.

In contrast, there are irregular spelling patterns that students will need to be familiar with to read any beginning reader (e.g., "*The* cat *was* on the mat"; "Can *you* spot *the* dog?"). As such, these irregular words need to be introduced to students early in the learning-to-read process. Teachers can use the *heart-word* approach to teach irregular words. Within the heart-word approach, students apply phonics knowledge to sound out parts of the word that reflect common grapheme-phoneme correspondence but learn other spelling-sound relationships by heart. In other words, great attention is given to the irregular parts of the word to help remember the irregularity. For example, the word *said* is an irregular word. Students can use their letter-sound knowledge for two letters, *s* and *d*, but they need to learn the *ai* vowel digraph by heart. To teach this, teachers would say, "Today, we will learn a new word. Some parts you know, and some parts you will need to learn by heart. Let's look at the word (see Figure 5.4). The word is *said*.

Figure 5.4. Heart Word Map for the Word "Said"

There are three sounds in the word said [point to the three symbols under the word] /s/ /ĕ/ /d/. There is a box under the sounds you know. Let's say those [point to *s*] /s/ and [point to *d*] /d/. The /ĕ/ in *said* is spelled *ai*. The *ai* part is the part we need to learn by heart. Let's sound the word out again /s/ /ĕ/ /d/. Now, let's spell the word. S-a-i-d spells *said*. What is the part we need to learn by heart? Ai spells the /ĕ/ in *said*."

The word *said* is considered permanently irregular, as the *ai* spelling is rarely used to spell the short *e* sound. In contrast, some words or parts of words are considered temporarily irregular. For example, among the first irregular words students need to know is the word *the*. They will not have been taught the *th* digraph within their phonics instruction scope and sequence.

Figure 5.5. Teaching the Word "the" as a Heart Word Prior to "th" Instruction

Therefore, when teaching the word *the*, teachers can treat both sound spellings within the word as irregular (see Figure 5.5). Teachers will directly teach students that the sound /th/ is spelled *th*, and the sound /ə/ is spelled with an *e*. The advantage of the heart-word approach over whole-word memorization is that the heart-word approach follows the same blending and segmenting routines students use for phonetic decoding and encoding. Students are taught to listen and look for word parts. In addition, when students apply a phonics approach to irregular words, they no longer confuse words such as *was* and *saw*, as they begin by sounding out known sounds (e.g., /w/ and /s/ in *was* and *saw*) and then add the part they need to know by heart (Farrell et al., 2019).

Reading Connected Text

Reading connected text also contributes to students' word-level reading skills. *Connected text* refers to a group of sentences that relate to one another. Thus, connected text can be a children's story, a poem, a brief passage of several sentences, or an entire novel. Reading connected text is different from reading words in isolation. Reading connected text provides several distinct advantages over reading words in isolation. First, reading connected text provides interleaved practice of target skills. For example, if students have been learning the *-igh* spelling pattern, reading a book that features that pattern will also include a variety of other patterns. Provided that students receive immediate corrective feedback on errors, the intermittent practice with the *-igh* pattern within the text will strengthen their connection between the *-igh* pattern and the pronunciation of words such as *sigh*, *might*, *high*, *flight*, and *knight*.

Second, connected text allows for self-monitoring of pronunciation in relation to word meaning. When reading words in isolation, students cannot ask themselves, "Does that word make sense in this context?" because there is no context. If students make an error when reading words in a list, there is nothing to alert them that they misread *best* as *bet*. If students misread the word *best* in the sentence "She picked her best dress," though, they would be more likely to notice the error and be prompted to self-correct. Self-monitoring also includes identifying the correct pronunciation of heteronyms. Recall from Chapter 4 that *heteronyms* are words whose pronunciation changes to indicate differences in meaning either by changing how the vowel is pronounced (e.g., *read/read*, *lĭve/līve*, *wĭnd/wīnd*) or by where the stress is placed (e.g., *Affect/aFFECT*, *COMpress/comPRESS*, *CONduct/conDUCT*). Reading connected text allows students to explore pronunciation changes that occur in relation to sentence structure and meaning.

Finally, reading connected text is essential for building oral reading fluency (Foorman et al., 2016). *Oral reading fluency* is the ability to read connected text accurately, at an appropriate rate, and with prosody (i.e., with appropriate expression). When text is read with prosody, the oral reading sounds like natural speech. Features of prosody include appropriate phrasing (e.g., the girl/walked/all the way home), stress (e.g., **the girl**/walked/all the way home; the girl/**walked**/all the way home; the girl/walked/**all the way home**), rise and fall patterns, and general expressiveness (Schwanenflugel et al., 2004). Oral reading fluency depends on students' word-level proficiency and metacognitive processing of the text. In other words, laborious single-word decoding impedes fluency, and a reader's lack of understanding of what is being read inhibits appropriate phrasing and expression during oral reading. Researchers have consistently demonstrated that once students have sufficient mastery of basic alphabetic skills, reading connected text has a positive effect on fluency and comprehension[5] (Foorman et al., 2016).

However, as was alluded to in the introduction of this chapter, not all connected text is the same. The type of text teachers have students read can influence the efficacy of the practice. Some text types promote bad habits, such as guessing words based on context or pattern, or encourage students to rely on picture clues rather than letter patterns for word reading.

Types of Connected Texts: Decodable, Leveled, Predictable, and Trade

Many terms are used to classify the types of connected texts used to support beginning reading instruction. Commonly used terms include *decodable*, *leveled*, *predictable*, and *trade*. A common misconception about structured literacy, or phonics-based approaches in general, is that such approaches do not involve reading connected text. In particular, many believe that phonics instruction means the absence of reading interesting stories. This is certainly not the case. As explained by Chall in 1997:

> Many fear that more *structured beginning reading methods* may mean dropping the reading of books—an unlikely occurrence since all reading methods have included connected reading. Even Noah Webster and McGuffey, whose programs taught phonics explicitly, included some of the finest children's literature in their readers 100 and 200 years before whole language was invented. [emphasis in the original] (p. 258)

---

5. The relationship between fluent reading and comprehension will be explored further in Chapter 6.

As such, all structured literacy approaches include the reading of connected text. Most structured literacy approaches include a particular kind of text within early reading instruction—*decodable texts*. Although a universal definition does not exist, a text is considered decodable if most phonics patterns included in the text have been previously addressed within a program's scope and sequence. As decodable texts are written for different programs, the scope and sequence of phonics skills may vary across different sets of decodable readers.

As a genre, though, *decodable texts* are designed to encourage students to apply their knowledge of grapheme-phoneme correspondence while reading simple stories. In particular, during the initial period of reading acquisition, decodable texts facilitate the deliberate practice of grapheme-phoneme correspondence (Castles et al., 2018; Hatcher et al., 1994). Decodable texts provide students with that first ah-ha, "I can read!" moment when they realize they can use their knowledge of letter-sound correspondence to sound out words on the page. In addition to providing ample, interleaved practice across previously learned and new grapheme-phoneme correspondences, decodable texts are noteworthy for the *absence* of unfamiliar or complex patterns. In other words, decodable readers would not include advanced phonics patterns (e.g., *weigh, gnome, judge, potion, nature*) or numerous multisyllabic words. Instead, the purpose of providing students with decodable texts is to have them gain fluency with independent reading. Further, the nature of decodable texts encourages students to apply their decoding strategies rather than rely on other sources of information, such as pictures or story structure, to guess words.

In contrast to decodable texts, *leveled texts* are commonly used within whole-language and balanced-literacy reading programs. Leveled texts differ in meaningful ways from decodable texts. Within leveled texts, the focus shifts from the word-level focus found within decodable texts to a broader text-level focus (Mesmer et al., 2012). Specifically, the sentence length, complexity, subject/verb order, and themes are controlled but the phonics patterns are not (Begeny & Greene, 2014). For example, a first-grade leveled text will include short sentences, words composed of a limited number of syllables, and words commonly found in the oral vocabulary of a first grader. In addition, early leveled books are picture heavy with a close correlation between pictures and print (i.e., look at the picture; say the word). With leveled books, teachers and parents may be confused about why a student is not progressing sequentially through a leveled series. These teachers and families assume that leveled books can be matched to students' reading skills, but that is not how leveled books work. Words like *pigeon, coyote*, and *machine* may appear within early leveled books. Therefore, leveled texts cannot be used to benchmark students' reading ability. A statement such as "My child is a level D reader" doesn't yield specific information about the phonics skills a child does and does not possess. It means that the child was able to read a short book with simple sentence structures on a familiar theme for the assessment.

Finally, the most significant limitation of leveled books stems not from the books themselves but from how they are used within reading instruction. Specifically, many teachers use leveled books as the primary teaching tool. Within a *guided reading* framework (Fountas & Pinnell, 1996), the teaching of reading occurs almost exclusively within the context of reading and discussing leveled books. Teachers are taught to assign and match students to reading levels. Then, as students attempt to read their *just-right-level* book aloud, teachers provide corrective scaffolding as students struggle with words. The scaffolding can include non-phonics or incomplete phonics guidance such as "Look at the picture" or "Look at the first letter. Do you know a word that begins with that letter?" or phonics-based guidance such as "The *ch* spells the /ch/ sound. Try that word again."

This type of instruction is problematic for several reasons. First, it reflects *incidental* rather than *explicit and systematic* instruction. Because the texts are not written to provide systematic practice with taught sound-spelling patterns, the amount of practice applying decoding skills can be limited. Repeated recall is a hallmark of systematic practice (Rosenshine, 2009). Second, because the text's phonics patterns are not controlled, students may encounter numerous words beyond their skill set, which can frustrate novice readers, inhibit fluency, and promote bad habits such as guessing. Third, the instruction is reactive rather than proactive. If instruction does occur outside of the *guided reading* time, it is more likely to reflect whole-word memorization. For example, *purple* may be taught as a whole word (look-say) prior to reading the text. The target word may be repeated within the text for the purpose of memorization but not for decoding practice, as the word-level features were not explicitly taught (e.g., the *r*-controlled *ur* spelling, the final stable syllable *-ple*). Finally, teacher feedback may or may not include attention to grapheme-phoneme correspondence. Many three-cueing curricula that make use of leveled texts recommend that teachers emphasize non-phonetic decoding strategies (e.g., looking at pictures, using context) over phonics strategies.

Predictable texts are another type of text that may be found within elementary classrooms. *Predictable texts* contain a repetitive structure, which facilitates student guessing of the word through the use of picture prompts (e.g., She looked in the *tub*. She looked in the *garden*. She looked in the *kitchen*. She looked in the *bedroom*.) or memorization of a word due to repetition (e.g., *Elephants* are gray. *Elephants* have long trunks. *Elephants* live in the grasslands.) Many adults may fondly remember predictable stories from their childhood, such as *Goodnight Moon* (Brown, 1947), *Are You My*

Mother? (Eastman, 1960), and *Brown Bear, Brown Bear* (Martin & Carle, 1967). Predictable books are excellent to read aloud to preschool children, as engaging young children with this type of text reinforces essential concepts of print. *Concepts of print* refer to a reader's awareness of how print works. It includes understanding that print represents speech and conveys a message, books have a particular orientation (top, bottom, front, back), English is read from left to right, and there is a distinction between letters, words, and sentences. These concepts can be reinforced via shared reading by having young children turn the pages, pointing to words as an adult or skilled reader reads them, and directing children's attention to familiar letters. All these skills are considered pre-reading skills. Given that the purpose of these books is for students to predict (i.e., guess) words, using predictable texts for *independent* reading during beginning reading instruction is not recommended. Unfortunately, many early leveled texts also follow a predictable pattern (Cunningham et al., 2004). Therefore, teachers and families should be aware of text patterns that promote guessing rather than attention to the letters and letter patterns.

Finally, books that are neither decodable nor leveled tend to fall into the category of *trade books*. *Trade books* refer to books published by a commercial publisher intended for a general readership. In other words, if you went to the children's section of any bookstore, the books found on those shelves would be trade books. The language within trade books is not strictly controlled as it would be with leveled books, nor are the books written to be decodable by adhering to a specific scope and sequence of phonics patterns. Instead, trade books typically contain rich vocabulary, varied sentence structure, and playful language patterns (e.g., rhyme, alliteration) and are written to entertain or inform.

Although great debate surrounds which type of texts should be used within early reading instruction, most reading scholars agree that the type of text selected should match the instructional purpose (Castles et al., 2018; Foorman et al., 2016). Specifically, as teachers introduce a new sound-spelling correspondence, students should practice with a decodable text that reflects the taught pattern and aligns with a structured instructional sequence. For example, a teacher may introduce a particular grapheme-phoneme correspondence (e.g., *ch*), next have students practice word reading in isolation along with a review of other taught patterns (e.g., *chip, mat, much, chat, fin*), and then use decodable texts to have students practice reading of connected text[6] (e.g., *Chad and His Chips*).

After basic alphabetic proficiency is acquired (i.e., students understand the alphabetic principle and can reliably map speech sounds with basic letter

---

6. In the next section, information on how spelling and writing are integrated within that sequence will be presented.

patterns), researchers have demonstrated the utility of having students read more complex texts (Castles et al., 2018). Engagement with more complex texts offers opportunities for the generalization of reading skills and for deeper language development. Specifically, through engagement with non-decodable, more complex texts, students can become more attuned to the statistical regularities within written language. As English is a deep orthography (i.e., no one-to-one correspondence between speech sounds and spellings), once students unlock the code and are familiar with basic grapheme-phoneme correspondences, exposure to varied sound spellings provides an opportunity for statistical learning. *Statistical learning* refers to the process of intuiting (i.e., figuring out without being explicitly told) relationships across concepts (Steacy et al., 2017). Students who understand the alphabetic principle and can reliably apply grapheme-phoneme correspondence to words are more likely to be sensitive to irregularities (i.e., novel pronunciations). Over time and through exposure to varied word structures, students can become sensitive to the statistical probability associated with various spelling patterns; hence, the term *statistical learning* is used to describe this phenomenon.

In addition to knowledge of word-level features that may be acquired via statistical learning, engagement with non-decodable texts can also provide opportunities for engagement with rich content and varied linguistic features (e.g., syntax, discourse structures). These elements that relate to meaning will be explored in further detail in the next chapter.

SPELLING

Finally, spelling makes a unique contribution to an individual's word-level knowledge. As such, within a structured literacy approach, spelling instruction is not considered separate from reading instruction but is integrated within instruction as a complementary and essential component of beginning reading acquisition. Instruction that integrates spelling and reading extends students' understanding of the reciprocal relationship inherent within alphabetic languages and is particularly important for opaque orthographies like English.

Learning to spell opaque orthographies is more complex than learning to read them. There are more ways to spell English phonemes than pronunciation variations for graphemes (e.g., there are more spelling variations of /ā/ than there are ways to pronounce most graphemes; Kessler & Treiman, 2001). In addition, an incorrect grapheme-phoneme pronunciation can be corrected when the resulting word does not map to a word in a reader's oral vocabulary (e.g., an incorrect pronunciation, /ēlĕphănt/, can result in a quick correction to /ĕləphənt/). Such a check is not available for spelling other than the squishy art of "Does this spelling look right?" In addition, spelling requires an explicit or implicit understanding of (a) morphology (i.e., affixes, bases) and the influence of affixes on the pronunciation of roots (e.g., *spir* → inspīre vs. insp*ə*ration; *bio* → biägraphy vs. biəgraphic); (b) spelling rules (e.g., *ck* will never appear at the beginning of a word), and (c) homophones (*ate/eight; do/due/dew*). As a result, spelling requires more than the phonological ability to separate phonemes within words. Specifically, researchers have found that unexpectedly poor spellers (i.e., relatively competent readers whose spelling is weak) experience difficulty attending to all the letters within a word (Frith, 1985; Holmes & Castles, 2001; Holmes et al., 2008; Holmes & Quinn, 2009). Within these studies, poor spellers appeared to sample letters when reading. Such spellers had difficulty noticing transposed letters within words (e.g., *turlte*) and took longer matching regularly spelled words (*happiness—happiness*). In addition, unexpectedly poor spellers were slower at reading long words or words with unexpected spelling patterns. Thus, orthographic processing appears to be distinct from phonological processing. For students with dyslexia, who are likely to have difficulty with phonology and orthography, the integration of reading and spelling instruction is of even greater importance (Weiser, 2013).

Students' spelling can provide valuable information about their phonological and orthographic abilities. Prior to formal instruction, preschool children experiment with writing using their limited alphabetic knowledge to spell words. A linguist, Charles Read (1971), was one of the first scientists to study this phenomenon, now commonly referred to as *invented spelling*. Read observed that young children move from writing scribbles to creating random letter sequences to represent words (e.g., BVG for *house*) to using letter sequences to represent the sound structure of words (e.g., *iz, wrk, prpul, difrint*) as they experimented with print. Once students were introduced to formal instruction in English orthography (i.e., how to spell words correctly), their spelling would change to reflect conventional spelling patterns.

Repeated engagement in the correct spelling of words facilitates a similar self-learning process that occurs with decoding. After repeated practice spelling words correctly, students internalize spelling patterns and are able to generalize those patterns to determine the spelling of novel words (Shahar-Yames & Share, 2008). However, students' inability to move from invented to formal spelling is a clear sign to teachers that focused orthographic instruction is needed. Either students are not being provided with appropriate spelling instruction (i.e., teachers are not teaching or correcting students' spelling errors), or students are experiencing difficulty that requires more intensive instruction.

Unfortunately, the value of invented spelling for understanding students' instructional needs was lost in the 1980s and 1990s, when it became part of whole language and subsumed within process-writing curricula (Calkins, 1986). As the goal of whole language was for students to read and write for meaning, precise spelling was not valued. As a result, teachers moved away from viewing invented spelling as a means to an end and embraced invented spelling as the desired end; the goal of writing was to put ideas on the page and not to spell words correctly. During this time, teachers would promote students' persistent use of invented spelling (e.g., "Don't worry about spelling." or "Spelling doesn't count."). Despite professional recommendations to move students from invented spelling to conventional spelling (e.g., International Reading Association, 1998), there was general acceptance of students' invented spelling long past when such errors should have been corrected (i.e., first grade and beyond).

In addition to the belief that students' use of invented spelling is not only acceptable but should be encouraged in the name of self-expression, the inefficacy of the prevailing approach to spelling instruction, namely, the weekly Friday spelling test, has done little to help convince teachers that spelling can and should be taught (McNeill & Kirk, 2014). A standard approach to spelling instruction is to provide students with a list of words on Monday, engage in extension activities (e.g., writing sentences, dictionary work, rainbow spelling—writing spelling words using different colored pencils) across the week, and test students on Friday. The Friday test approach often fails to include several features of instruction found essential for robust learning (Roediger & Karpicke, 2006). Specifically, the approach fails to take advantage of (a) testing effects, which would be in the form of brief assessments or low-stakes practice testing occurring multiple times during the week; (b) interleaved practice in which previously taught words would be integrated within currently assessed concepts; and (c) direct, systematic instruction as the majority of spelling activities rely on incidental learning. Lacking these features, the Friday spelling test approach is not likely to result in sustained improvements in students' spelling. For teachers, the practice *feels* as ineffective as it is. Given this backdrop, confusion about the importance of accurate spelling and the utility of spelling instruction continues within schools today. As a result, many teachers downplay its significance, limit spelling instruction to incidental methods, and have abandoned traditional methods of explicit instruction (Pan et al., 2021).

Unfortunately, the consequences of not learning to spell are significant. Despite the prevailing sentiment that technology (e.g., spell-check) has solved the spelling conundrum, evidence suggests this is not the case. Externally, the ability to spell correctly is viewed by others as an indicator of intelligence, competence (e.g., perceived attention to detail), and overall writing ability (Figueredo & Varnhagen, 2005; Kreiner et al., 2002). Internally, difficulty with spelling affects self-esteem and confidence and reduces engagement via writing on the part of the writer. As a result, students who struggle with spelling often view themselves as poor writers, produce less writing, and avoid engaging in writing tasks. Thus, despite popular notions that conventional spelling is passé, little evidence demonstrates its demise has come.[7] As a result, when teachers and school systems decide not to prioritize or directly teach students to spell, they place limitations on students that have far-reaching consequences.

Thankfully, the lost art of teaching spelling can easily be re-integrated within the curriculum. Researchers have demonstrated that systematic, explicit instruction can ameliorate students' difficulty with spelling (Galuschka et al., 2020; Moats, 2005; Weiser, 2013). After reviewing 53 studies, Graham and Santangelo (2014) found that direct spelling instruction was superior to incidental approaches, and more instruction was associated with even greater gains. Further, robust teaching methods resulted in spelling gains that generalized to students' writing and were maintained over time. Similar findings were found when researchers examined effective spelling instruction for students with dyslexia. Galuschka et al. (2020) found spelling instruction that addressed phonics, orthographic patterns, and morphology had a moderate to high impact on the maintained spelling performance of students with word-level reading difficulties.

Within a structured literacy approach, spelling instruction is aligned and integrated with decoding instruction. Instruction will stress phonemic relationships (i.e., sound-letter correspondence) as well as attention to morphological and etymological features of words. In addition, instruction will be systematic (i.e., it will follow a planned scope and sequence). For example, in the early elementary grades, instructional activities may include the following:

- Phoneme-grapheme correspondence work (e.g., hearing a phoneme pronunciation and writing learned spelling variations)
- Word mapping (e.g., segmenting a word by sounds and mapping graphemes to the sounds via a grid [Elkonin box] or sound lines)
- Word sorting (e.g., -*dge* [*judge*] and -*ge* [*age*] words)
- Word dictation (i.e., practice testing)

Once foundational spellings are taught, direct teaching of common inflectional endings and the spelling conventions associated with adding affixes (e.g., doubling the final consonant if the vowel is short, dropping the *e* in bases if the suffix begins with a vowel, changing the *y* to *i*) is appropriate. In the upper elementary grades and higher, explicit instruction in advanced morphology has been shown to help students learn to spell more complex words (Henry, 2003). Finally, given the rich etymological roots of English, teaching students about word origin can also enhance their spelling (Levesque et al., 2021). For example, Greek-based words use the *ch* spelling for /k/ (e.g., *chorus*), the *ph* spelling for /f/ (e.g., *phone*), and *y* for /ĭ/ or /ī/ (e.g., *gymnasium* and *cycle*).

---

7. Ask anyone who has made a spelling error on a social media post or any online forum.

The value of morphological instruction to enhance students' understanding of word meaning will be addressed in the next chapter.

CONCLUSION

The Simple View of Reading is a useful heuristic for conceptualizing two broad aspects of reading: word recognition and language comprehension. Within this chapter, we explored how a structured literacy approach can be used to promote students' ability to read words accurately and quickly—the word-recognition component of the reading equation. The concept of a *structured* approach to beginning reading instruction is not new, but whole-word and meaning-focused philosophies of reading that became prevalent in the 20th century shifted the focus of reading instruction away from direct teaching of the alphabetic principle. As a result, teachers came to believe that reading and spelling abilities could be caught (i.e., picked up naturally through exposure to text and writing opportunities), and the act of direct teaching was detrimental to students' development. Even if teachers were incorporating elements of alphabetic instruction within their teaching, the methods often reflected haphazard rather than planned and systematic exposure to concepts moving from basic to more complex.

A structured literacy approach is inclusive of a variety of methods and curricula. The key differentiators between reading instruction that aligns with structured literacy and instruction that does not are attention to (a) content that reinforces students' understanding of the alphabetic principle and (b) methods that reflect a systematic, explicit, and cumulative instructional focus. To enhance students' word-level reading skills, structured literacy means attending to the relationships between speech sounds and spelling patterns (i.e., grapheme-phoneme/phoneme-grapheme correspondences); learning how to blend sounds for decoding and segment sounds for spelling; reading connected text with a focus on building accuracy, speed, and prosody; and knowing advanced spelling patterns.

Despite the critical and foundational role of word-level reading in students' reading proficiency, reading words and connected text with ease and prosody is insufficient for reading comprehension. Similarly, while spelling words correctly may boost students' confidence in writing, learning to write coherent, meaningful pieces of writing requires direct teaching of syntax, language forms, ideation, punctuation, and transcription. Therefore, to help students address the language comprehension aspect of The Simple View of Reading, meaning-focused instruction must also occur. In the next chapter, we will examine how to build the knowledge and skills needed to bring understanding to what students read and clarity to what students write.

Chapter Six

Structured Literacy: Language Comprehension

As all definitions of dyslexia[1] affirm, a primary characteristic of students with dyslexia is difficulty with word-level reading. Specifically, students with dyslexia experience difficulty hearing and manipulating the sounds of language (phonology) and mapping these sounds to written language (orthography). Despite this well-documented relationship between word-level difficulty and dyslexia, a growing body of research has also demonstrated that (a) students with dyslexia do not reflect a monolithic group (i.e., students with dyslexia have a diversity of reading profiles), and (b) multiple factors, including internal (e.g., students' oral language, executive functioning, and other cognitive factors) and external (e.g., instruction, the language environment) interact to influence reading ability (Catts & Petscher, 2020; Snowling, Hulme, & Nation, 2020). In fact, over the past several decades, researchers have consistently identified that students with the most significant reading needs have both word-level reading and language comprehension deficits (Brasseur-Hock et al., 2011; Catts et al., 1999; Capin et al., 2021; Capin et al., 2022; Clemens et al., 2017). Although students' profiles may differ in terms of severity (e.g., some students may have significantly weaker phonological processing skills and less severe language comprehension difficulties or more severe language needs with less severe word-level reading challenges), students who struggle with reading are likely to benefit from word-level reading *and* language comprehension instruction (Capin et al., 2022; Gillam et al., 2023).

The connection between young children's language acquisition and later reading ability has been firmly established. Specifically, young children with language-based difficulties, such as difficulties with vocabulary, morphology, syntax, and discourse skills (e.g., conversing, storytelling), are far more

---

1. See Chapter 1 for a comparison of definitions.

likely to experience reading disability in the later grades. Further, oral language skills independently contribute to reading comprehension beyond that of phonological processing (Catts et al., 1999; Duff et al., 2022; Snowling, Hayiou-Thomas, et al., 2020), confirming the important role linguistic ability plays in students' ability to comprehend text.

Notably, the influence of language comprehension on students' ability to understand text changes as they progress through school. In the early elementary years, students' ability to read words (i.e., word recognition) is closely tied to reading comprehension. As students move into upper elementary and secondary grades, the texts get more complex and content-rich. Therefore, for older students, language skills account for more of the variance associated with reading comprehension (Catts et al., 2005; Foorman et al., 2018). Given the significant influence of linguistic knowledge on later reading achievement, attention to language comprehension should begin at the earliest stages of literacy instruction.

In this chapter we will examine how teachers can address the language comprehension component of the Simple View of Reading (Hoover & Gough, 1990; Hoover & Tunmer, 2022). Language comprehension involves understanding word meanings (semantics) and facility with language structure. Instructional elements that contribute to students' language comprehension include vocabulary, morphology, background knowledge, and discourse writing (see Figure 6.1).

The relationship between vocabulary knowledge and reading comprehension has a long and rich research history. Specifically, researchers have consistently found a strong correlation between vocabulary knowledge and reading comprehension (Beck et al., 1982; Cain & Oakhill, 2011; Tannenbaum et al., 2006; Torgesen et al., 1997; Perfetti, 2017)—that is, students who know more words perform better on reading comprehension tasks. The question for reading researchers has been: Does vocabulary knowledge *cause* better reading comprehension, or do other factors, such as students' general knowledge,

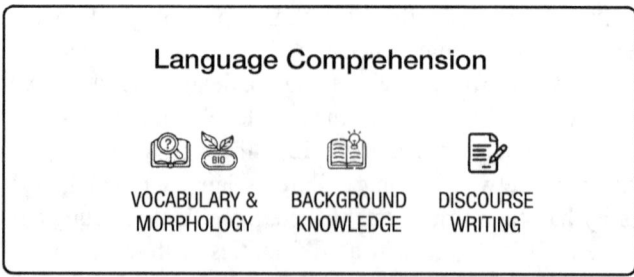

Figure 6.1. The Language Comprehension Component of *The Simple View of Reading*

verbal ability, or automaticity and depth of word knowledge, explain differences in students' comprehension? Likely, a combination of these factors (i.e., students' knowledge of specific words, background knowledge, verbal ability, and verbal efficiency) contribute to reading comprehension (Elleman et al., 2009; Perfetti & Stafura, 2014).

Therefore, to address the first factor—students' knowledge of specific words—structured literacy approaches include the direct teaching of vocabulary words. Notably, when students are learning specific content, directly teaching vocabulary is particularly important (O'Connor et al., 2019). Researchers have found that effective vocabulary instruction involves providing students with multiple and varied experiences with word meanings (Beck et al., 2013). Additionally, teaching *morphology* can also contribute to gains in students' overall vocabulary knowledge (Bowers et al., 2010). *Morphology instruction* involves teaching students to attend to word parts (prefixes, suffixes, and base elements). Taken together, the direct teaching of vocabulary words and morphology instruction serve as one way teachers can build students' linguistic comprehension (i.e., the first instructional component in Figure 6.1).

Although knowledge of specific words contributes to comprehension, knowing word meanings is insufficient, in and of itself, for understanding connected text. Comprehension is primarily built on a reader's capacity to make inferences. Further, the more one knows about a topic, the easier it is not only to read and understand the content but also to remember the content. Another name for topic familiarity is *background knowledge*. Studies have demonstrated that individuals with greater background knowledge are more likely to comprehend text than peers with weaker word recognition skills (Smith et al., 2021). In other words, if a person knows all the words in a passage in isolation but does not bring any background knowledge to the reading, that person will likely comprehend less than a person who had difficulty reading some of the words within the passage but has greater topic familiarity. Of course, limited to no decoding skills provide no opportunity for comprehension, but knowing more about a topic allows a reader to bridge ideas, even if some words are missed. Therefore, an essential component of a comprehensive, structured literacy approach includes attention to building students' background knowledge (i.e., the second instructional component in Figure 6.1).

Finally, the production of connected text also contributes to comprehension. Just as decoding and spelling share a reciprocal relationship that contributes to word recognition, comprehending written text and producing written text share a similar mutually beneficial relationship. Writing allows students to use their vocabulary, explore morphological structures, and extend their background knowledge. Specifically, *discourse writing*, when students are asked to produce writing that reflects an orderly expression of thought on a topic, has been shown to boost their comprehension (Graham & Hebert, 2010). Thus, a final contributing element of instruction that can increase students' linguistic knowledge is discourse writing instruction (i.e., the third instructional component in Figure 6.1).

Recall that a structured literacy approach reflects two elements of instruction—the *what* and the *how*. In the last chapter, we explored content such as alphabetics, grapheme-phoneme correspondence, reading connected text, and spelling that constituted the *what* of a structured literacy approach to word-recognition instruction. In this chapter, the *what* will change, but the *how* will remain remarkably consistent. Content will be planned (i.e., systematic), taught directly (i.e., explicit), and continuously reviewed.

SEMANTICS

At this point in the book, it should be clear that reading comprehension is impossible without the ability to decode a word. But what is necessary for students to bring meaning to the text they are reading? *Semantics*, an understanding of the meaning of language and language structure, is required for reading comprehension. Understanding the meaning of what is being read requires knowledge of words (vocabulary) and word parts that convey meaning (morphology) but also general knowledge of the topic (background knowledge). Within this section, we will explore how teachers can strengthen students' ability to construct meaning from text through explicit attention to vocabulary, morphology, and knowledge building.

Vocabulary

The depth and breadth of a person's word knowledge contribute directly to reading comprehension. Familiarity with many words (i.e., extensive breadth) allows access, whereas depth (i.e., thorough and complete knowledge) contributes to understanding. As such, word knowledge does not fall into an either/or category of known or unknown but occurs along a continuum (Beck et al., 2013). Word knowledge can range from zero familiarity (i.e., never heard or seen the word) to limited familiarity (i.e., have a vague sense that it is positive or negative or has to do with a particular context such as automobiles) to deep familiarity (i.e., can use the word or recognize its use across multiple contexts; Beck et al., 1987). Perfetti (2007) characterized the extensiveness of word knowledge as *lexical quality*. A person possessing a rich lexical representation of a word knows its pronunciation (phonology); meaning across multiple contexts (semantics); spelling (orthography); and parts, such as prefixes, suffixes, and/or bases (morphology) and can use the word within a sentence (syntax). The higher the lexical quality, the more rapidly word meaning can be retrieved. Teachers can enhance students' word knowledge by systematically planning for numerous and varied experiences with words.

One way to build students' word knowledge is through the direct teaching of vocabulary. Explicit vocabulary instruction offers several distinct benefits over incidental learning that may occur as a result of independent reading. First, context does not always provide clear information about a word's meaning. When attempting to determine a word's meaning from context alone, the meaning can be ambiguous (e.g., "She found the house in *disarray* and wondered if anyone had lived there recently." Was the house *orderly*, *dusty*, *messy*, or *empty*?); contradictory ("As she handed him the cake, he smiled *ruefully* back at her." Isn't a smile a signal of pleasantry?); or facilitative ("They were *bewitched* with her performance and jumped to their feet for a standing ovation as a sign of their delight when she had finished."). As these examples demonstrate, although context can facilitate understanding of word meaning, context alone may be insufficient for vocabulary development.

Second, students who struggle with decoding experience far fewer opportunities for contextualized vocabulary development. In contrast to avid readers, who regularly seek out new books to read, struggling readers tend to avoid books and reading. Further, when struggling readers are forced to engage with texts, their lack of fluency and sufficient prior experience with complex texts limit their ability to extract meaning from the novel words they encounter.

Finally, although independent reading can provide students with nuanced information about words and specific examples of word use, the direct teaching of new vocabulary has the benefit of engaging students in instructional exercises that promote phonological, orthographic, semantic, morphological, and syntactic learning. As a result, the words are more likely to be incorporated into students' mental lexicons.

Elements of Effective Vocabulary Instruction

Beck et al. (2013) refer to high-quality vocabulary instruction as *robust*, and they believe robust instruction includes not only instructional features associated with long-term retention (i.e., repeated recall and application across various learning opportunities) but also elements that reflect the joy of learning. Students love to learn, experiment with, and stretch their use of new vocabulary. Vocabulary instruction that embraces students' affinity for expanding avenues of self-expression will likely include elements of joy and fun. A kindergartener is delighted to express, "I am so *famished* right now. Is it almost lunch?" Similarly, the middle schooler likes to flex newfound word knowledge by stating: "I don't mean to *contradict*, but didn't you say there would be no homework tonight?" Finally, the high schooler is delighted to apply a subject-specific word and concept to the everyday experience of high-school life, "Changes to the cafeteria menu should not be done without appropriate *representation* from students." The joyful integration of new vocabulary can come about only as a result of active exploration and use.

Unfortunately, typical vocabulary instruction lacks the critical features of *robust* instruction. Within standard vocabulary instruction, students are provided a list of words, directed to write a dictionary definition, and asked to create sentences that include the word (Apthorp et al., 2012). In addition, students may be required to identify the part of speech or even draw a picture of the word, but each activity is fraught with potential pitfalls. First, dictionary definitions can be confusing (e.g., *exception* = a person or thing that is excluded; this definition does not help a student understand the sentence, "She made an *exception* and allowed him to turn in his homework late."); circular (e.g., *intention* = a thing intended); or contain words or phrases students don't understand (e.g., *condescension* = a patronizing attitude or behavior; Nagy & Stahl, 2002). In addition, dictionary definitions were written to be concise rather than to convey nuanced meaning. As a result, students might only learn one aspect of a word's meaning but fail to gain a deeper understanding of a word's use across multiple contexts. In short, having students look up or write dictionary definitions does not likely facilitate a deep understanding of the words' meanings.

Second, having students write a sentence containing the word lacks two essential components of robust vocabulary instruction—active thinking about word meaning and a variety of contexts in which to apply word meaning. Simply writing a complete and correct sentence does not require a student to understand the word (e.g., "She was an *entrepreneur*."). Even if a student produces a sentence that is closer to the definition (e.g., "The *entrepreneur* opened a new store."), this does not mean that the student understands the essential features of the word (e.g., starting a new business that involves *risk*, *innovation*, and *unknowns*). Further, having students compose one sentence limits students to one particular use of the word. What does it mean to be *entrepreneurial* or to have an *entrepreneurial spirit*? Are entrepreneurs more likely to be associated with words like *ambitious*, *passionate,* and *open-minded* or words like *cautious*, *introverted*, and *uninterested*?

Finally, like the Monday spelling list, the weekly vocabulary list fails to capitalize on frequent, varied recall and continuous review of previously taught words. In particular, if students are tested only once on the words, it is not likely they will retain the information for any length of time and certainly not incorporate the word into their oral or written vocabularies (Dunlosky et al., 2013). In addition, if previously taught words are not regularly integrated into students' weekly vocabulary practice, definitions students may have learned will be quickly forgotten.

These limitations can be addressed by incorporating the principles of robust vocabulary instruction championed by Beck et al. (2013) and other vocabulary researchers (Archer & Hughes, 2011; O'Conner et al., 2019). Robust instruction begins with the selection of high-utility words—words that add dimension or are foundational for comprehending a text selection. Beck et al., conceptualized a three-tiered framework to aid in the selection of high-utility words. Within their framework, Tier 1 words are common words whose meaning will likely be known by most students (e.g., *book*, *girl*, *happy*, *jump*). At the other end of the spectrum, Tier 3 words reflect highly specialized words that are likely to appear only in subject-specific contexts (e.g., *igneous*, *preamble*, *quotient*). In the middle are Tier 2 words, which are more likely to occur in written rather than everyday oral language and have multiple meanings (e.g., *industrious*, *benevolent*, *reluctant*). Tier 2 words reflect the sweet spot of vocabulary instruction. Not only do these words add nuance and specificity to context, but they also appear across many different genres, including narrative and expository texts. Therefore, the first step to implementing robust vocabulary instruction is to select a handful of Tier 2 words drawn directly from classroom reading materials to be the focus of instruction.

Next, Nagy's (1988) three elements of effective instruction—*integration*, *meaningful use*, and *repetition*—can be applied. *Vocabulary integration* can occur through oral or scaffolded reading, class discussion, and vocabulary exercises. When vocabulary instruction is integrated, it is not relegated to a Monday list and a Friday test. Instead, vocabulary instruction occurs multiple times and in multiple contexts. For example, as Tier 2 words are more likely to occur within complex texts that may be beyond the reading abilities of struggling readers, teachers can read passages aloud to their students or provide scaffolded oral reading opportunities. During scaffolded reading, teachers may read a text selection and have students engage in echo reading (i.e., repeated reading of the text selection the teacher just read) or direct students to read only specific, accessible sentences or passages within the text. Integration is also facilitated by engaging students in vocabulary exercises or class discussions related to the text reading. For example, a teacher can ask students to describe or write about how specific characters do or do not reflect certain character traits (e.g., *charismatic, carefree, irrational, manipulative*).

Meaningful use occurs when students must apply their knowledge of word meaning or experience others using it in context (e.g., an author, a teacher, or peers). As explained previously, writing a sentence containing the word can fall short of the meaningful-use threshold. In contrast, if students are provided with sentence starters such as "The first grader was *reluctant* to . . . " or "The teacher demonstrated her *benevolence* by . . . ," and students are prompted to apply their knowledge of the word to complete the task, that exercise will require the meaningful application of target words. Similarly, asking students to match a word with associated terms (e.g., Does *intrepid* go with *courageous* and *spunky* or *cowardly* and *timid*?) draws upon their conceptual understanding of the word. Teacher modeling of the word both during class instruction and more spontaneously outside of that instructional period (e.g., "I saw some *intrepid* third graders take on a group of fourth graders in basketball today at recess.") can further boost students' access to meaningful use of new vocabulary. Likewise, meaningful use occurs when students encounter the word in varying contexts. For example, students can encounter the word *intrepid* in *Flat Stanley's Worldwide Adventures: The Intrepid Canadian Expedition* (Brown, 2009) but also come across the word in a social studies unit on World War II. Multiple informative encounters with words enable flexibility—students' ability to deduce word meaning in novel contexts and integrate words into their oral or written vocabularies.

Finally, repetition, a foundational element of all structured literacy instruction, is the key to long-term retention of vocabulary. *Repetition* involves repeated encounters with words across multiple contexts across multiple days. Repetition is more powerful when students are asked to recall, apply, classify, generate, explain, compare, and otherwise actively engage around word meaning. The beauty of distributed practice is that instruction does not need to be lengthy to promote long-term learning (Benjamin & Tullis, 2010). A quick do-now prompt at the start of class (e.g., "Describe one way you can demonstrate *intrepidness* this week."); a brief discussion during a text reading (e.g., "Why would the *USS Intrepid* be a good name for a warship?"); or expeditious transition prompts (e.g., "Everyone, stand, push in your chairs, and stand *intrepidly* to show me who is ready to go to lunch.") all require students to engage with word meaning. Cumulative review is another example of repetition. *Cumulative review* occurs when teachers integrate previously taught terms within exercises, discussions, activities, and quizzes.

In summary, robust vocabulary instruction will include rich and varied experiences with Tier 2 words. Planning for the systematic integration of vocabulary instruction requires teachers to identify words in advance and plan where, when, and how engagement with words will occur. The use of explicit vocabulary routines can facilitate that integration.

Explicit Vocabulary Routines

Explicit vocabulary routines include the essential elements of robust vocabulary instruction (Archer & Hughes, 2011; see Table 6.1). Explicit instruction begins with the teacher modeling a word's correct pronunciation and pairing that pronunciation with its spelling. Connecting phonology with orthography helps build students' mental representation of the word. This representation can serve as an anchor to which students will attach meaning (Rosenthal & Ehri, 2008). Recall the orthographic mapping or connectionist framework described in Chapter 4. When spellings are paired with word pronunciations, those concepts become fused and can be accessed automatically. Further, researchers have found that awareness of spelling aids in pronunciation recall (Ehri & Wilce, 1979); if students hear a word but do not see or learn its spelling, they are less likely to remember its pronunciation. Even if irregular (e.g., Wed-nes-day), learning the spelling facilitates word pronunciation. Therefore, the foundational first step in vocabulary instruction is to create the pronunciation and spelling anchor.

The next step is to provide a student-friendly explanation of the word. In contrast to the sometimes problematic dictionary definition, student-friendly explanations offer information about a word's meaning and use (Archer & Hughes, 2011; Beck et al., 2013). Student-friendly explanations use everyday language to express critical elements associated with the meaning of a word. For example, a dictionary definition of *reluctant* is "feeling or showing aversion or hesitation; assuming a specified role unwillingly" (Merriam-Webster, n.d.). Students may be unfamiliar with the words *aversion* and *hesitation*. Therefore, a student-friendly explanation includes terms students are likelier to know and highlights how the word differs from others. In addition, the explanation consists of information about how the word may be used. Thus, a student-friendly explanation of *reluctant* could be, "When someone is not willing or enthusiastic about doing something. The person may be afraid or nervous to try something like tasting a new food or going on a roller coaster."

Although it is common practice for teachers to begin vocabulary instruction by asking students what they already know about a word, querying students about what they *think* about a word is often unproductive and can even be counterproductive. The provision of near-correct guesses sends students' thinking in the wrong direction, and the provision of incorrect guesses can

Table 6.1. An Explicit Vocabulary Routine

Introduce the Word	• Present the word on the board. [reluctant] • Read the word. Students repeat. [What word?] • Segment the word for spelling. [/r/ /ə/ /l/ /ə/ /k/ /t/ /ə/ /n/ /t/] • Spell the word. [reluctant]
Present a Student-Friendly Explanation	When someone is not willing or enthusiastic about doing something. The person may be afraid or nervous to try something like tasting a new food or going on a roller coaster.

Illustrate the Word	• Create a visual mnemonic.

	• Create sentences.
	  ◦ Many people are *reluctant* to jump off the high dive.
	  ◦ If your friend asks you to try a new food, you might be *reluctant* to try something new.

Deepen Students' Understanding Through Concept Development Work	• Check for meaning.
	  ◦ Why might a person be *reluctant* to do something?
	• Examples and non-examples.
	  ◦ In which of the following sentences could you use the word *reluctant*? (a) He had looked forward to the trip all day, and now he was excited/reluctant to go! (b) She deeply feared spiders, so she felt excited/reluctant about going into the abandoned cabin in the woods.
	• Sentence starters.
	  ◦ The young child was *reluctant* to . . .
	• Student-generated examples.
	  ◦ Create three sentences about something you are *reluctant* to do.

result in students recalling those incorrect guesses later (Beck et al., 2013). Therefore, rather than asking students what they think they know about a word, it is better to directly provide a student-friendly explanation.

Although student-friendly explanations may make the meaning more accessible, students need context to build a conceptual understanding of the word. Context helps students situate where, when, and how the word can be used. Techniques for building contextual understanding include creating a visual mnemonic for the word, generating examples and non-examples, using sentence starters, mapping word associations, and creating application exercises related to text materials. A visual mnemonic pairs a word and its definition with a picture or visual image. In the case of *reluctant*, a visual image of a dog pulling away from its owner (see the third row in Table 6.1) can provide an example of what someone or something may do when feeling *reluctant*. Students can be taught, "Lucky, the dog, was *reluctant* to go to the vet." The dog's name provides a hook for remembering the term *reluctant*, and the image offers a hook for remembering that Lucky was unwilling to go. The teacher can then guide a discussion about the visual mnemonic (e.g., "Why might Lucky be *reluctant* to go to the vet?"), which can lead to expanded uses for the word in other contexts (e.g., "Why might someone be *reluctant* to jump off a high dive? Visit an unfamiliar place? When have you ever felt like Lucky?").

Finally, teachers can engage students in various vocabulary exercises to build, extend, and firm students' understanding of the word. Although one or two exercises may be completed immediately following the initial introduction of the word, distributing engagement across multiple learning sessions needs to occur for the instruction to be truly robust. Vocabulary exercises can range from low-level knowledge tasks such as recognition (e.g., Which word makes sense in this sentence?) to higher-level cognitive tasks such as generation (e.g., Describe three situations where a person may feel *reluctance*.). Informal assessment of student understanding can come from in-class choral responses using gestures (e.g., "Show me thumbs up if what I say is an example of when someone may be *reluctant* and thumbs down if it is not an example of when someone might be *reluctant*: Being asked to . . . eat a live bug, go to an amusement park, rewatch a favorite movie, watch a scary movie).

Vocabulary knowledge is an important predictor of reading comprehension. Unfortunately, many students who struggle with reading have reduced vocabularies (Hock et al., 2009). Researchers have found that robust vocabulary instruction can positively and significantly affect students' ability to learn taught words (Elleman et al., 2009; Wright & Cervetti, 2017). Targeted vocabulary instruction can increase students' comprehension of passages containing taught words. In addition, active-processing techniques, such as those associated with robust vocabulary instruction, are more effective than standard dictionary definition exercises (Wright & Cervetti, 2017). Despite these positive findings related to vocabulary instruction, scholars also found that studies examining the effects of vocabulary instruction failed to demonstrate improvements in general comprehension as a result of the vocabulary interventions (Elleman et al., 2009; Wright & Cervetti, 2017). These findings may signal that short-term interventions are insufficient—students may require focused vocabulary instruction across multiple years beginning in the early elementary years—and/or that additional, complementary instructional components are necessary. One promising complementary area of language comprehension instruction is morphology instruction.

Morphology

Recall that English is a morphophonemic language. Word spellings reflect phonology (i.e., this sound is represented by this spelling; /s/ = *s*) and morphology (i.e., this word meaning is represented by this spelling; before = *pre*). The phonological aspect of reading was addressed in Chapter 6 and falls under the *word recognition* component of the Simple View of Reading. Morphology instruction, in contrast, deals with the meaning of parts of words—prefixes, suffixes, and bases—and reflects students' linguistic comprehension. When students are sensitive to the morphological components of words (e.g., recognizing *un-* means *not* [*unafraid*, *unhelpful*] or knowing *-er* means *more of* something [*taller*, *smarter*] or a *person who* [*teacher*, *writer*]), they can deduce word meaning using morphological information. Morphological sensitivity also allows students to create and spell word variations (e.g., *walk* → *walked* or *walks* or *walker*). Researchers have demonstrated that morphology instruction increases students' word recognition, spelling, and vocabulary knowledge (Bowers et al., 2010; Goodwin & Ahn, 2013).

Morphology instruction also expands students' understanding of words and flexibility with words. For example, a *morphological word family* consists of words that share a common meaning and structure but vary in terms of the specific affixes (e.g., *read*, *read•er*, *mis•read*, *un•read•able*). As students' facility with morphemes increases, they are better able to understand morphologically complex words and change known words into syntactically correct forms when speaking or writing. Thus, morphology instruction involves teaching students the structure of words. As was addressed in Chapter 5, awareness of morphemes can facilitate decoding as students "peel off" meaningful chunks when sounding out words (e.g., undoable → *un•do•able*), but the teaching of morphemes directly addresses word meaning. Further, just as knowledge of consonants and vowels provides the background knowledge necessary for teachers to explain to students how to sound out words, knowledge of morphological structure can help teachers plan for and scaffold morphology instruction.

Understanding Morphemes

Morphemes are broadly classified as free or bound (see Figure 6.2). *Free morphemes* can stand alone and consist of only one morpheme (i.e., meaningful unit; e.g., *cat, purple, the, house, weak*). *Bound morphemes*, in contrast, cannot stand alone, but each part contributes to the meaning of a complete word. Bound morphemes are affixes (i.e., prefixes and suffixes) and bound roots (i.e., word parts that cannot stand alone; e.g., *aqua* = water as in *aquarium, subaquatic, nonaquatic; dent* = tooth as in *dentist, dental, dentures*). Affixes can be further divided into two types, derivational and inflectional. *Inflectional morphemes* are suffixes that do not change the meaning of a word but change the grammatical property of a word, such as tense (e.g., *walk<u>s</u>, walk<u>ed</u>, walk<u>ing</u>*), number (e.g., *bird<u>s</u>, house<u>s</u>*), possession (e.g., *Fredrick<u>'s</u>*) or comparison (e.g., *happ<u>ier</u>, strong<u>est</u>*).

In contrast, *derivational morphemes* can be prefixes or suffixes that do result in a change in the meaning of a word. For example, adding the prefix *un-* to the word *do* results in a new word, *undo*. One way to think about the difference between inflectional and derivational morphemes is that derivational morphemes result in a new dictionary entry. In contrast, inflectional morphemes are variations of the same word.

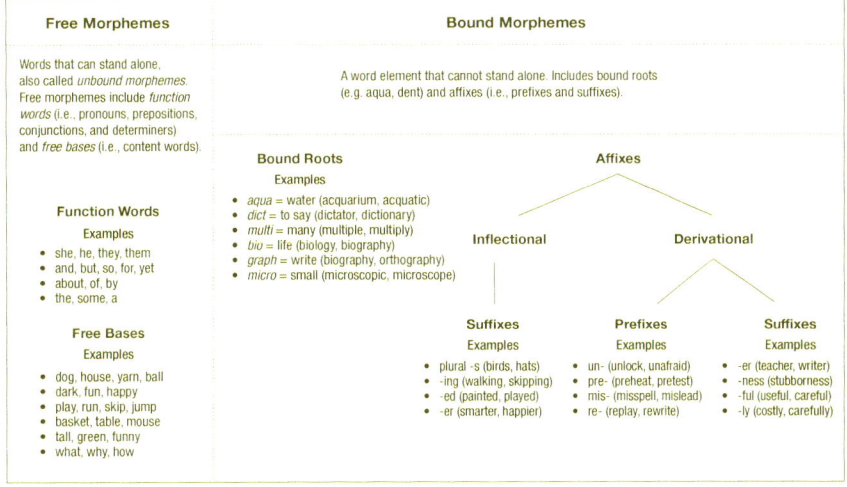

Figure 6.2. Classification of Morphemes

Morphology Instruction

Similar to teaching students vocabulary words, teaching students morphemes can and should include elements of joy. Joyful instruction occurs when students realize they possess the skills necessary to accomplish a task and gain fluency. For example, consider the third-grade classroom described by Manyak et al. (2018) in which the teacher handed out cards with words sharing the same free base (e.g., *do* = *doable, undo, redo, overdo*; *play* = *played, replay, playful, misplay*). The task for students was to find their peers with cards with the same base, identify the affixes, and discuss word meanings. As students had been taught the common prefixes and suffixes in previous lessons, the lesson activity was designed to support students' application and generalization of their knowledge. Following the word analysis discussion, the students engaged in a fluency exercise—a Jeopardy-style quiz wherein students responded to fill-in-the-blank questions such as "The name of the *test* you take *before* you start studying a subject is ____."

Engaging instruction is made possible when students are provided with a structured introduction to the material. A structured approach to morphology instruction involves teaching (a) the meaning of affixes and bases; (b) morphological analysis (i.e., how to break words into morphological parts); (c) spelling patterns for adding or changing morphemes (e.g., *happy* → *happiness*); and (d) how to change the morphological structure of words to create syntactically correct sentences (e.g., *She did not study. She was* _____ *[prepare]*.)

Moreover, morphology instruction is strengthened when teachers provide a context for students to explore word meaning and syntactical use (Kieffer & Lesaux, 2010). Varied contexts allow students to engage with morphologically related words, promoting a deeper understanding of words and word families. Varied contexts can include a range of reading materials (e.g., news articles, websites, narrative texts, textbooks), class discussions, and multiple application activities. Thus, the guiding principles for morphology instruction include planned and frequent encounters with words across contexts, direct engagement with morphological analysis, and instructional exercises that allow for distributed practice and varied applications of morphological knowledge.

Morphology Matrices

One instructional tool that can be used within a structured approach to morphology instruction is a morphology matrix (Bowers & Kirby, 2010; Ng et al., 2022). On a morphology matrix, words are divided into possible parts—prefixes, bases, and suffixes (see Figure 6.3). Matrices are particularly useful for helping students explore the changes in meaning and spelling that occur as a result of changes in affixes. Using a morphology matrix, students create word sums (e.g., *re* + *move* + *ed* = *removed*) and then explain the component

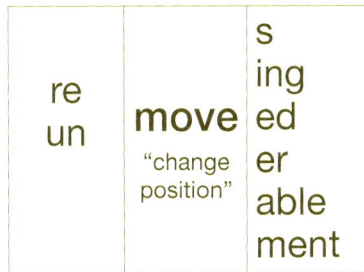

Figure 6.3. Morphology Matrix

parts. For example, for the word *removed*, students would explain the prefix *re-* means "again" (as in to do again) or "back" (as in withdrawal or backward motion), and the suffix *-ed* indicates past tense. In the case of *removed*, the *re-* with *move* means that something was taken back, and *-ed* demonstrates that the moving back already occurred. Students can then practice applying the concept through cloze activities (e.g., "The bookcase was so heavy it was [removable/unmovable].") or by creating their own sentences based on sentence prompts (e.g., base = *move*; prompt = Use the base *move* to write sentences about [a] something stinky, [b] something heavy, and [c] something fast).

As students learn to make word sums, they learn how adding affixes changes word spelling. Thankfully, there are only a few spelling patterns students need to learn for the addition of suffixes (see Table 6.2). In first grade, students can work with word sums that do not require spelling changes, such as inflectional suffixes added to single-syllable bases (e.g., *help, helps, helped, helping*). By second grade, students can begin working with word sums that require consonant doubling, dropping the silent *e*, and changing *y* to *i* for suffix additions.

Table 6.2. Suffix Spelling Patterns and Word Sums

Spelling Patterns	Word Sum
If the base ends with a short vowel followed by a single consonant, double the consonant before adding a vowel suffix.	run + ing = run**n**ing sad + est = sad**d**est skip + er = skip**p**er
If the base ends with a silent *e*, drop the *e* before adding a vowel suffix.	wave + ing = waving hike + able = hikable bake + ed = baked
If the base ends with a silent *e*, keep the *e* if adding a consonant suffix.	peace + ful = peaceful skate + s = skates sprite + ly = spritely
If the base ends in a *ce* or *ge*, keep the *e* when the vowel suffix begins with an *a* or *o*.	courage + ous = courageous trace + able = traceable advantage + ous = advantageous
If the base ends with a consonant followed by a *y*, change the *y* to *i* unless the suffix begins with an *i*.	cry + es = cr**i**es silly + er = sill**i**er fly + ing = fly**i**ng
If the base ends with a *y* vowel team, keep the *y*.	toy + ing = toying gray + ish = grayish repay + ment = repayment

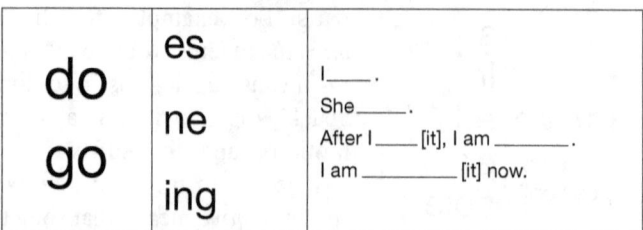

Figure 6.4.   Morphology Matrix for the Words *Do* and *Go*

Morphology matrices, in particular, provide an excellent visual tool to help students understand the relationships across words as pronunciation changes occur due to affix changes. For example, the connection between the words *do* and *done* or *go* and *gone* may not be apparent for early elementary students. A morphology matrix can help students see how the meaning relationship is preserved even though pronunciation changes (see Figure 6.4).

For older students, the word *sign* provides an excellent example of phonological changes due to affix additions (see Figure 6.5). The root *sign* comes from the Latin word *signum,* meaning "an identifying mark or symbol." When people *sign* letters, they leave their mark. A *signal* is an indicator or mark, alerting someone about what to do. An *assignment* is a task requiring someone to leave their mark. As affixes are added, the pronunciation of *sign* changes. For example, the long /ī/ in *sign* becomes a short /ĭ/ in *signal,* and the *g* becomes pronounced /g/. The pronunciation of *s* can also change (e.g., the /s/ in *sign* becomes a /z/ in *design*). Matrices provide a concrete, visual representation of word structure that students frequently do not understand unless they actively add and change affixes through structured instruction.

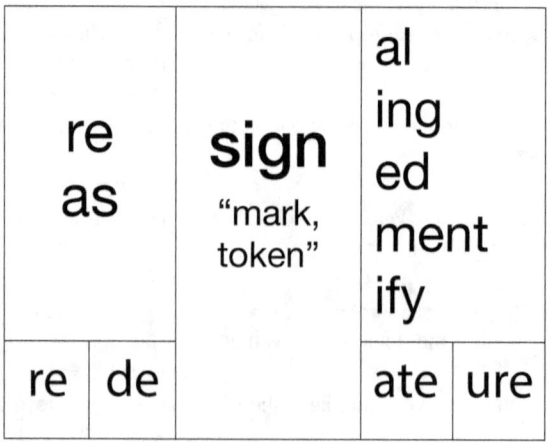

Figure 6.5.   Sign Word Matrix

Because morphology instruction is a component of vocabulary instruction, the same principles for word selection and many of the same features of instruction apply. Specifically, words selected for morphology instruction should be high-utility, academic words (i.e., Tier 2 words; Beck et al., 2013). Morphology instruction in kindergarten and first grade will focus on inflectional endings—adding -*s* to make words plural, -*ed* to indicate past tense, and -*ing* to demonstrate action. By second grade, though, common prefixes and suffixes can be introduced (e.g., *un-, re-, dis-, -er, -est*). Prefix and suffix work will continue and be expanded upon in third and fourth grade, leading to focused work with Latin and Greek roots in the upper elementary grades.

The academic word list (AWL) generated by Coxhead (2000) can be an excellent tool for word selection. The AWL is a compilation of words used frequently across content-area texts (e.g., *define, estimate, interpret, vary*). Thus, words on the AWL list reflect the type of high-utility, versatile words found across academic disciplines—science, social studies, mathematics, and English–language arts—recommended for instruction by vocabulary scholars. Many academic words have extensive word families (e.g., *interpret, interpretation, interpretative, misinterpret, misinterpretation, reinterpret, misinterpreting*). Instruction includes oral and written activities following the structured framework of explicitly teaching root meaning, followed by varied engagement with word families. For example, teachers may lead students in reading text passages that contain keywords, followed by a discussion of word meanings across the contexts and extension questions (e.g., "What are some reasons people or animals may *migrate*?) or writing exercises (e.g., "Discuss two other examples of *migration* we have studied").

For example, in a structured sequence of lessons on the root *migr* (Latin, meaning "move"), students would read a passage about immigration and engage in a class discussion on the word. Then, students would be prompted to use a matrix to create word sums such as *im + migr + ant*, *e*m + *migr + ate*, *migr + ate +ion*, and *migr + ant + s*. Using their word sums, students would then be asked to develop sentences using those words. Researchers have demonstrated a particular advantage of having students focus on the base, which drives the word's meaning, and then exploring changes in meaning or syntactical use by adding affixes (i.e., word families; Crosson et al., 2021; Ng et al., 2022).

Finally, systematic morphology instruction can improve students' writing. Specifically, recent research has demonstrated positive effects of morphology instruction on students' spelling and sentence-level production (Goodwin & Ahn, 2013; Kieffer & Lesaux, 2010; McCutchen et al., 2022). As morphology instruction involves attention to spelling and word meaning, explicit attention to morphemes can support students' ability to select words that capture the meaning they are trying to express during writing (i.e., text generation) and spell those words with greater accuracy and fluency (i.e., transcribe the word[2]).

Knowledge Building: Background Knowledge

Although vocabulary and morphology knowledge are important components of language comprehension, word knowledge alone is insufficient for reading comprehension. Even if students can read every word in a passage, and they know the meanings of those words, other factors within the reader and external factors associated with the text itself will affect their ability to extract and retain meaning from the text (see Table 6.3; Snow, 2002). One important within-reader factor is background knowledge. *Background knowledge* refers to all the knowledge about the world a person possesses. Background knowledge extends beyond definitional knowledge to encompass what a person knows about a specific topic (e.g., trains), broader but related knowledge (e.g., transportation, infrastructure, energy usage), and general knowledge (e.g., concepts such as economics and politics; cultural references such as Agatha Christie's *Murder on the Orient Express;* and idioms such as *train wreck* or *the train has left the station*).

Background knowledge is of particular importance because of how text is written. Writers don't include every detail of a story, explanation, or factual account. If too much explanation is provided, the reader can become overwhelmed trying to process the onslaught of information. If you have ever listened to someone tell a story and thought, "Just get to the point," you have experienced explanation overload. Therefore, writers rely on readers' ability to make inferences while reading. *Inferences* are logical guesses based on the provided information. For example, if students read: "The long-awaited field trip was tomorrow. Judy knew she would not be able to sleep tonight," they must (a) know that when people are excited, they have difficulty sleeping and (b) infer that the cause of Judy's sleep trouble was excitement and not some other cause. The more inferences readers need to make, the more readers will need to draw on background knowledge to fill in the gaps. Whereas readers with strong background knowledge may be able to use their knowledge to

Table 6.3. Factors Associated with a Student's Ability to Gain Knowledge from Texts

Within-Reader	External
• Current background knowledge (specific, broad, general) • Fluency, Attention, and Working Memory	• Text Cohesiveness and Coherence • Text Structure: Narrative and Expository

---

2. Information about text generation and transcription is presented in the Discourse Writing section of this chapter.

make sense of complex or ambiguous texts, readers with less background knowledge will struggle to make the inferences demanded by the text. Further, research has demonstrated prior knowledge about a topic directly contributes to understanding during reading and retention after reading (Cervetti & Wright, 2020). Thus, background knowledge contributes to the stickiness of learning; adding knowledge to existing knowledge makes learning easier. The additive value of knowledge was aptly captured by Stanovich's (1986) description of the phenomenon as *The Matthew Effect*, which harkens back to the biblical expression, "For to everyone who has, will more be given" (Matthew 25:29). Knowledge is cumulative. Therefore, building background knowledge is an essential component of high-quality literacy instruction.

Thus, a person's current background knowledge is one element that will influence the quality and quantity of reading comprehension that can occur during text reading. Still, external factors, such as text features, and internal factors, such as working memory and attention, will also influence the reading experience. A structured approach to knowledge building will take all these factors into account.

Text Features and Cognitive Load

Cognitive load refers to the mental processing demands imposed by a particular task. All texts will require readers to make some inferences and, therefore, place cognitive load demands on them, but some texts are more reader-friendly than others. Two elements of writing that contribute to cognitive load are cohesion and coherence (Smith et al., 2021). *Cohesion* refers to the way vocabulary and grammatical structures are used to convey ideas within a text. Highly cohesive texts make strategic use of linking words (e.g., *however*, *therefore*) and the repetition and expansion of key terminology (e.g., using the term *president* three times in a text and then weaving in synonymous terms such as *leader* and *head of state* to provide alternatives to the term *president*). In addition, cohesive texts remove distracting redundancy (e.g., Franklin D. Roosevelt was first elected as president in 1932. **He** was reelected [as president] in 1936, 1940, and 1944.). The judicious use of pronouns and elimination of redundant phrases (e.g., *as president*) results in more cohesive writing. Thus, highly cohesive texts reduce the cognitive demands placed on the reader by way of strategic word use.

Coherent texts also facilitate reading comprehension. *Coherence* refers to how logically concepts are presented within a text. Within coherent texts (a) ideas are presented logically; (b) main ideas are evident; and (c) signposting (i.e., telling readers what to expect by using phrases such as "In this essay ...," "Having established ...," and "The findings demonstrate...") is used to connect ideas within and across paragraphs. In addition, examples and non-examples may be provided in highly coherent texts to reinforce concepts. Finally, if the overall structure, outline, or theme of a piece of writing is evident, the text is considered to have high coherence. High coherence, similar to strong cohesiveness, reduces the cognitive demands placed on readers by clearly demonstrating how ideas are connected rather than requiring readers to determine the connections on their own.

Students primarily encounter two types of texts within school—narrative and expository. *Narrative* texts are stories that relate a series of events. Narratives can be fictional stories (e.g., the story of the three pigs) or non-fictional stories (e.g., a story about Amelia Earhart). Narrative texts dominate early elementary grades (Moss, 2008). Narrative texts employ structural features that make comprehension easier. Specifically, stories tend to (a) follow a temporal sequence (e.g., *first, once upon a time, one day; second, then, next, after that, suddenly, later; finally, last, in the end, eventually, as a result*); (b) adhere to a predictable sequence; and (c) use familiar language (Medina & Pilonieta, 2006). Given the nature of the narrative structure, narrative texts are naturally more cohesive and coherent. However, as students move to fourth grade and beyond, they are increasingly expected to read and understand expository texts. *Expository* texts are texts designed to impart information and facts about a topic. As expository texts are written to inform, the structure of texts varies according to the topic (e.g., cause and effect; compare and contrast; problem and solution; sequence). These structures are less transparent than the familiar beginning, middle, and end structure of narrative writing, making it more challenging for readers to identify relationships across ideas. Expository and narrative texts also differ in the language used; expository texts feature more academic and technical terms, whereas narrative texts feature more high-frequency words.

Researchers have consistently found that all students and struggling readers, in particular, experience far more difficulty comprehending expository texts than narrative texts (Best et al., 2008; Jitendra et al., 2011; McNamara et al., 2013). Because expository texts are written to build new knowledge, they are often written in such a way that assumes some background knowledge. For example, a book on whales may not provide explanatory information about the ocean, endangered species, hemispheres, or migration. As a result, students with less background knowledge will experience increased difficulty comprehending these texts (Beck & McKeown, 2016).

Other critical within-reader factors contribute to building background knowledge and, by extension, students' ability to extract meaning from text. Those factors are fluency and working memory. Unfortunately, for many students with dyslexia or who struggle with reading, limitations with these processing tasks will further impede their ability to gain knowledge from reading.

Other Within-Reader Factors: Fluency and Working Memory

Reading fluency is the capacity to read with speed, accuracy, and expression. The first aspect of reading fluency is speed. Even if a student is reading accurately, slow reading impedes the student's ability to make sense of connected text by placing too much demand on working memory. *Working memory* is the amount of information that can be held in an accessible state. In other words, working memory is the amount of information a person can be actively thinking about at one time. For example, working memory allows readers to remember what was read at the beginning of a sentence and connect it to what is read at the end. In addition, working memory processing involves recalling information stored in long-term memory and relating it to a text being read. Drawing upon known concepts allows inferences and new information to be connected to known concepts. Thus, *active thinking* involves processing external stimuli—in the case of reading, processing printed words—and connecting that material with ideas from long-term memory. When reading is slow, the ability to think about what one is reading during the reading process is lost. Working memory is bogged down with decoding processes.

In turn, inaccurate reading is problematic, because incorrect words are either inserted or missed—thus altering or confusing the meaning—but also because attempts to decipher unknown words can reduce reading speed and tax working memory. As a result, inaccurate reading is a word-recognition problem and a meaning-interfering problem. LaBerge and Samuels's (1974) automaticity theory and Perfetti's (1985) verbal efficiency theory reflect this relationship between word fluency (i.e., word-reading efficiency) and the capacity for text processing. LaBerge and Samuels noted that thinking (i.e., actively processing information in working memory) requires attention. However, when a skill is automatic, like driving a car or tying one's shoes, attention can be directed elsewhere. Students who are not automatic must devote limited attention to word recognition. Similarly, according to Perfetti's *verbal efficiency theory*, readers who struggle with word recognition recruit working memory resources for word recognition, which reduces their working memory capacity for processing text meaning and integrating ideas.

Finally, a reader's ability to bring expression to reading reflects reading fluency. *Expression*, also called *prosody*, involves using appropriate phrasing, intonation, and voice when reading. Disfluent readers have difficulty grouping words into meaningful phrases (e.g., She ran / across the street) and applying the necessary intonation to convey the particular meaning of a sentence (e.g., She **ran** /across the street, or She ran / across **the street**?). Thus, expressiveness is an important component of reading fluency and reflects a reader's processing of meaning while reading.

Fluent reading is the hallmark of strong reading and the strongest predictor of reading comprehension (Kim et al., 2012). Fluent reading is a result of word-reading skills but is also a reflection of knowledge. Thus, one way to improve reading fluency is through knowledge building.

The Need for Knowledge

What students need in order to understand the text they are reading is, ironically, knowledge. As has been emphasized in this chapter, knowledge begets knowledge. Unfortunately, schools are more likely to focus on content-free instructional exercises rather than knowledge-building ones. Comprehension is often considered a skill that can be taught independently of knowledge building. In other words, comprehension is taught as if it is a specialized thinking skill that can be applied to any piece of writing. For example, teachers commonly attempt to teach students a strategy for how to "find the main idea" of a piece of text. Students may be instructed to look for repeated words or at the topic and concluding sentences to determine the focus of the text. To practice this skill, students may be given several brief passages on different topics (e.g., sharks' teeth, global warming, what makes a good pet) and asked to identify the main idea and three supporting details. Unfortunately, this type of practice is unlikely to change students' ability to comprehend most expository texts they will encounter in school.

The primary and most problematic reason for this is that there is no such thing as a "general thinking skill." Cognitive psychologists have repeatedly demonstrated that thinking is domain-specific (Hirsch, 2019; Willingham, 2009). The quality of thinking is directly related to what a person knows about a topic. Recall that inferences can only come from background knowledge. A reader cannot read a text carefully or even *closely* to glean an inference. The reader must possess sufficient background and vocabulary knowledge to determine the main ideas,[3] the author's intent, explicit and implicit messages, and so on. I recall reading a passage about a rugby match last year and laughing as I struggled to comprehend almost every sentence in the article. I lacked the vocabulary (e.g., *advantage, blindside, pitch, blood bin*) and sufficient background knowledge. Specifically, to make sense of what I was reading, I needed to understand the historical context between the rival

---

3. Contrary to how "find the main idea" is taught in school, complex pieces of writing typically have more than one main idea.

teams and individual players, and I needed to know the game well enough to understand why a particular player walking off the pitch at a specific moment in the game was an affront to the other team. No graphic organizer or summarizing strategy would have helped me make sense of the text, nor am I a deficient critical thinker. I simply lacked the background knowledge and vocabulary needed to understand the information provided.

The second major problem with teaching comprehension as a context-free skill is that the exercises fail to build the knowledge students need for comprehension. Instead, they give teachers and students the illusion that a skill is being learned due to the nature of the passages. That is, the brief passages used for the comprehension exercises tend to be highly coherent and cohesive. This means the texts have been pre-processed—the links between ideas are explicitly stated. In addition, the texts are written to support the activity rather than facilitate a deep understanding of a concept. As a result, detailed and nuanced information about the topic is likely not present. Instead, one main idea and several supporting details will be included in each passage, whether the passage is on the Constitution or the availability of chocolate milk in the cafeteria. In contrast, the types of expository texts students are expected to read and make sense of in upper elementary, middle, and high school are complex texts with multiple ideas interwoven.

Finally, the strategies themselves offer some but limited utility. Researchers have found that although teaching students reading comprehension strategies can increase self-regulation (e.g., monitoring, checking for understanding while reading, using visual imagery while reading), the benefit of the strategy is still constrained by background knowledge (Filderman et al., 2022; Gajria et al., 2007). In other words, once students are taught to monitor their understanding, they do not gain an additional, universal comprehension boost from extended practice with discrete passages on topics with which they have varying familiarity. Willingham and Lovette (2014) liken reading comprehension strategies to general advice like "drive safely" or "think before you speak." Reading comprehension strategies remind students to check to ensure they understand as they read. Sometimes, though, it is not obvious that the message or writer's intent is being missed. Or, a strategy may direct students to create a visual image. Again, the image can stick and be helpful for remembering the content, or the image could be incorrect and lead the reader astray. Researchers have found that the general, good advice offered by reading comprehension strategies is helpful to students (see NICHD, 2000) but can be quickly learned and does not require instruction beyond a handful of sessions (Willingham & Lovette, 2014).

Unfortunately, state standards perpetuate the false notion that critical thinking skills can be taught independently of content and that there is benefit in repeated practice. Hirsch (2019) found the same standard, "Identify the main idea," repeated verbatim at every grade level from second through eighth grade in Virginia's state standards. Notably, the standard was not connected to any specific content; thus, the only guidance for teachers was to have students practice finding the main idea, reinforcing the notion that critical thinking is domain independent. Virginia is not an exception. Most states do not specify English–language-arts–related content; instead, skills such as "determining central ideas," "providing an objective summary," or "evaluating a summary for accuracy" are offered. Even worse, many elementary schools have reduced or eliminated content-rich instruction (i.e., social studies, science, and the arts) in a concentrated effort to devote more instructional time to English–language arts (Banilower et al., 2018; Wexler, 2019). As a result, the content students are exposed to in school is haphazard and not guaranteed.

Like vocabulary and morphology instruction, knowledge-building instruction should be robust. Concepts and themes should be explored via multiple sources and reviewed. Rather than having students spend hours practicing an elusive skill of "making inferences" on brief (sometimes vapid) passages, extended engagement with one theme or unit of study is recommended. Under those conditions, repeated and varied engagement with vocabulary and concepts are more likely to build knowledge that sticks and can be used in the service of future reading comprehension.

Finally, many scholars view systematic and deliberate engagement in knowledge building as an *equity imperative* (Knowledge Matters Campaign, n.d.). In striking contrast to the progressive ideal that students will naturally be drawn to content that interests them and teachers should follow students' lead, advocates of knowledge building hold that students with less access to knowledge do not know what they do not know, which precludes students' ability to lead or make informed choices. In addition, students may think they do not have an interest in something, but once they experience success—their vocabulary and conceptual understanding grows—they are delighted to have acquired new knowledge. Finally, allowing students who do not understand how a lack of knowledge will limit their ability to learn in the future to make such a choice is the equivalent of allowing children to decide for themselves matters of health or safety. Systematic knowledge building ensures that all students have *equal access* to information, which will expand rather than limit their future options.

Knowledge-Building Instruction

Dan Willingham, a cognitive psychologist, has written extensively about the relationship between knowledge and comprehension (Willingham, 2011).

He points out that comprehension requires knowing facts and concepts. Unfortunately, fact-learning is commonly disparaged in education.[4] Yet, it is an indisputable cognitive truth that knowing things facilitates learning even more things. Thus, the cultural resistance to the systematic and deliberate acquisition of knowledge (i.e., "Why memorize it if I can just Google it?") is detrimental to building a literate society. Indeed, to be genuinely literate means that a person possesses sufficient background knowledge to access most texts. But, of course, background knowledge does not consist of knowledge of isolated facts. Instead, conceptual understanding requires that students understand relationships across ideas and situate those relationships within contexts (Kintsch, 1988).

Therefore, an instructional focus on background knowledge development goes hand in hand with vocabulary and morphology instruction recommendations. Namely, student engagement with the content should be extended (i.e., occur over multiple days or weeks), varied (i.e., multiple sources used), and involve the features of structured literacy important for all learning (i.e., it should be systematic, explicit, and cumulative; Connor et al., 2017; Kim et al., 2021; Romance & Vitale, 2001). Knowledge building can begin as early as kindergarten and first grade and should continue throughout upper elementary, middle, and high school. Instruction should involve organizing content into units or themes and systematically planning for repeated engagement with content that introduces, builds, and expands knowledge. For example, teachers can identify a specific topic (e.g., space) and then design a series of lessons during which vocabulary (*orbit, astronaut, terrestrial, solar system*), morphology (e.g., *sol* = "solar, *terra* = "earth"), and connective concepts are systematically explored.

Various text sources can be used to support such knowledge building (Cervetti & Hiebert, 2019). By selecting sets of related texts, teachers can systematically build requisite background knowledge while extending students' understanding of the content (Cervetti et al., 2015; Lewis et al., 2014; Lupo et al., 2020). The most frequent recommendation for building knowledge is wide reading. *Wide reading* involves reading a great volume and diversity of material (Cunningham & Stanovich, 2001). Within a structured approach to literacy, wide reading is strategic. Teachers carefully select a range of texts that scaffold the vocabulary and conceptual knowledge students require to access text.

---

4. Quotes like "Education is not the filling of the pail, but the lighting of a fire" and "Imagination is more important than knowledge" fuel the misconception that factual knowledge can be separated from critical thinking. On the contrary, Einstein (the source of the imagination quote) was referring to intuition, which was only made possible by deep knowledge of the issue at hand. Insights cannot occur in a vacuum.

When planning for scaffolded wide reading, the primary text is considered the target text (Lupo et al., 2020). The target text is the most rigorous and complex; it reflects the pinnacle texts the other texts are in service of. Target texts may be a grade-level textbook, a primary source document, or a novel. Next, teachers can select a range of other texts that provide vocabulary knowledge, contextualization, or even a motivational hook that will be read in conjunction with the target text. For example, teachers may select a below-grade-level informational book with straightforward explanations of key concepts and terminology to build the necessary background information students need to access the target text. These texts may be more accessible and allow for independent student reading.

In addition, teachers may also use non-text-driven materials such as picture books, videos, or even experiences such as experiments, field trips, and simulations. As students can experience difficulty making sense of unfamiliar concepts, videos or visual diagrams can aid initial concept development (Mayer, 1989). Finally, teachers can provide materials to drive interest. Such motivational hook materials may include a current-event article, a pop-culture reference, or the source of an allusion within a text. For example, a text may allude to a fairy tale (e.g., "It was a classic *Cinderella* story"), novel (e.g., "Her *Scrooge*-like behavior was cause for concern"), play (e.g., "He was quite the *Romeo*"), historical event (e.g., ". . . the *crash* hit them hardest" in *To Kill a Mockingbird*), Greek myths (e.g., "Public speaking is my *Achilles heel*"), or historical figure (e.g., "He was betrayed like *Julius Caesar*"). As the class reads the target text, the teacher can pull in the complementary texts to help fill in gaps in background knowledge and create moments of interest and new connections for students.

Using multiple texts to support background knowledge development can begin as early as kindergarten. Connor et al. (2017) successfully designed and implemented a content-rich curriculum for elementary students (kindergarten through fourth grade) around science and social studies content. Over the course of a two- or three-week unit, students would *connect* (i.e., engage with a motivational hook); *clarify* (i.e., learn from secondary sources); *research* (i.e., explore primary sources); and *apply* (i.e., create projects or write about content). Students who participated in the knowledge-building curricula demonstrated improved science and social studies knowledge and, most notably, positive effects on oral and reading comprehension.

In addition to teachers creating knowledge-rich environments through text selection, several published curricula at the elementary level reflect a knowledge focus. One freely available curriculum is the Core Knowledge curriculum (https://www.coreknowledge.org/). In addition, the Knowledge Matters Campaign (https://knowledgematterscampaign.org/) is an organization composed of reading scholars whose mission is to promote knowledge-rich instruction within K–12 classrooms. On their website, they provide reviews of curricula that have a knowledge-building focus.

One way to amplify the benefits of wide reading is through writing. Writing provides an opportunity for students to integrate information from across text sources. In addition, the reciprocal relationship between writing and reading comprehension means that as students learn to write more complex sentences, they will better comprehend complex sentences. And the more content they can extract from the texts they read, the more the quality and depth of their writing will improve. Finally, grounding writing in meaningful content has the additional benefit of increasing students' motivation for learning (Guthrie et al., 2006). Thus, the final instructional tool that can be used to increase students' understanding and use of language is discourse writing.

DISCOURSE WRITING

Discourse writing is the orderly and extended expression of written thought on a subject. Unfortunately, by and large, students in the United States do not receive adequate instruction in writing (Brindle et al., 2016; Graham, 2019). Yet writing is one of teachers' most powerful tools to get students to learn and understand language. When students write, they must reflect on their thinking, retrieve what knowledge they have on the topic, organize words to express their ideas, and represent their thoughts through orthography (i.e., the writing system of their language). In short, writing is a complex cognitive task. Yet when students are provided with a *structured approach* to instruction in writing, this complex task can be broken down into parts, systematically practiced to gain automaticity, and strategically employed to help students remember and retain content while strengthening language comprehension.

If a structured approach to writing involves strategic, incremental instruction in the component parts of writing, the type of writing practice students are most likely to receive in school can be characterized as the polar opposite. Specifically, over the past several decades, the writer's workshop model has been the predominant approach to teaching writing in the United States (Gilbert & Graham, 2010). The driving philosophy behind the workshop model is that the purpose of writing is self-expression, and the best avenue for promoting writers is to provide students with extended time to engage in independent writing. Within a workshop framework, the ultimate goal of writing is not to produce a coherent, cohesive, and grammatically correct piece of text but to convey one's writing voice. Although ideation (i.e., coming up with novel thoughts) and personal expression are valuable aspects of writing, ideas come from knowing things. Personal expression is best achieved when students are familiar and fluent with various linguistic structures that allow them to use language appropriately and creatively.

LIMITATIONS OF A WORKSHOP APPROACH FOR WRITING INSTRUCTION

There are several reasons why a workshop approach is particularly problematic for struggling readers and writers. First, in a typical writer's workshop framework, more time is allocated to independent writing than direct teaching. Teacher-provided instruction consists of 5 to 10 minutes of explanation regarding the focus of the day's writing (e.g., write about a small moment, how to use a mentor text for inspiration). Notably, during this period of instruction, teachers do not teach *how* to write (e.g., do this first, then do this); instead, they describe *what* the concept is and may model, via a think-aloud, how *they* would go about the writing process. For example, a teacher might explain, "Let me think about a small moment that happened to me. Oh, yes, the other day, just as I walked out of a store, I heard a clap of thunder, and a downpour of rain descended on me. I can write about what I saw, felt, and experienced at that moment." The teacher may prompt students to reflect on how they might feel in such a situation or even ask students to generate examples of their small moments. The teacher may even provide a graphic to help students understand the difference between a big topic and a small moment (think *mountain* versus *pebble*). After a brief discussion, students have 20 or 30 minutes (sometimes as much as 45) for independent writing. Teachers can roam the room and provide as-needed support, but the goal is for students to do what writers do—wrestle with their thoughts and craft a piece of writing. In some cases, teachers also sit down to engage in their own writing as the ultimate model of what a writer looks like!

I have observed this lesson in action several times, and many students struggle with it. As we have explored, a fundamental challenge of writing is knowledge. Even though students are ostensibly drawing from personal experience and, therefore, should have lots of knowledge about the event, consider the knowledge required for the teacher to describe her unfortunate encounter with the rain. Thus, even when writing about a personal experience, many students will struggle with vocabulary, the knowledge needed to provide explanatory details, or even the knowledge needed to figure out what the prompt asks them. As a result, rather than engaging in deliberate, focused writing practice, students will sit stumped about what to write about or dive into a stream-of-consciousness retelling of something that happened to them, which will undoubtedly be about an event involving getting wet. In other words, this creative writing exercise is not as creative as most teachers might believe.

The imbalance between teacher instruction (5 to 10 minutes) and independent student work is particularly problematic for students who lack world and word knowledge and writing skills. No knowledge is built or drawn upon during the mini-lessons; glaringly, no writing skills are introduced or taught. Let's tackle the knowledge issue first. First, the concept of big versus small is abstract and arbitrary. Is losing my tooth a small moment or a big one? Second, as soon as the students are released for independent writing, the hands pop up, or a line begins to form around the teacher's desk. Some students will request guidance for topic selection, while others will get stuck ("How do I spell . . . ?"), only to be assured, "Spelling doesn't count," or directed to "Look at the word wall to see if it is there." As was discussed at length in Chapter 5, spelling does count. Students are more likely to avoid using words they do not know how to spell, and spelling words incorrectly reinforces poor spelling. Perhaps the teacher will move from desk to desk, providing a mini-conference and directing students to think about ways to describe their particular moment. In short, the lesson is riddled with inefficiencies.

The tragedy of the lesson is the opportunity cost of haphazard instruction. Consider the differences in learning outcomes if the instruction had been structured and embedded within an instructional unit. For example, if the students had been studying marine mammals and taken a field trip to a local aquarium or watched a video on dolphins and whales, they could have been asked to write about something that surprised them or identify which marine mammal was their favorite and why. During instruction, key vocabulary terms could have been reviewed. As students were writing, the teacher may have noticed many students having difficulty remembering facts, which would have provided an opportunity to stop the writing and provide a mini-review of the content.

In addition to the lost opportunity to build knowledge, students do not learn new writing skills as a result of the lesson. Instead, old habits are continually reinforced—sentence after sentence, workshop after workshop. In contrast, imagine if the mini-lesson consisted of specific guidance on how to write strong topic sentences. For example, students could have been taught to use different sentence types (e.g., declarative, exclamatory, or interrogative) to craft their introductory sentences (Hochman & Wexler, 2017a). Or, students could have been directed to use an appositive (e.g., My favorite marine mammal, the blue whale, is the largest animal on Earth.) or begin their sentence with a subordinating conjunction (e.g., *before, although, when, even though, unless*) to compose interesting topic sentences (Hochman & Wexler, 2017a). Thus, the structure of the workshop model fails to capitalize on opportunities to build knowledge and skills, but that is not the only limitation of the approach.[5]

A final limitation of the workshop model is the focus on quantity over quality. Within workshop models, students are encouraged to write first, get all their ideas on paper (i.e., a flash draft), and edit later. There are several problems with the flash draft. First, as students have not been systematically taught to write coherent and grammatically correct sentences, initial drafts will likely be riddled with errors. Editing, particularly for struggling readers and writers, is not a quick clean-up process but an overwhelming task of rewriting and reorganizing most sentences. Second, fast writing means that students are not practicing the thoughtful construction of complex sentences. Crafting a meaningful, meaty sentence requires thought. Although students may be able to fix their run-on sentences created in fast drafts by sprinkling periods throughout the draft, they are less likely to rewrite sentences to create new, syntactically complex sentences. Finally, and most problematic, when students repeatedly write long, poorly constructed run-on sentences, this type of writing becomes habitualized. Breaking a bad habit is more difficult than building strong writing habits from the start. Not surprisingly, studies have demonstrated that students with dyslexia or other language-based disabilities or who are language learners make fewer gains within a writing workshop model of instruction (Al-Hroub, et al., 2019).

One of the reasons teachers continue to use a workshop approach to writing, even though they do not see gains in students' writing as a result of the approach, is lack of knowledge. Just as an understanding of the alphabetic principle helps teachers recognize the necessity of teaching *words have parts*, knowledge about the structure of written language can help teachers understand what students need to learn in order to write. Writing is a complex behavior involving mechanics and conventions (e.g., handwriting, spelling, capitalization, punctuation, and syntax); content knowledge (i.e., knowledge about the topic of the writing, whether that is a downpour or a dolphin); and the processes involved in producing longer pieces of text (planning, monitoring, revising, and editing). Knowing what and how to teach can help demystify writing instruction and move teachers away from general guidance such as, "Does that sound right?" or "Add more detail," to specific guidance that students can deliberately practice.

The Content of Writing Instruction: Mechanics and Conventions, Knowledge, and Composing Connected Text

Most teachers do not know how to teach writing because they have never been taught to teach it (Myers et al., 2016). As such, they do not know how

---

5. More information on how to directly teach writing skills is provided in the following section.

to systematically teach the elements of (a) mechanics and conventions, (b) knowledge, and (c) composing connected text. Nor do they place equal value on each of these components. Part of the appeal of the workshop approach is its rejection of formal grammar instruction. Teachers may have bad memories of the sentence diagramming exercises they were forced to do in school or first-hand knowledge of assigning worksheets requiring students to underline subjects and predicates or change fragments into complete sentences. Neither the diagramming nor the worksheets appeared to affect the quality of students' writing. Thus, many teachers do not view the absence of grammar instruction as a loss (Myhill et al., 2012). Likewise, as has been explored extensively in this chapter, teachers have placed less value on the role of knowledge when it comes to students' writing. Many teachers believe that skilled writing, similar to reading comprehension, can be separated from knowledge. That is, writing is a content-independent skill. Of course, anyone who has tried to write about something they know very little about knows this is not true. Finally, although many teachers will directly teach the writing process as a method for creating connected text, such instruction is often done without structured instruction in mechanics, conventions, and knowledge. As such, many process-writing exercises are as ineffective for building students' ability to write well as find-the-main-idea exercises are for aiding students' comprehension.

Mechanics and Conventions

The appropriate use of writing conventions and mechanics facilitates clear communication in writing. As such, strong instruction in writing will address grammar, punctuation, and capitalization. In addition, attention will be provided to bolstering students' transcriptions skills—handwriting and spelling. Direct instruction and practice with these foundational skills promote automaticity, freeing up the working memory necessary for the thoughtful expression of ideas.

Grammar. *Grammar* refers to the structure of English and encompasses the rules for how language elements are organized. Grammar is an umbrella term that encompasses many aspects of language— morphology, phonology, semantics, and syntax. Phonology (i.e., how speech sounds are represented by print) was addressed in Chapter 5. Morphology and semantics were addressed within this chapter's sections on vocabulary and knowledge. Within this section, we will explore the syntax component of grammar. *Syntax* instruction encompasses learning about the parts of speech (subject, predicate, direct object); phrases (groups of words without a subject or predicate); clauses (groups of words with a subject and verb); and sentence structure (simple, compound, complex, or compound-complex). When students learn syntax, they learn how to organize words to express ideas. In addition to syntax, students also need to learn the mechanics of writing—punctuation and capitalization. Many grammatical rules involve the use of punctuation (when to use commas, semicolons, and so on) and capitalization (i.e., which words require capitalization and when).

When teachers employ a workshop approach to writing instruction, they rely on students' use of internalized grammatical knowledge. Most writers are unaware of formal rules of sentence construction or names of sentence elements (hence, the pain associated with sentence diagramming). Yet, they can apply the rules and constructs within their writing. When teachers ask students to check their writing to see if it *sounds right*, teachers rely on students' implicit knowledge of language structure. Unfortunately, many students lack "the ear" for determining what sounds right, because they have limited tacit knowledge of syntax. Thus, most students cannot check their or their peer's work by rereading it. The task for the teacher is to build students' knowledge and, therefore, their capacity to write syntactically correct sentences.

Researchers have found limited utility in teaching grammar in isolation (Graham, 2019). As most teachers suspect, completing worksheets wherein students must change fragments to sentences, correct subject-verb agreement, add or delete commas, change verb tense, add possessive apostrophes, and correct end punctuation rarely generalizes to students' independent writing. In contrast, evidence points to the value of embedding grammar instruction within students' own writing (Jones et al., 2013; Myhill et al., 2018). Moreover, teaching mechanics and conventions in conjunction with student writing offers several advantages over instruction in isolation.

First, as the purpose of grammar is to help writers communicate clearly, having students apply grammar to their personal writing allows them to explore different ways to express their ideas. Second, the fundamental utility of grammar is for the transfer of information. Therefore, grounding grammar instruction within familiar content enhances students' ability to check if their writing matches the information they are trying to express. Finally, all writers have default writing patterns. When grammar is taught within the context of students' writing, students are forced to mix up their writing by adding new elements (e.g., introductory clauses, modifiers, complex sentence structures). Deliberate practice using varying sentence structures will help students break out of old writing habits and increase their options of ways to express their ideas.

Handwriting and Spelling. A frequently overlooked aspect of writing is transcription. Students' ability to transcribe—that is, generate written words through handwriting or typing and to spell words—is directly related to the quality and quantity of their writing (Santangelo & Graham, 2016). Difficulty with transcription skills places demands on working memory and can be physically draining. When students have to switch attention from what they are planning to write to thinking about letter formation or spelling, they can forget what they were going to write. Poor pencil grip, such as holding a writing instrument too tightly or bearing down too hard, can cause muscle fatigue. Similarly, writing slowly can mean that students lose track of what they intended to write. Students with dyslexia and other learning disabilities are more likely to have difficulty with handwriting and spelling (Carretti et al., 2016; Hebert et al., 2018). As such, direct, systematic instruction in transcription skills is vital for these students.

Researchers have found that elementary students' handwriting and spelling skills account for up to 42% of the variance in writing quality (Graham et al., 1997). Therefore, whereas a lack of background knowledge may be an obvious constraint on writing output, teachers may overlook the important role transcription skills play in determining writing quality. Yet teachers rarely receive training in how to teach transcription skills (Graham et al., 2007). Therefore, even if they are using a handwriting curriculum, they are likely not well-versed in how to promote fluency and generalization of handwriting skills within students' everyday writing. For example, attention to pencil grip and form may be limited to handwriting exercises but not reinforced in daily activities. Similarly, although keyboarding is frequently identified as an accommodation for students with dyslexia, teachers rarely provide direct instruction or allocate time for keyboarding practice (Freeman et al., 2005). As a result, students' hunt-and-peck approach to keyboarding is simply reinforced with each assignment completed; keyboarding skills will not improve without direct attention and practice in correct positioning.

In addition to handwriting and keyboarding, spelling is considered a transcription skill. Every time writers have to stop to think about how to spell a word, their thinking is interrupted. Within a structured approach to literacy, spelling is addressed within decoding instruction and vocabulary and morphology instruction. Unfortunately, this multipronged and systematic approach to spelling instruction is not the norm. Correct spelling will not be automated without systematic and distributed practice in spelling. Furthermore, because writing tasks are typically divorced from content instruction, teachers lose an opportunity for students to practice their spelling of key vocabulary words when spelling is not an explicit component of writing instruction. Students may avoid including words they do not know how to spell when writing. Despite teachers' insistence that spelling errors can be addressed during the editing process or that points will not be deducted for such mistakes, students save themselves the hassle by using words they know or think they know how to spell.

Given the importance of transcription skills, a structured approach to writing instruction includes direct attention to these lower-level processing skills. Through spaced and deliberate practice, students will gain automaticity in handwriting, keyboarding, and spelling, freeing up the necessary processing capacity for thinking about the content of their writing.

Knowledge for Writing

When it comes to writing, the greatest gift teachers can give students is to provide them with something to write about. Writing is the expression of one's thoughts. Recall that *thinking* involves the processing of information that has been stored in long-term memory. Students can't think and write about what they do not know. The solution to the knowledge problem has been to have students write about their personal experiences. Certainly, students are very familiar with that. But are they? When retelling an experience, do students possess a firm grasp on who, what, where, when, how, and why? Do they have the vocabulary they *want* to use to explain the event? Although teachers could help students fill in their knowledge and vocabulary gaps, it can be challenging with a classroom of students all writing about different experiences. That type of ad hoc instruction also fails to capitalize on the distributed practice benefits of writing about a topic over an extended period.

Despite these limitations, the personal narrative dominates most writing conducted at the elementary level. Within a *personal narrative*, students write about their life, experiences, or thoughts. In contrast, students rarely engage in expository writing (i.e., writing about content, or fact-based writing). Within *expository writing*, the purpose of writing is to explain (i.e., *expose*) information to readers. Narrative writing can provide a rich opportunity for exploring different writing structures and is not without its merits. However, not asking students to engage in expository writing means that teachers miss out on a powerful knowledge-building tool. In addition, narrative writing does not reflect the writing required in college, the workplace, or even at home (Hull & Schulz, 2002).

The solution, of course, is to build students' knowledge. Embedding writing within content areas provides natural opportunities for writing. For example, within English–language arts instruction, students can write about what they are reading—on multiple occasions distributed over a period of days or weeks. Numerous distributed opportunities to write about the same content, but with different purposes and multiple information sources, provide the same rich benefits as distributed and varied knowledge-building instruction. Repeated writing practice increases students' familiarity with the content.

Students can make connections and have the knowledge necessary to think critically about the content—the ultimate goal of writing!

Composing Connected Text

Ultimately, the goal of writing instruction is for students to produce coherent and cohesive connected text. Thus, the final component of writing instruction involves the types of instructional activities that best support students' ability to create connected text in which they inform, persuade, argue, evaluate, or entertain. The writing process is one aspect of writing instruction that teachers may be the most well-versed in and is strongly recommended by scholars (Graham et al., 2012). The *writing process* is the ideal series of steps or stages writers follow when producing a piece of text—from prewriting to text generation to revision (Hayes & Flower, 1980). For the vast majority of teachers, the way to build students' capacity for creating connected text is through the writing process.

Despite its ubiquity in education classrooms, this notion of how writers write may not be the most appropriate model for developing or struggling writers. The writing process model is based on models of expert writers and focuses on macrolevel writing processes (i.e., planning, organization, and self-monitoring) while diminishing the role of foundational skills such as handwriting, grammar, and mechanics (Furey et al., 2017; Wakely et al., 2006). Rather than building students' fluency with foundational skills as a prerequisite for writing longer pieces of text, within a writing process approach, students are encouraged to compose lengthy essays *first* (i.e., the draft) and clean up issues with syntax, spelling, and punctuation *after* writing (i.e., during the revision and editing stages). In other words, students compose sentence after sentence that reflect their default sentence structures (e.g., the repeated use of *and* to connect events or ideas; simple rather than complex sentence structures; missing punctuation or punctuation limited to the use of periods) and are then expected to clean up the myriad issues they created during the revision process. Of course, struggling writers are less likely to make such revisions due to a lack of knowledge of how to improve their writing and the overwhelming nature of the task. Researchers have found that struggling writers make fewer and lower quality revisions (e.g., revisions that do not change sentence structure) than their more capable peers (Graham et al., 1995). If a peer or teacher provides feedback or corrections, the struggling writers are not likely to internalize the feedback or gain the capacity to apply the feedback in future writing.

Next, as has been a theme throughout this chapter, process writing instruction will likely give short shrift to knowledge, particularly in the elementary grades, where students are first learning and building their writing habits. Even though extended time (e.g., days or weeks) may be spent on a piece of writing, the content of the writing is likely to stem from either personal experience or a brief, superficial coverage of some content. Although some writing curricula do explicitly recommend and demonstrate how to use a process approach within the context of content-rich instruction (see, for example, Hochman & Wexler, 2017a), most process-writing recommendations do not emphasize or reflect an emphasis on content integration (Atwell, 1987; Calkins, 1986; Graves, 1983).

More important, though, when it comes to writing ability, most process-writing approaches fail to emphasize the sentence as the foundation of writing. Poorly developed sentence-level skills impede students' ability to engage in more complex writing tasks. Thus, a shift in instruction is necessary to move away from having students write long pieces of text to having students practice developing strong, singular sentences.

In sentence-level focused instruction, students spend time crafting single sentences (e.g., work on creating strong topic sentences) rather than spending large amounts of time on the independent writing of longer pieces of text. Focused instruction at the sentence level helps build students' fluency in creating syntactically and mechanically correct sentences. Sentence-focused approaches involve directly teaching students ways to construct complex sentences (e.g., using grammatical features such as subordinating clauses, appositives, and coordinating conjunctions other than *and*; using question prompts for sentence expansion; employing sentence-combining techniques; Greene & Enfield, 1997; Hochman & Wexler, 2017a, 2017b; Saddler et al., 2019). In addition, students receive immediate feedback that can be applied (practiced) in the revision of a single sentence. During sentence-level instruction, students move systematically through sentence-building activities that facilitate fluency with simple, compound, and complex sentence construction (Hochman & Wexler, 2017a; Saddler, 2018). Further, when sentence-level instruction is integrated with content instruction, the knowledge benefits are reciprocal. Crafting a singular, complex sentence on a topic of study can reveal gaps in understanding—sending the writer back to the text—and writing a sentence helps students remember and retain content.

Studies have demonstrated the effectiveness of focused, systematic sentence-level writing instruction on students' capacity to create complex and grammatically correct writing (Furey et al., 2017; Saddler, 2012, 2018). In addition, sentence-focused instruction can be integrated within a process-writing structure (Furey et al., 2017; Hochman & Wexler, 2017a). As students gain proficiency with writing sentences, they can be systematically taught how to plan for and construct longer pieces of writing, such as a paragraph or essay.

The bridge between sentence-level instruction and connected-text instruction occurs naturally as students move from using their notes to create topic sentences to translating notes to linear outlines for writing paragraphs and essays. In addition, sentence-level instruction on using transition words and phrases to connect two sentences becomes a transferrable skill creating cohesion within longer pieces of connected text. In sum, although the goal is to engage students in the writing process, moving students too quickly into composing longer pieces of text can be counterproductive. In contrast, building fluency at the sentence level means that students can focus on meaning creation and monitoring rather than sentence construction as they shift to writing longer pieces of text.

A Structured Approach to Writing Instruction

As with all structured approaches, effective instruction involves identifying what to teach and then applying the principles of learning—the *how*—for the delivery of instruction. The *what* of writing instruction involves (a) directly instructing students in mechanics and conventions, (b) building students' knowledge so they have something to write about, whether that be content-aligned material (e.g., social studies, science, mathematics, the arts) or expanding students' understanding of personal experiences by teaching them associated vocabulary and concepts, and (c) teaching students to write connected text that is cohesive and coherent. In terms of the *how*, several themes shape the delivery of a structured approach to writing instruction: quality over quantity, frequency over duration, purposeful practice over vague guidance, and content-integrated rather than content-free. One way to address each of these themes is through purposeful, often brief, writing exercises.

Although the goal of writing instruction is to build students' capacity to produce longer pieces of connected text, students do not learn by simply writing. Learning is an iterative process of feedback and deliberate practice (i.e., practice during which the learner applies specific guidance). In their book, *The Writing Revolution*, Hochman and Wexler (2017a) offer numerous examples of how teachers can provide quality-focused, sentence-level instruction that is then smoothly transitioned to instruction in developing paragraphs and compositions.

For example, if a third-grade class has been studying habitats and the environment, a teacher could have students work on creating complex sentences by using an exercise referred to as "Because, but, so." For this exercise, the teacher may provide the stem, "All organisms benefit from being in their natural habitat," to which students will use the three conjunctions *because*, *but*, and *so* to create three novel and complex sentences. For example, one student may write, "All organisms benefit from being in their natural habitat, because it provides the ideal temperature, food, and protection for the plant or animal." A different student may write, "All organisms benefit from being in their natural habitat, because desert animals would not be able to survive in the tundra." For the second sentence, students must juxtapose two concepts, "All organisms benefit from being in their natural habitat, *but* changes in the environment can force animals to look for new places to live." Or, a student may write, "All organisms benefit from being in their natural habitat, but some animals migrate from one habitat to another during the year." For their final sentences, students may write: "All organisms benefit from being in their natural habitat, so it is important to protect habitats to avoid endangering some animals." Or they may write, "All organisms benefit from being in their natural habitat, so the destruction of habitats can cause animal extinction." As you can see, this focused writing exercise requires students to synthesize the content and use a complex sentence structure to express a thought. Students struggle the most with creating a juxtaposition using the conjunction *but*. Their struggle creates a rich teaching opportunity, which may include reviewing the content and additional practice using the conjunction in a sentence.

Likewise, to have students work on creating information-rich, complex sentences, the teacher may use questions to have students expand simple sentences (i.e., the type of sentence students are more likely to write). For example, after learning about lionfish, the teacher may construct a kernel (simple) sentence such as "It causes problems." Then she may ask the students to use their notes to answer the following questions: *What? Where? How?* Using their notes, students identify *the what*: "the introduction of red lionfish"; *the where*: "in the Atlantic Ocean"; and *the how*: "they have no known predators and will prey on native fish." Students are then asked to combine all the content to create one complex sentence, such as "The introduction of red lionfish in the Atlantic Ocean causes problems for native fish, because lionfish have no known predators, and they will prey on native fish." As you can see, through repeated practice with this exercise, students will learn how to use a variety of questions to expand their simple sentences across different academic areas. They will also practice using correct punctuation and receive immediate feedback and the opportunity for revision, a key aspect of deliberate practice.

Brief, focused writing exercises such as these are likely to yield greater benefits than providing students with extended periods of independent writing, as is common to most writing workshop models. One way to increase writing frequency is to distribute writing across the academic day. For example, students can be asked to complete writing exercises (one to three sentences) as a warm-up before class for review, a summary activity after reading, an exit ticket at the end of class, or for preparation for class discussion.

As students gain fluency with sentence-level writing, teachers can introduce paragraph writing. As students were taught how to take notes and use them to create single sentences during the sentence-writing exercises, students will be well prepared for instruction on transferring notes to a linear paragraph outline. At this point, students formally engage in the writing process—planning, generation, and revision (Hayes & Flowers, 1980). The difference between this structured, sequential introduction of the writing process and many workshop approaches is that students already (a) know how to take notes, (b) know how to use notes to create sentences, and (c) are familiar with various strategies (e.g., changing the sentence type, using various conjunctions, adding an appositive) to create complex, grammatically correct sentences. They have also learned how to revise sentences to make them complete or apply the correct punctuation—commas and end marks, for example. As a result, students have the foundational skills necessary to create coherent pieces of connected text. Of course, even as students progress to constructing paragraphs and compositions, continued daily practice of sentence-level exercises will facilitate knowledge-building, fluency in sentence writing, and automaticity with mechanics.

CONCLUSION

The Simple View of Reading serves as a powerful reminder that a person's ability to comprehend text is a complex and multifaceted endeavor. Students with dyslexia or who experience persistent difficulty with reading will benefit from attention to elements associated with word recognition *and* those associated with language comprehension. However, in the push and pull of the Reading Wars, language-related instruction was overshadowed by arguments between whole-language and phonics camps. For advocates of phonics and families of struggling readers, getting students to accurately identify printed words was primary; getting students to figure out what the words meant or dive into social studies and science content felt more like a luxury than a priority. However, over the past few decades, as our understanding of reading comprehension has expanded, the essential—not luxury or secondary—role of knowledge has come to the forefront.

Within this chapter, we explored how direct and systematic instruction in vocabulary, morphology, conceptual knowledge, and discourse writing contribute to students' ability to understand, retain, and think critically about the texts they read. Although the components of language-rich instruction can be separated, within a structured approach to writing, they are integrated and inseparable. In the final chapter, we explore how an understanding of reading acquisition and elements of a structured literacy approach can be used for advocacy and action.

Chapter Seven

Advocacy and Action

The purpose of this book was to disentangle the complex, knotty challenge of learning to read English. Some people do not recall how they learned to read; it just seemed to happen. They may recall a book series used within their elementary schools or a particular teacher, but for them, reading did seem to unfold naturally—although spelling may have taken some effort. For others, learning to read was a process. These individuals recall bits and pieces of that process, such as the way different spellings were taught, moving through reading groups or levels, or how a teacher or parent would sit and help them work through reading a passage. They may even recall specific words that vexed them and tricks they developed to help them remember how to read or spell those tricky words.

Finally, though, there are those who will never forget their experiences with reading. For them, reading casts a dark cloud over their memories of school. As was stated in the introductory chapter, their difficulties with reading were not trivial. These difficulties significantly affected their quality of life—from their feelings of self-worth to their ability to engage fully in P–12 schooling. This book was written for them, the teachers who work with them, and the families who help them navigate school.

With information comes insight and the confidence to engage in meaningful action. This book is filled with information about the development of English orthography and its implications for instruction, the history of reading instruction and the theories and assumptions that undergird the various approaches employed in schools over the years, and structured approaches to word-recognition and language-comprehension instruction that meet the learning needs of students with dyslexia. In this final chapter, we will explore how to use this information to advocate and navigate for services for students with dyslexia in public schools in the United States.

DYSLEXIA IN THE PUBLIC SCHOOLS

Instruction and intervention options for students with dyslexia vary. As pointed out in Chapter 1, many people still believe that school personnel are banned from even using the word *dyslexia* with parents or in any form of written communication (e.g., 504 plans, IEPs, evaluation notifications; Mitchell, 2020; Yudin, 2015). Despite this persistent misunderstanding, students with characteristics of dyslexia or dyslexia have a variety of service options available to them within the schools. Accessing and advocating for support requires knowledge of the early signs of reading difficulty, features of effective reading instruction, and the differences across the available service options.

Early Intervention and Reading Difficulty

As Catts and Hogan (2021) noted, an ounce of prevention is worth a pound of treatment. The early identification of reading difficulty and delivery of timely and powerful instruction can change the reading trajectory for many students who demonstrate early signs of risk (Fletcher et al., 2007). Specifically, effective instruction that incorporates attention to the alphabetic principle and knowledge building has the power to reduce the number of poor readers who are simply instructional casualties and elevate reading-related outcomes of students with significant, persistent reading-related needs (Lovett et al., 2017; National Early Literacy Panel, 2008). However, the delivery of effective early intervention is contingent upon adequate teacher preparation, universal screening for the identification of students in need, and the provision of effective interventions.

Teacher Knowledge

Without a knowledgeable and skilled workforce, it is unlikely that students will receive the type of high-quality, early reading instruction required for reading success. Notably, teachers' lack of understanding of how the alphabet works and how systematic instruction in reading and writing can be used for prevention and intervention is the root cause of ineffective, inefficient reading instruction in the United States. In testifying before Congress, Reid Lyon (2002) stated: "Put another way, does the education profession create *instructional casualties* by inadequately preparing both general education and special education teachers to address learning differences among children?" Relatedly, in the UK, Sir Jim Rose (2009) came to three important conclusions related to teacher knowledge of instruction for students with dyslexia:

1. There should be up-to-date, accessible information about literacy difficulties available for all teachers so they can adjust their teaching for children with dyslexia;
2. There should be courses that enable schools to develop expertise in improving outcomes for children with literacy difficulties; and
3. Children who need intensive support should have access to a specialist teacher.

Rose's conclusions remain true, yet unrealized for many teachers. These professionals report not being taught about the basic structure of the English language nor provided with training in methods for teaching reading that went beyond a superficial coverage of letter names, sounds, and immersion within children's literature as a means to awaken the necessary motivation required for learning to read (Moats, 2020b; Snow, 2021). Worse, some teachers were explicitly taught to dismiss systematic instruction in phonics as tedious, boring, and counter-productive to reading achievement (Luscombe, 2022). For these teachers, the false dichotomy of teaching reading as either teaching the code or teaching for meaning was firmly entrenched within the rhetoric of their preparation.

Further, differences in student performance were dismissed with the equally damaging hokum: "All children learn differently." Although it is true that meaningful differences in students exist—stemming from biological and environmental influences—the phrase is often employed to dismiss or diminish concerns about differences in reading performance. Specifically, differences in students' reading performance are either interpreted from a developmentalist perspective of "the child will catch up later/there is no need to intervene" or as "there are multiple ways to learn to read/learning the alphabetic code is not the only way to learn to read." However, research on reading illuminates these as false beliefs. Early intervention can be transformative, and good readers process individual letters and letter patterns within words, fluently mapping phonology with orthography (Ehri, 2020). What the biological and environmental differences in students do mean is that instruction will need to be more direct, more intense (i.e., more opportunities for deliberate practice distributed over a longer period), and more systematic for those students who exhibit signs of reading difficulty. Despite these differences, there are universal principles associated with learning to read: To read well requires that all learners break the code and possess the requisite knowledge to bring meaning to what they are reading.

Thus, the incumbent role of teachers is trifold, consisting of prevention, identification, and intervention. Prevention aims to reduce the number of instructional casualties, those students whose difficulties with reading arise due to not understanding how the alphabet works and the failure of schooling to help students learn the code. Once these students receive appropriate instruction, their reading ability takes off. In contrast, there remain those students whose difficulties are more profound. For them, early identification holds great promise. Over the past decade, 46 states passed legislation to ensure the systematic screening and identification of students for early signs of reading difficulty (i.e., screening for characteristics of dyslexia; Dyslegia.com; Gearin et al., 2022; Youman & Mather, 2018). One reason for the emphasis on screening was to counter firmly held beliefs that impeded the delivery of direct intervention at the first sign of student difficulty.

Universal Screening

Although the systematic screening of students for early indicators of reading difficulty is to be applauded and should be standard practice within all schools (Catts & Hogan, 2021), having a dyslexia screening system in place is not the panacea some teachers and parents believe it is (Heubeck, 2023). First, the skills assessed by dyslexia screeners are not novel. Most schools likely already collect the type of data most dyslexia screeners yield. Therefore, dyslexia screeners do not tap into some mysterious behaviors or symptoms of dyslexia that exist outside of what can be readily observed and measured in regard to reading and reading-related behaviors (e.g., phonological processing, graphophonemic knowledge, rapid automatized naming, decoding and encoding skills, and oral reading fluency). In many cases, the benefit of requiring screening is that states or districts (a) require the systematic collection of data on those behaviors, which may otherwise be happening haphazardly, and (b) codify what should happen in terms of instruction or intervention as a result of the screening (e.g., students who perform below certain benchmarks should receive focused instructional support). In this way, the requirement for a screener creates a more transparent structure for teachers and administrators to follow, which can be a tremendous benefit for teachers and families wanting to know where, when, and how to look for and address signs of risk.

Additionally, it is important to keep in mind that screening for a condition differs from conducting diagnostic testing. The goal of screening for any condition, whether it be cancer or dyslexia, is for early detection or monitoring. In contrast, a diagnostic test or battery of assessments is used to confirm the presence of a condition. Thus, the purpose of dyslexia screening is to identify students who may be demonstrating signs of risk and who would benefit from monitoring and possibly more in-depth assessment. Single-point-in-time screeners will likely over-identify students. But if screening data are paired with ongoing progress monitoring, a more complete picture of student risk can be attained. Further, schools can make use of existing data to complement screening data. For example, assessing students' mastery and retention of reading-related skills can provide the information needed to direct and inform reading instruction. Once students move beyond kindergarten, end-of-year tests yield important information about their reading performance that should inform the delivery of instruction for the following school year (VanDerHeyden & Burns, 2017). Thus, screeners are not a substitute for diagnostic data, nor are they intended to be, but, particularly when paired with direct skill-level data and progress monitoring, they can serve a critical role in a comprehensive approach to reading instruction and intervention.

Finally, simply having a universal screening system does not guarantee that the data collected by schools will result in timely and effective intervention (Heubeck, 2023). Assessment is not intervention. Screening practices are only as effective as a school's prevention and intervention efforts. As such, the quality of response to screening data will directly reflect teacher knowledge and the curricula schools have in place. For teachers with foundational knowledge of English orthography and expertise in effective reading practices (i.e., those that address word recognition and language comprehension), the screening will provide the data necessary for planning responsive instruction. Beyond teacher knowledge and skills, schools that have comprehensive curricular options for teachers to use will enhance teachers' likelihood of successful instruction and intervention.

What are early indicators of risk? Most dyslexia screeners assess students' phonemic awareness (i.e., their ability to unglue the spoken sounds of language), letter-sound knowledge (i.e., the graphophonemic awareness necessary for decoding), letter name and/or rapid automatized naming fluency (i.e., an indicator of processing speed), decoding accuracy and fluency, spelling, and oral reading fluency. For second-grade students and older, a measure of reading comprehension will also likely be included. As you can see, each element assessed aligns with specific components of The Simple View of Reading (Hoover & Tunmer, 2022) and related processing skills (e.g., attention, working memory, processing speed). Teachers or families interested in advocacy and action should become familiar with the screening assessments used within their schools. What type of data are collected? Is there a cut score used to determine who receives additional services or specialized instruction? Knowing what skills are being assessed and what the cut scores are will provide the necessary information for understanding individual students' level of risk.

In summary, the fact that the majority of state dyslexia laws include a requirement for universal dyslexia screening is an important first step in the identification and treatment of dyslexia. The requirement for screening reflects a shift away from developmentalist thinking (i.e., students develop at different rates; therefore, early differences are not a sign of risk but of developmental maturity) and toward the notion that delays are an indicator of instructional need—whether those needs are a sign of dyslexia, lack of opportunity, or both—that should be addressed. At a minimum, an early screening system creates an inflection point for decision-making. Therefore, advocacy for universal screening is not ineffectual or misplaced, but advocacy for screening should be aligned with advocacy for effective early intervention for it to be transformative.

Effective Early Intervention

The greatest avenue for prevention is universal, high-quality primary reading instruction (Foorman et al., 1998; Torgesen et al., 1999). Yet, even with robust early reading instruction, students will enter school with different skills, which will require a certain degree of differentiated instruction. In other words, no one-size-fits-all beginning reading curriculum will address the needs of all incoming students. For example, English language learners may enter school with relative weaknesses in vocabulary and oral comprehension (Kieffer & Vukovic, 2013; Mancilla-Martinez & Lesaux, 2011). In addition, students from low-income households are more likely to enter school with less alphabet knowledge, decreased phonological awareness, and weaker spelling than students from higher-income households (Lee & Al Otaiba, 2015). As such, students entering school with below age-level reading and reading-related skills due to differences in early childhood language and learning environments will benefit from targeted instruction in these areas. However, beyond the differentiation demands that are well within the purview of early elementary settings, either through systematic, whole-group instruction paired with small-group remediation support or other forms of targeted instruction, some students will require more direct and intense intervention support. These students are those identified by dyslexia screeners as having the most significant risk and needing specialized support.

For students identified as having the greatest risk, early intervention is critical. Researchers have found that starting intervention early (e.g., first grade rather than second or third) can result in greater gains for students (Lovett et al., 2017; Wanzek & Vaughn, 2007). In addition, interventions of longer duration are likely to yield stronger effects (Vadasy et al., 2002). Given the interwoven skills required for accurate and efficient reading, researchers have found particular success in providing multicomponent early interventions (Connor et al., 2013; Lovett et al., 2017; Torgesen, 2004). Specifically, effective early intervention will include systematic, intense instruction in phonology, decoding (i.e., grapheme-phoneme correspondence), encoding (i.e., orthography), fluency, vocabulary, morphology, and knowledge building.

However, once students are identified as at risk or below grade level in their reading performance, several service delivery options become available. Knowledge of the various laws and policies that shape support for students with disabilities can help teachers and families navigate the systems in place.

Service Options

Data collection should begin at the first signs of reading difficulty or below age-level performance. Data can include samples of student work, screening data, and any reading-related assessment data (e.g., curriculum-based measures, benchmark data, interim assessments). Creating a binder to hold samples of student work, assessment reports, and any school-home communication can be particularly important for documenting the history of difficulty as well as progress a student may be experiencing. Entry into the delivery of specialized services typically begins within a response-to-intervention (RTI) framework.

Response-to-Intervention

The concept of RTI was built into the 2004 reauthorization of the Individuals with Disabilities Education Act (IDEA, 2004). Originally conceived as a model for identifying students with *specific learning disabilities*, RTI has morphed into a tiered instructional delivery service model used by schools with all general education students. Within a school-wide RTI framework, also referred to as a multi-tiered system of support or MTSS, schools provide tiered levels of support. Tiered instruction begins with Tier 1, which is high-quality instruction provided to all general education students. Students identified as at risk or below grade level will receive Tier 2 services, which reflect additional, targeted support in the form of specialized programs, strategies, or instruction. Students who do not respond or fail to make expected progress with Tier 2 supports are moved to Tier 3. For most states, formal evaluation for special education begins at this time.

Although RTI was initially conceived as an alternative to traditional special education identification practices, which often included waiting until students were significantly behind their peers—second or third grade—to begin formal evaluation for special education, evaluations of RTI implementation have found mixed results in terms of its capacity for early identification and intervention (Balu et al., 2015; Nagro et al., 2019). Theoretically, within an RTI framework, intervention services are provided at the first sign of delay or difficulty. Although some schools offer robust and targeted instructional support within their RTI processes, considerable variation in the quality and specificity of interventions exists (Fuchs & Fuchs, 2017). As such, some teachers and families find that students fail to make gains with a school's standardized tiered framework. In addition, some schools or districts have established specific timelines to guide their RTI processes, leaving teachers and families to believe that students must be in a particular tier for a predetermined amount of time before referral to special education can occur (Braun et al., 2020).

To clarify the confusion between school-wide models of tiered instruction and special education, the Office of Special Education and Rehabilitative Services issued the following statement: "the use of MTSS, such as RTI, may not be used to delay or deny a full and individual evaluation . . . of a child suspected of having a disability." In other words, at any time during the RTI process, families have the right to request a formal, comprehensive evaluation for eligibility for special education services.

Special Education Services

Students with dyslexia may be eligible to receive special education services under the category of *specific learning disabilities*. To qualify for special education services, students must meet two basic conditions: (a) They must be identified as having a disability that falls under one of the 13 categories of disability listed within the IDEA, and (b) they must have a demonstrated educational need that is not being met by general education. For example, if a student exhibits signs of dyslexia but is not performing significantly below grade level, an evaluation team may not find the student eligible for special education services. In these cases, teachers or families may want to pursue non–special education service options, which are addressed in the next section. However, students whose reading difficulties persist despite high-quality Tier 1 instruction or early intervention support will likely be identified as having a disability and qualify for special education services.

The IDEA ensures that students with disabilities receive federal education protections. Specifically, students with disabilities are entitled to a free, appropriate public education (FAPE). Under the IDEA, students with disabilities are eligible to receive specially designed instruction (SDI), which is instruction intended "to meet the unique needs of a child with a disability" (20 U.S.C. § 1401(29) (2018); § 300.39(a)(2)). SDI is further defined in the regulations:

[SDI] means adapting, as appropriate to the needs of an eligible child under this part, the *content, methodology*, or *delivery* of instruction—

(ii) To address the unique needs of the child that result from the child's disability; and
(iii) To ensure access of the child to the general curriculum, so that the child can meet the educational standards within the jurisdiction of the public agency that apply to all children. ([emphasis added]; 34 C.F.R. § 300.39(b), 2019)

Therefore, special education means that *what* a student is learning or *how* a teacher presents information may be adapted to meet a student's unique educational needs. As such, the delivery of SDI aligns well with a structured literacy approach. Assessment data collected as part of the evaluation process will be used to develop annual IEP goals, statements that describe what knowledge, skills, or behaviors a student is expected to achieve over a year. IEP goals are based on a student's present levels of academic achievement and functional performance (PLAAFP). To determine a student's unique performance levels, IEP teams use data from valid and reliable assessments (e.g., standardized assessments, curriculum-based measurements) and observations, parent interviews, or evaluations of student work to develop specific PLAAFP statements (Spiel et al., 2014). For students with dyslexia, PLAAFP statements reflect the underlying knowledge and skills associated with word-level reading (e.g., letter-sound knowledge, phonic decoding, spelling, handwriting, vocabulary knowledge, irregular word knowledge, language skills, and oral reading fluency). IEP teams may develop PLAAFP statements that indicate areas of strength, but teams are required to identify students' academic and functional needs. Further, any area of need identified in a PLAAFP statement requires a corresponding IEP goal (34 C.F.R. § 300.320, 2019).

Although educator and parental advocacy are important at each stage of the process, from the awareness of early signs of language or reading difficulty through engagement with the delivery of early intervention, once a student has been identified as eligible for special education services, establishing a student's IEP goals reflects a pivotal point for advocacy. Students' progress in special education will be measured in light of their IEP goals. IEP goals hold teachers and schools accountable for working on the specific skills identified within the goals. To put it another way, what gets measured, gets managed. Observable, measurable goals create transparency for the delivery of targeted instruction and are the backbone of special education.

To this end, IEP goals should reflect the primary reading-related needs of the student. Secondary goals may address access and accommodation needs, such as the provision of alternative texts or formats, but the purpose of special education is not solely or even primarily to provide workarounds for students' instructional needs; it is to provide direct instruction to build students' knowledge and skills (Sayeski et al., 2022). Recall that the IDEA guarantees FAPE. Therefore, IEP goals constitute an individual student's FAPE. Given the relationship between the IEP and the delivery of FAPE, failure to measure and report progress toward annual goals reflects a substantive violation of the law (Yell et al., 2020). The more specific and measurable IEP goals are, the easier it is for teachers and families to track students' progress. In short, having clear, specific goals increases the likelihood of students receiving the instruction needed to meet those goals. If students do not progress toward those goals, clear targets create the transparency necessary for reevaluating the type of intervention students receive.

Given the historical tension between whole language/balanced literacy approaches to reading and code-based, structured approaches, some families want to specify a particular (often branded) approach to reading instruction within the IEP (e.g., an Orton-Gillingham approach; Sayeski & Zirkel, 2021). In these situations, families want to ensure that the instruction and intervention their children receive reflect a systematic, code-based approach. The legal term for the inclusion of a specific instructional approach or program is *methodology*. When a family requests that a particular program be written into an IEP, they are asking to add a methodology to that IEP. Analysis of case law has demonstrated that families are not likely to prevail in methodology requests (Rose & Zirkel, 2007; Sayeski & Zirkel, 2021). Several reasons account for the poor outcomes.

First, schools are likely to be providing some level of evidence-based reading instruction, even though the level of specificity may not be to the degree desired by the parents. In these situations, the courts will show "significant deference to the choices made by school officials" (*Ridley School District v. M.R.*, 2012, p. 277). In other words, the courts are likely to defer to the instructional decisions made by professional educators within schools. Second, the courts tend to engage in a holistic review of the case, examining the quality of the IEP under the relatively relaxed substantive standard for FAPE. Specifically, courts will attempt to determine: "Is the [IEP] developed through the Act's procedures reasonably calculated to enable the child to receive educational benefits?" (*Board of Education of Hendrick Hudson Central School District v. Rowley*, 1982, p. 207). In addition, the courts will look to see if the school "offer[ed] an IEP reasonably calculated to enable a child to make progress appropriate in light of the child's circumstances" (*Endrew F. v. Douglas County School District RE-1*, 2017, p. 999). Thus, the standard courts use to determine an IEP's appropriateness represents the fairly low bar of *reasonably calculated for appropriate progress* (Zirkel, 2022).

Despite historical trends that do not favor parental requests for specific methodology, a handful of recent cases have tied the use of a particular methodology to the delivery of FAPE (*Albuquerque Public Schools Board of Education v. Armstrong*, 2021; *Preciado v. Board of Education of Clovis Municipal Schools*, 2020; *Rogich v. Clark County Schools*, 2021). In these cases, however, the methodology was either not the sole issue (i.e., there were other procedural or complicating factors the courts considered) or the issue of concern was not the use of a particular program or approach (e.g., Orton-Gillingham, SPIRE), but in the district's poor implementation of the methodology (Zirkel, 2022). Given these factors, costly legislation will not be the most expeditious or promising route for advocacy and action.

The take-home message for families and school district personnel is that although the IDEA established federal protections for the education of students with disabilities, those protections reflect floor-level standards. Above and beyond these legal obligations, schools have a professional obligation to implement instruction that reflects what is known about effective reading instruction for students with reading disabilities (Foorman et al., 2016; Kilpatrick, 2015; Moats, 2020b; Seidenberg, 2017) and communicate with parents about these practices and the rationale for their implementation. In turn, active, collaborative parental involvement will include providing child-specific information and the capacity to partner with schools in the implementation of special education services (Gearin et al., 2018; Lichtenstein, 2019). Again, establishing clear, concrete IEP goals is one of the most compelling demonstrations of school–home collaborative problem-solving.

As noted previously, though, not all students with characteristics of dyslexia will qualify for special education services. For these students, there are non–special education service options available to them.

Non–Special Education Service Options

The primary non–special education service option for students with characteristics of dyslexia is a 504 plan. Specifically, Section 504 of the Rehabilitation Act of 1973 prohibits discrimination of individuals based on disability: "No otherwise qualified individual with a disability in the United States . . . shall, solely by reason of her or his disability, be excluded from participation in, be denied the benefits of, or be subjected to discrimination under any program or activity receiving Federal financial assistance." Therefore, under Section 504, students with dyslexia may be identified as having an impairment that substantially limits major life activities and be afforded *reasonable accommodations*. The accommodations a student is to receive will be specified in a 504 plan. Accommodations can include audiobooks, speech-to-text software, text-to-speech software, extended time, alternative texts, test-readers, note-taking supports, and so on. In addition, accommodations can include access to remedial reading instruction (see, for example, *Campbell v. Board of Education of Centerline School District*, 2003). The goal of a 504 plan is to delineate changes in the learning environment that will enable students to learn alongside their peers (Understood, n.d.). In other words, if a student with dyslexia is experiencing difficulty learning in the general education environment, a 504 plan will specify the accommodations, supports, or services the student will receive. Similar to an IEP, 504 services are provided at no cost to the parents.

Section 504 plans differ from special education in several important ways. First, states receive funding under the IDEA for the delivery of special education services; no such funding is provided for Section 504. Second, the IDEA offers more procedural safeguards than Section 504. For example, although notice to parents is required under Section 504, that notice does not necessarily have to be in writing. In contrast, specific procedural and substantive requirements are formally specified under the IDEA. Procedural safeguards include (a) a complete explanation of all procedural safeguards provided in writing; (b) the right of the parents to review all educational records; (c) the right of the parents to participate in all meetings; (d) the right of parents to obtain an independent educational evaluation of their child "at public expense"; (e) the right to receive prior *written* notification on matters related to identification, evaluation, or placement; (f) the right to consent to or deny services; (g) the right to disagree with service decisions; and (h) the right to use the IDEA's mechanisms for resolving disputes. Substantive requirements ensure that IEP goals align with PLAAFP statements and are designed to confer educational benefit, student progress is monitored and regularly communicated to parents, and a continuum of placement options is available to students.

Although the IDEA offers more formal protections, a 504 plan may be the best fit for a student with dyslexia who is performing relatively well within the general education environment but would benefit from specific accommodations or support. Typically, parents seeking to have their child receive services under Section 504 will submit a written request to the school. Forms and guidelines are located on a district's website or can be obtained by contacting the school or district office. The Office of Civil Rights (OCR) of the U.S. Department of Education holds responsibility for enforcing Section 504. Similar to IDEA concerns, concerns about 504 implementations are best handled at the local level. However, if families experience frustrations with 504 implementation, formal complaints can be handled through OCR state or regional offices.

Other non–special education services schools may provide may be in the context of MTSS (e.g., Tier 2 intervention) or remedial instruction provided to general education students (e.g., leveled, small-group instruction). As noted previously, such intervention services can be particularly beneficial for students whose difficulties result from lack of opportunity due to ineffective early reading instruction or lack of exposure to language and literacy within early childhood environments. However, if students' difficulties persist, even with these additional services, families will want to pursue more intensive intervention services by requesting an evaluation for special education.

CONCLUSION

Dyslexia is one of the most well-researched learning conditions, with evidence demonstrating neurobiological and environmental influences. Individuals with dyslexia experience difficulties with word-level reading and spelling, which can directly affect their overall quality of life (Snowling, Hulme, & Nation, 2020). Researchers have found that families do not need to wait until students experience years of failure before intervening. Early signs of difficulty with reading and reading-related behaviors can be addressed through early intervention. Multicomponent early interventions addressing all aspects of the Simple View of Reading will likely yield the greatest benefit. For older students whose reading needs were not identified early or whose reading difficulties persist in upper elementary and secondary settings, intensive, structured approaches to literacy can result in the transformative, life-altering benefit of learning to read.

The enduring legacy of the Simple View of Reading lies in its power to reduce the complex behavior of reading into a powerful tool for guiding instructional decision-making. Although decades of research on dyslexia consistently identify phonological processing as one of the most robust indicators of reading difficulty, phonological processing consists within a constellation of other reading-related behaviors. As such, narrowly focused instruction and intervention on phonology alone is unlikely to elevate general reading outcomes. Failing to address the interrelated components of word recognition and language comprehension will not result in students' ability to read fluently and make sense of the various print they will encounter in and out of school. Structured approaches to literacy will embrace both components of the Simple View of Reading, placing literacy instruction within a rich environment of code-based practices (i.e., decoding and spelling) and meaning-based practices (i.e., knowledge building, vocabulary, morphology, and writing). The methods used for instruction will reflect principles derived from cognitive psychology, neuroscience, and behavioral research. Specifically, effective instruction will involve direct teaching; deliberate, distributed practice; cumulative review; planned opportunities for transference or generalization; and meaningful engagement. Additionally, learning can and should be fun. Success creates the opportunity for joy within classrooms.

The history of dyslexia reveals several important lessons. First, interest stems from personal connection. As such, demands for services and continued research on dyslexia are not likely to diminish. Families of struggling students will continue to seek avenues of support, teachers who work with struggling readers will continue to explore the most effective methods for instruction and intervention, and policymakers will continue to put systems in place necessary to identify and serve the most vulnerable learners. Second, advocacy persists within a social justice framework. Individuals with access to social capital will advocate for resources and support to be put in place for those who do not have such access. Informed and broad-minded advocates have the power to elevate conversations. To move beyond historical dichotomies requires knowledge and an openness to letting go of firmly held assumptions. Research and practice will shed new light on dyslexia, reading instruction, and reading intervention. A blend of curiosity, humility, and skepticism is necessary to avoid pendulum swings between false dichotomies and move thinking and action forward.

Finally, although new insights are around the corner, there is no need to wait. Teachers, families, interventionists, and researchers experience success in teaching students with dyslexia to read every day. Somewhere a lightbulb is going off in a student's head, "Ah! Words have parts." A different student has just finished decoding an entire book independently and is grinning from ear to ear. And a middle school student with dyslexia just volunteered to read a passage aloud (with expression!) in class. The perfect curriculum or teacher is not necessary to teach students with dyslexia to read. However, research has illuminated elements of instruction that contribute to expeditious and effective outcomes. Keeping the elements of instruction that directly contribute to word recognition (e.g., grapheme-phoneme correspondence, decoding and encoding, connected-text reading) and language comprehension (e.g., vocabulary and morphology, knowledge building, discourse writing) in mind and teaching those components in a structured manner will inevitably result in untangling the knot that holds students back from achieving literacy.

Glossary

Affricates: Consonants produced by a combination of a stop and fricative; /ch/ and /j/

Alphabet: A standardized set of letters or symbols used to represent the basic sounds of a language

Alphabetic principle: Words are composed of letters that represent speech sounds

Articulatory gestures: The movements of the mouth used during phoneme production

Background knowledge: All the knowledge about the world a person possesses; the knowledge a reader has about a topic

Balanced literacy: A method of teaching reading in which teachers guide students through the reading of leveled texts; students are taught to use cues (context, syntax, and letters) to read words

Base element: A morpheme from which words are created by adding affixes; can stand alone in English (e.g., *cycle*, *civil*), but affixes can be added to change the meaning of the word (*bicycle*, *uncivilized*)

Cognitive load: The mental processing demands imposed by a particular task

Connected text: Group of sentences that relate to one another

Consonant: A speech sound produced by complete or partial constriction of airflow through the vocal tract (i.e., lips, tongue, throat, and/or nose)

Consonant blends: Consonant strings that retain their individual sounds but are co-articulated (e.g., *bl, str, st, gr*)

Continuant: A speech sound that can be produced uninterrupted for the duration of a breath (e.g., /mmmmm/, /ŏŏŏŏ/, /ssssss/); consonants and vowels can be continuants

Continuous blending: A process for sounding out words without stopping between the sounds (e.g., /mmmmaaaaat/)

Continuous review: The provision of regular practice sessions distributed over time in which new and review concepts are interspersed

Decodable texts: Simple stories designed to encourage students to apply grapheme-phoneme correspondence knowledge to the reading of connected text; connected text that contains phonics patterns previously addressed within a reading program's scope and sequence of instruction

Decode/ing: The ability to phonologically recode a written word

Developmental disorders: Groups of conditions due to an impairment that begin during initial development (i.e., initiating in childhood) and are typically present throughout the lifespan; different from acquired disorders

Diagraphs: Two consonants that represent one speech sound; e.g. *ch*, *sh*, *th*

Diphthongs: Vowels that glide from one sound to another (e.g., /oy/ and /ou/)

Discourse processing: The inferences needed to understand

Discourse writing: A formal and orderly expression of thought on a subject in written form

Encode/ing: Spelling; the ability to assign graphemes to phonemes

English orthography: The spelling system of English

Explicit instruction: A systematic method of teaching students that involves breaking a complex process into small steps, providing direct feedback during learning, and facilitating high levels of student engagement

Expository texts: Texts designed to impart information and facts about a topic; nonfiction texts

Fricatives: A consonant produced by friction caused by the partial obstruction of airflow

Glides: Consonants produced by gliding into the vowel sounds that follow; /wh/, /w/, and /y/

Grapheme: A letter or group of letters that represents a phoneme

Heart-word instruction: A method for teaching irregular words that combines the application of grapheme-phoneme correspondence with the memorization of low-frequency sound spellings (i.e., parts that need to be learned by heart)

High-frequency words: Words that occur most frequently in written material; includes regular and irregular words

Inferences: Drawing a conclusion based on provided information

Interleaved practice: The mixing of multiple subjects or topics when learning content or practicing a skill; differs from blocked practice, which involves focusing on one topic or skill exclusively during practice

Irregular words: Words whose spelling-sound relationships do not reflect the most common sound-spelling correspondences

Language or linguistic comprehension: The ability to understand spoken language

Leveled texts: Texts written specifically to control for sentence length, sentence complexity, average number of syllables, and themes; phonics patterns are not controlled

Lexical quality hypothesis: The ability to comprehend text is dependent on the quality of the reader's mental dictionary, which includes access to phonetic and semantic information

Lexicon: The vocabulary of a person, language, or branch of knowledge

Liquids: Consonants produced when the tongue creates a partial closure in the mouth, resulting in a resonant, vowel-like consonant

Logograph: A letter, symbol, or sign that reflects a whole word or phrase; etymology: Greek, *word + writing*

Mental lexicon: A mental dictionary that contains the pronunciation and meaning of a word

Morphemes: The smallest units of words that contain meaning; prefixes, suffixes, and roots and bases

Morphological awareness: An understanding of how words can be broken down into smaller units of meaning, including prefixes, suffixes, and roots and bases

Morphological word family: Words that share a common meaning and structure

Multiple deficit model: Developmental disabilities are caused by the interaction of multiple factors, including genetic and environmental risk and protective factors

Narrative texts: Stories that relate a series of events; can be fiction or nonfiction

Nasals: Consonant produced by allowing air to flow through the nasal cavity

Neuroplasticity: The ability of the brain to form and reorganize synaptic connections, especially in response to learning or experience or following injury

Oral reading fluency: The ability to read connected text accurately, at an appropriate rate, and with prosody

Orthographic mapping: The mental process by which individuals connect speech sounds to word spellings; during mapping, sound-spellings are bonded and become available for automatic retrieval

Orthography: The writing system of a language; a set of conventions for writing that includes spelling, hyphenation, capitalization, and emphasis

Pedagogy: The method and practice of teaching

Phoneme: A speech sound

Phonemic awareness: The ability to identify and manipulate individual sounds in spoken words

Phonetically regular words: Words in which letters represent their most common sounds

Phonics: The correlations between sounds and symbols in an alphabetic writing system; a method for teaching reading that involves directly teaching sound-symbol correspondences

Phonological recoding: The process of mapping letter sounds to letters and letter combinations; can be assessed by nonword reading

Phonology: The study of the sounds of language; the sound system of language

Predictable texts: Books that contain a repetitive structure

Rapid automatized naming (RAN): The ability to quickly name aloud a series of familiar visual stimuli (e.g., letters, numbers, colors, or objects) presented as a group

Reading: The translation of print to speech

Regular words: Words that reflect the most common grapheme-phoneme correspondences

Root words: Greek or Latin words that cannot stand alone in English; they require affixes; e.g., *aud* ("related to hearing") or *cyc* ("circle")

Semantics: The study of the meaning of language

Set for variability: The ability to self-correct the mispronunciation of a word through the use of partial decoding along with context and existing vocabulary knowledge

Share's self-teaching hypothesis: The process of applying grapheme-phoneme correspondences to novel words results in the acquisition of orthographic memories, or new sight words

Short vowel sounds: A name used to refer to lax vowels; lax vowels are produced with little tension in the vocal cords; they primarily occur in syllables that end with a consonant (e.g., *a* [/măt/], *e* [/fĕd/], *i* [/sĭt/], *o* [/mŏp/], *u* [/ŭp/])

Sight-word instruction: A method of teaching reading through whole-word memorization; look-say method

Sight-word recognition: The ability to accurately and quickly recognize whole words; achieved through orthographic mapping (see also *Orthographic mapping*).

Stop: A consonant speech sound that is produced by stopping airflow; a plosive phoneme

Structured literacy: An approach to teaching reading that reflects instructional features and content associated with gains in reading development; instruction is planned, direct, and systematic and addresses the content elements of phonemic awareness, phonics, orthography (i.e., spelling), morphology, syntax, and semantics

Syllabification (Syllabication): The separation of words into spoken or written syllables

Syllable: A unit of speech that consists of at least one vowel sound, with or without consonants

Syntax: The arrangement of words and phrases in a language governed by rules

Synthetic phonics: A method of teaching students to read that involves teaching them to blend the sounds in words that are represented by graphemes

Testing effect: The finding that long-term memory is improved by the retrieval of information from memory

The Simple View of Reading: A framework of reading proposed by Gough & Tunmer in 1986 that suggested reading comprehension was the product of decoding and language comprehension expressed by the formula $R = D \times C$

Trade books: Books published by a commercial publisher intended for a general readership; the books are written to entertain or inform

Transcription skills: Transforming speech into written symbols by spelling words via handwriting or typing

Vowels: Phonemes produced via an open vocal tract; classified by tongue position and height, specifically high/low or front/middle/back

Vowel digraphs: Groups of two letters that represent a single sound; vowel digraphs commonly represent long vowels

Vowel-*r* or *r*-controlled: When the letter *r* immediately follows the letters *a*, *e*, *i*, *o*, or *u*; the presence of the *r* influences the pronunciation of the vowel

Whole language: A philosophy of reading acquisition based on the notion that learning to read develops naturally like learning to speak; students are taught to use context and minimal graphophonic cues to determine words

Wide reading: Reading from material that reflects various genres, formats, and topics

Word recognition: The ability to recognize words accurately; word recognition can be achieved through decoding (sounding words out) or through sight-word recognition

Working memory: The amount of information that can be held in an accessible state

References

20 U.S.C. § 1401(29) (2018)

34 C.F.R. § 300.39(b) (2019)

Adams, M. J. (1990). *Beginning to read: Thinking and learning about print*. MIT Press.

Albuquerque Public Schools Board of Education v. Armstrong, 80 IDELR 42 (D.N.M. 2021).

Al-Hroub, A., Shami, G., & Evans, M. (2019). The impact of the "writers' workshop' approach on the L2 English writing of upper-primary students in Lebanon. *Language Learning Journal*, 47(2), 159–171. https://doi.org/10.1080/09571736.2016.1249394

American Academy of Ophthalmology. (2014). *Joint statement: Learning disabilities, dyslexia, and vision—2014*. https://www.aao.org/education/clinical-statement/joint-statement-learning-disabilities-dyslexia-vis

American Psychiatric Association. (2013). *Diagnostic and statistical manual of mental disorders (5th ed.)*. American Psychiatric Publishing. https://doi.org/10.1176/appi.books.9780890425596

Anderson, R. C., & Nagy, W. E. (1993). The vocabulary conundrum. *American Educator: The Professional Journal of the American Federation of Teachers*, 16(4), 14–18.

Apthorp, H., Randel, B., Cherasaro, T., Clark, T., McKeown, M., & Beck, I. (2012). Effects of a supplemental vocabulary program on word knowledge and passage comprehension. *Journal of Research on Educational Effectiveness*, 5(2), 160–188. https://doi.org/10.1080/19345747.2012.660240

Archer, A. L., & Hughes, C. A. (2011). *Explicit instruction: Effective and efficient teaching*. Guilford Publications.

Ashman, G. (2019). *The truth about teaching: An evidence-informed guide for new teachers*. SAGE Publications Ltd.

Associated Press (2022, June 22). *He was knocked out of the National Spelling Bee, but appeal gives him another chance.* National Public Radio. https://www.npr.org/2022/06/02/1102714379/national-spelling-bee-appeal

Atwell, N. (1987). *In the middle: Writing, reading, and learning with adolescents.* Heinemann Publishing.

Austin, M. C., & Morrison, C. (1961). *The torch lighters: Tomorrow's teachers of reading.* Harvard University Press.

Balu, R., Zhu, P., Doolittle, F., Schiller, E., Jenkins, J., & Gersten, R. (2015). *Evaluation of response to intervention practices for elementary school reading.* US Department of Education. http://ies.ed.gov/ncee/pubs/20164000/pdf/20164000.pdf

Banilower, E. R., Smith, P. S., Malzahn, K. A., Plumley, C. L., Gordon, E. M., & Hayes, M. L. (2018). *Report of the 2018 NSSME.* Horizon Research.

Battistella, E. L. (2019, October 6). *Reading, writing, and readability: Appreciating Rudolph Flesch.* Oxford University Press.

Bazis, P. S., Hebert, M., Wambold, B., Lang, D., & Burk, M. (2022). Integration of reading and writing instruction to increase foundational literacy skills: Effects of the "write sounds" intervention on handwriting, decoding, and spelling outcomes. *Learning Disabilities: A Contemporary Journal, 20*(2), 151–174.

Beck, I. L., McKeown, M. G., & Omanson, R. C. (1987). The effects and uses of diverse vocabulary instructional techniques. In M. G. McKeown & M. E. Curtis (Eds.), *The nature of vocabulary acquisition.* (pp. 147–163). Lawrence Erlbaum Associates, Inc.

Beck, I., & McKeown, M. G. (2016). *Conditions of vocabulary acquisition.* In R. Barr, M. L. Kamil, P. B. Mosenthal, and P. D. Pearson (eds). *Handbook of Reading Research,* 789–814. https://10.4324/9780203447772.CH28.

Beck, I., McKeown, M. G., & Kucan, L. (2013). *Bringing words to life: Robust vocabulary instruction* (2nd ed.). The Guilford Press.

Beck, I., Perfetti, C., & McKeown, M. (1982). Effects of long-term vocabulary instruction on lexical access and reading comprehension. *Journal of Educational Psychology, 74,* 506–521. https://doi.org/10.1037/0022-0663.74.4.506

Begeny, J. C., & Greene, D. J. (2014). Can readability formulas be used to successfully gauge difficulty of reading materials? *Psychology in the Schools, 51,* 198–215. https://doi.org/10.1002/pits.21740

Benjamin, A. S., & Tullis, J. (2010). What makes distributed practice effective? *Cognitive Psychology, 61*(3), 228–247. https://doi.org/10.1016/j.cogpsych.2010.05.004

Berlin, R. (1884). Über dyslexie. *Archiv für Psychiatrie, 15,* 276–278.

Best, R. M., Floyd, R. G., & McNamara, D. S. (2008). Differential competencies contributing to children's comprehension of narrative and expository texts. *Reading Psychology, 29*(2), 137–164.

Bhattacharya, A., & Ehri, L. C. (2004). Graphosyllabic analysis helps adolescent struggling readers read and spell words. *Journal of Learning Disabilities, 37*(4), 331–348. https://doi.org/10.1177/00222194040370040501

Binks-Cantrell, E., Washburn, E. K., Joshi, R. M., & Hougen, M. (2012). Peter effect in the preparation of reading teachers. *Scientific Studies of Reading, 16*(6), 526–536. https://doi.org/10.1080/10888438.2011.601434

Bishop, D. V. M. (2009). Genes, cognition, and communication. *Annals of the New York Academy of Sciences, 1156*, 1–18. https://doi.org/10.1111/j.1749-6632.2009.04419.x

Blevins, J. (2017). Areal sound patterns: From perceptual magnets to stone soup. *The Cambridge Handbook of Areal Linguistics, 5587.*

Bloom, B. S. (1971). Mastery learning. In J. H. Block (Ed.), *Mastery learning: Theory and practice* (pp. 47–63). Holt, Rinehart & Winston.

Board of Education of Hendrick Hudson Central School District v. Rowley, 458 U.S. 176 (1982).

Bosman, A. M. T., & Van Orden, G. C. (1997). Why spelling is more difficult than reading. In C. A. Perfetti, L. Rieven, & M. Fayol (Eds.), *Learning to spell: Research, theory, and practice across languages* (pp. 173–194). Lawrence Erlbaum Associates.

Bourassa, D.C., Treiman R., & Kessler B. (2006). Use of morphology in spelling by children with dyslexia and typically developing children. *Memory & Cognition, 34*(3), 703–714. https://doi.org/10.3758/bf03193589

Bowers, P. N., & Kirby, J. R. (2010). Effects of morphological instruction on vocabulary acquisition. *Reading & Writing, 23*(5), 515–537. https://doi.org/10.1007/s11145-009-9172-z

Bowers, P. N., Kirby, J. R., & Deacon, S. H. (2010). The effects of morphological instruction on literacy skills: A systematic review of the literature. *Review of Educational Research, 80*(2), 144–179. https://doi.org/10.3102/0034654309359353

Boyer, N., & Ehri, L. C. (2011). Contribution of phonemic segmentation instruction with letters and articulation pictures to word reading and spelling in beginners. *Scientific Studies of Reading, 15*(5), 440–470. https://doi.org/10.1080/10888438.2010.520778

Brasseur-Hock, I. F., Hock, M. F., Kieffer, M. J., Biancarosa, G., & Deshler, D. D. (2011). Adolescent struggling readers in urban schools: Results of a latent class analysis. *Learning and Individual Differences, 21*(4), 438–452. https://doi.org/10.1016/j.lindif.2011.01.008

Braun, G., Kumm, S., Brown, C., Walte, S., Hughes, M. T., & Maggin, D. M. (2020). Living in tier 2: Educators' perceptions of MTSS in urban schools. *International Journal of Inclusive Education, 24*(10), 1114–1128. https://doi.org/10.1080/13603116.2018.1511758

Brindle, M., Graham, S., Harris, K., & Hebert, M. (2016). Third and fourth grade teachers' classroom practices in writing: A national survey. *Reading & Writing, 29*(5), 929–954. https://doi.org/10.1007/s11145-015-9604-x

Brown, J. (2009). *Flat Stanley's worldwide adventures# 4: The intrepid Canadian expedition.* Harper Collins.

Brown, M. W., (1947). *Goodnight moon.* Runaway Bunny.

Brysbaert, M. (2022). Word recognition II: Orthography-phonology. In M. Snowling, C. Hulme, & K. Nation (Eds.) *The Science of Reading: A Handbook* (2nd ed.). Wiley.

Brysbaert, M., Stevens, M., Mandera, P., & Keuleers, E. (2016). How many words do we know? Practical estimates of vocabulary size dependent on word definition, the degree of language input, and the participant's age. *Frontiers in Psychology, 7*(1116), 1–11.

Byrne, B. (2005). Theories of learning to read. In M. J. Snowling & C. Hulme (Eds.), *The science of reading: A handbook* (pp. 104–119). Blackwell.

Cain, K., & Oakhill, J. (2011). Matthew effects in young readers: Reading comprehension and reading experience aid vocabulary development. *Journal of Learning Disabilities, 44*, 431–443. https://doi.org/10.1177/0022219411410042

Calkins, L. M. (1986). *The art of teaching writing*. Heinemann.

Calkins, L., Louis, N., Hartman, A., Franco, E., Wears, K., Cronin, R, Báez, A., Martinelli, M., Holley, C., Moore, E., & Teachers College Reading & Writing Project (2015). *Units of study for teaching reading, kindergarten*. Heinemann Publishers.

Campbell v. Board of Education of Centerline School District, 58 F. App'x 162 (2003)

Campbell, T. (2011). From aphasia to dyslexia, a fragment of genealogy: An analysis of the formation of a medical diagnosis. *Health Sociology Review, 20*(4), 450–461.

Capin, P., Cho, E., Miciak, J., Roberts, G., & Vaughn, S. (2021). Examining the reading and cognitive profiles of students with significant reading comprehension difficulties. *Learning Disability Quarterly, 44*(3), 183–196. https://doi.org/10.1177/0731948721989973

Capin, P., Gillam, S. L., Fall, A. M., Roberts, G., Dille, J. T., & Gillam, R. B. (2022). Understanding the nature and severity of reading difficulties among students with language and reading comprehension difficulties. *Annals of Dyslexia, 72*(2), 249–275. https://doi.org/10.1007/s11881-022-00255-3

Caravolas, M. (2022). Reading and reading disorders in alphabetic orthographies. In M. J. Snowling, C. Hulme, & Nation K. (Eds.), *The science of reading: A handbook* (2nd ed.). Wiley Blackwell. https://doi.org/10.1002/9781119705116.ch15

Carle, E. (1969). *The very hungry caterpillar*. World Publishing Company.

Carnine, D., Silbert, J., & Kame'enui, E. J. (1997). *Direct instruction reading* (3rd ed.). Merrill.

Carretti, B., Motta, E., & Re, A. M. (2016). Oral and written expression in children with reading comprehension difficulties. *Journal of Learning Disabilities, 49*(1), 65–76. https://doi.org/10.1177/0022219414528539

Castles, A., Rastle, K., & Nation, K. (2018). Ending the reading wars: Reading acquisition from novice to expert. *Psychological Science in the Public Interest, 19*, 5–51.

Catts, H. W., & Hogan, T. (2021). Dyslexia: An ounce of prevention is better than a pound of diagnosis and treatment. *Reading League Journal, 2*(1), 6–13. https://doi.org/10.31234/osf.io/nvgje

Catts, H. W., & Petscher, Y. (2020). *A cumulative risk and protection model of dyslexia*. PsyArXiv Preprints.

Catts, H. W., Adlof, S. M., Hogan, T. P., & Weismer, S. E. (2005). Are specific language impairment and dyslexia distinct disorders? *Journal of Speech, Language & Hearing Research, 48*(6), 1378–1396. https://doi.org/10.1044/1092-4388(2005/096)

Catts, H., McIlraith, A., Bridges, M., & Nielsen, D. (2017). Viewing a phonological deficit within a multifactorial model of dyslexia. *Reading & Writing, 30*(3), 613–629. https://doi.org/10.1007/s11145-016-9692-2

Catts, H. W., Fey, M. E., Zhang, X., & Tomblin, J. B. (1999). Language basis of reading and reading disabilities: Evidence from a longitudinal investigation. *Scientific Studies of Reading, 3*, 331–361.

Cepeda, N. J., Pashler, H., Vul, E., Wixted, J. T., & Rohrer, D. (2006). Distributed practice in verbal recall tasks: A review and quantitative synthesis. *Psychological Bulletin, 132*(3), 354–380. https://doi.org/10.1037/0033-2909.132.3.354

Cervetti, G. N., & Hiebert, E. H. (2019). Knowledge at the center of English language arts instruction. *The Reading Teacher, 72*(4), 417–543.

Cervetti, G. N., & Wright, T. S. (2020). The role of knowledge in understanding and learning from text. In E. B. Moje et al. (Eds.), *Handbook of reading research*. Taylor and Francis Group.

Cervetti, G. N., Kulikowich, J. M., & Bravo, M. A. (2015). The effects of educative curriculum materials on teachers' use of instructional strategies for English language learners in science and on student learning. *Contemporary Educational Psychology, 40*, 86–98. https://doi.org/10.1016/j.cedpsych.2014.10.005

Chall, J. S. (1967). *Learning to read: The great debate; an inquiry into the science, art, and ideology of old and new methods of teaching children to read, 1910–1965*. McGraw-Hill.

Chall, J. S. (1996). *Learning to read: The great debate* (3rd ed.). Harcourt Brace & Company.

Chall, J. S. (1997). Are reading methods changing again? *Annals of Dyslexia, 47*, pp. 257–263.

Chen, O., Paas, F., & Sweller, J. (2021). Spacing and interleaving effects require distinct theoretical bases: A systematic review testing the cognitive load and discriminative-contrast hypotheses. *Educational Psychology Review, 33*(4), 1499–1522. https://doi.org/10.1007/s10648-021-09613-w

Church, J. A., Grigorenko, E. L., & Fletcher, J. M. (2021). The role of neural and genetic processes in learning to read and specific reading disabilities: Implications for instruction. *Reading Research Quarterly*. Advance online publication. https://doi.org/10.1002/rrq.439

Clemens, N. H., Simmons, D., Simmons, L. E., Wang, H., & Kwok, O. (2017). The prevalence of reading fluency and vocabulary difficulties among adolescents struggling with reading comprehension. *Journal of Psychoeducational Assessment, 35*(8), 785–798. https://doi.org/10.1177/0734282916662120

Coltheart, M., & Rastle, K. (2001). DRC: A dual route cascaded model of visual word recognition and reading aloud. *Psychological Review, 108*(1), 204–256. https://doi.org/10.1037/0033-295X.108.1.204

Connor, C. M., Dombek, J., Crowe, E. C., Spencer, M., Tighe, E. L., Coffinger, S., Zargar, E., Wood, T., & Petscher, Y. (2017). Acquiring science and social studies knowledge in kindergarten through fourth grade: Conceptualization, design, implementation, and efficacy testing of content-area literacy instruction (CALI). *Journal of Educational Psychology, 109*(3), 301–320. https://doi.org/10.1037/edu0000128

Connor, C. M., Morrison, F. J., Fishman, B., Crowe, E. C., Al Otaiba, S., & Schatschneider, C. (2013). A longitudinal cluster-randomized controlled study on the accumulating effects of individualized literacy instruction on students' reading from first through third grade. *Psychological Science, 24,* 1408–1419. http://dx.doi.org/10.1177/0956797612472204

Connor, C. M., Morrison, F. J., Fishman, B., Crowe, E. C., Otaiba, S. A., & Schatschneider, C. (2013). A longitudinal cluster-randomized controlled study on the accumulating effects of individualized literacy instruction on students' reading from first through third grade. *Psychological Science, 24*(8), 1408–1419. https://doi.org/10.1177/0956797612472204

Cottrell, J. M., & Barrett, C. A. (2016). Defining the undefinable: Operationalization of methods to identify specific learning disabilities among practicing school psychologists. *Psychology in the Schools, 53*(2), 143–157. https://doi.org/10.1002/pits.21892

Coxhead, A. (2000). A new academic word list. *TESOL Quarterly, 34*(2), 213–238. https://doi.org/10.2307/3587951

Cremin, L. (1964). *The transformation of the school: Progressivism in American education, 1876–1957.* Alfred A. Knopf.

Crosson, A. C., McKeown, M. G., Lei, P., Zhao, H., Li, X., Patrick, K., Brown, K., & Shen, Y. (2021). Morphological analysis skill and academic vocabulary knowledge are malleable through intervention and may contribute to reading comprehension for multilingual adolescents. *Journal of Research in Reading, 44*(1), 154–174. https://doi.org/10.1111/1467-9817.12323

Cruttenden, A. (2014). *Gimson's pronunciation of English.* Routledge.

Cunningham, A. E., & Stanovich, K. E. (2001). What reading does for the mind. *Journal of Direct Instruction, 1*(2), 137–149.

Cunningham, J. W., Koppenhaver, D. A., Erickson, K. A., & Spadorcia, S. A. (2004). Word identification and text characteristics. In J. V. Hoffman & D. L. Schallert (Eds.), *The texts in elementary classrooms* (pp. 21–37). Erlbaum.

Darling, J. (1993). Rousseau as progressive instrumentalist. *Journal of Philosophical Education, 27*(1), 27–39. https://doi.org/10.1111/j.1467-9752.1993.tb00294.x

DeFord, D. E., Lyons, C. A., & Pinnell, G. S. (1991). *Bridges to literacy: Learning from reading recovery.* Heinemann Publishers.

Dehaene, S. (2009). *Reading in the brain: The new science of how we read.* Penguin.

Dehaene, S. (2011). The massive impact of literacy on the brain and its consequences for education. *Human neuroplasticity and education, 117,* 19–32.

Dehaene, S. (2020). *How we learn: Why brains learn better than any machine . . . for now.* Viking.

Dehaene, S., Cohen, L., Morais, J., & Kolinsky, R. (2015). Illiterate to literate: Behavioural and cerebral changes induced by reading acquisition. *Nature Reviews Neuroscience, 16*(4), 234–244. https://doi.org/10.1038/nrn3924

DeWalt, D. A., Berkman, N. D., Sheridan, S., Lohr, K. N., & Pignone, M. P. (2004). Literacy and health outcomes. *Journal of General Internal Medicine, 19*(12), 1228–1239. doi: 10.1111/j.1525-1497.2004.40153.x

Dewey, J. (1897). My pedagogic creed. *School Journal, LIV*(3), 77–80.

Dewey, J. (1898). The primary-education fetish. *School Journal, 66(15),* 315–328.

Dewey, J. (1938/1963). *Experience and education.* Collier Books.

Diliberto, J. A., Beattie, J. R., Flowers, C. P., & Algozzine, R. F. (2009). Effects of teaching syllable skills instruction on reading achievement in struggling middle school readers. *Literacy Research & Instruction, 48*(1), 14–27. https://doi.org/10.1080/19388070802226253

Dilnot, J., Hamilton, L., Maughan, B., & Snowling, M. J. (2017). Child and environmental risk factors predicting readiness for learning in children at high risk of dyslexia. *Development and Psychopathology, 29*(1), 235–244. https://doi.org/10.1017/S0954579416000134

Dolch, E. W. (1936). A basic sight vocabulary. *Elementary School Journal, 36*(6), 456–460.

Duff, D. M., Hendricks, A. E., Fitton, L., & Adlof, S. M. (2022). Reading and math achievement in children with dyslexia, developmental language disorder, or typical development: Achievement gaps persist from second through fourth grades. *Journal of Learning Disabilities*, 1–21. Advance online publication. https://doi.org/10.1177/00222194221105515

Dunlosky, J., Rawson, K. A., Marsh, E. J., Nathan, M. J., & Willingham, D. T. (2013). Improving students' learning with effective learning techniques: Promising directions from cognitive and educational psychology. *Psychological Science in the Public Interest, 14*(1), 4–58. https://doi.org/10.1177/1529100612453266

Dyson, H., Best, W., Solity, J., & Hulme, C. (2017). Training mispronunciation correction and word meanings improves children's ability to learn to read words. *Scientific Studies of Reading, 21*, 393–407.

Eastman, P. D. (1960). *Are you my mother?* Beginner Books.

Ehri, L. C. (1998). Grapheme-phoneme knowledge is essential for learning to read words in English. In J. L. Metsala, & L. C. Ehri (Eds.), *Word recognition in beginning literacy* (pp. 3–40). Routledge.

Ehri, L. C. (2004). Teaching phonemic awareness and phonics: An explanation of the national reading panel meta-analyses. In P. McCardle & V. Chhabra (Eds.), *The voice of evidence in reading research* (pp. 153–186). Paul H. Brookes Publishing Co.

Ehri, L. C. (2014). Orthographic mapping in the acquisition of sight word reading, spelling memory, and vocabulary learning. *Scientific Studies of Reading, 18*(1), 5–21. https://doi.org/10.1080/10888438.2013.819356

Ehri, L. C. (2020). The science of learning to read words: A case for systematic phonics instruction. *Reading Research Quarterly, 55*, S45–S60. https://doi.org/10.1002/rrq.334

Ehri, L. C., & Wilce, L. S. (1979). The mnemonic value of orthography among beginning readers. *Journal of Educational Psychology, 71*(1), 26–40. https://doi.org/10.1037/0022-0663.71.1.26

Ehri, L. C., Nunes, S. R., Stahl, S. A., & Willows, D. M. (2001). Systematic phonics instruction helps students learn to read: Evidence from the National Reading Panel's meta-analysis. *Review of Educational Research, 71*(3), 393–447. https://doi.org/10.3102/00346543071003393

Eide, D. (2012). *Uncovering the logic of English: A common-sense approach to reading, spelling, and literacy.* Logic of English.

Elbro, C., de Jong, P. F., Houter, D., & Nielsen, A. (2012). From spelling pronunciation to lexical access: A second step in word decoding? *Scientific Studies of Reading, 16*(4), 341–359.

Ellefson, M. R., Treiman, R., & Kessler, B. (2009). Learning to label letters by sounds or names: A comparison of England and the United States. *Journal of Experimental Child Psychology, 102*(3), 323–341. https://doi.org/10.1016/j.jecp.2008.05.008

Elleman, A. M., Lindo, E. J., Morphy, P., & Compton, D. L. (2009). The impact of vocabulary instruction on passage-level comprehension of school-age children: A meta-analysis. *Journal of Research on Educational Effectiveness, 2*, 1–44. https://doi.org/10.1080/19345740802539200

Elliott, J., & Grigorenko, E. (2014). *The dyslexia debate*. Cambridge University Press.

Endrew F. v. Douglas County School District RE-1, 137 S. Ct. 988 (2017).

English-Language Arts Curriculum Framework and Criteria Committee (1987). *English-language arts framework for California public schools kindergarten through grade twelve*. California State Department of Education.

Ericsson, K. A. (2005). Recent advances in expertise research: A commentary on the contributions to the special issue. *Applied Cognitive Psychology, 19*(2), 233–241. https://doi.org/10.1002/acp.1111

Ericsson, K. A. (2008). Deliberate practice and acquisition of expert performance: A general overview. *Academic Emergency Medicine, 15*(11), 988–994. https://doi.org/10.1111/j.1553-2712.2008.00227.x

Fälth, L., Gustafson, S., & Svensson, I. (2017). Phonological awareness training with articulation promotes early reading development. *Education, 137*(3), 261–276.

Farrell, L., Hunter, M., & Osenga, T. (2019). *A new model for teaching high-frequency words*. Reading Rockets. https://www.readingrockets.org/article/new-model-teaching-high-frequency-words

Fawson, P. C., & Reutzel, D. R. (2000). But I only have a basal: Implementing guided reading in the early grades. *Reading Teacher, 54*(1), 84–97. http://www.jstor.org/stable/20204881

Figueredo, L., & Varnhagen, C. (2005). Didn't you run the spell checker? Effects of type of spelling error and use of a spell checker on perceptions of the author. *Reading Psychology, 26*(4/5), 441–458. https://doi.org/10.1080/02702710500400495

Filderman, M. J., Austin, C. R., Boucher, A. N., O'Donnell, K., & Swanson, E. A. (2022). A meta-analysis of the effects of reading comprehension interventions on the reading comprehension outcomes of struggling readers in third through twelfth grades. *Exceptional Children, 88*(2), 163–184. https://doi.org/10.1177/00144029211050860

Firth, J., Rivers, I., & Boyle, J. (2021). A systematic review of interleaving as a concept learning strategy. *Review of Education, 9*, 642–684. https://doi.org/10.1002/rev3.3266

Flesch, R. (1955). *Why Johnny can't read: And what you can do about it* (1st ed.). Harper & Brothers.

Flesch, R. (1981). *Why Johnny still can't read: A new look at the scandal of our schools* (1st ed.). Harper & Row.

Flesch, R., & Gould, A. J. (1949). *The art of readable writing* (1st ed.). Harper & Row.

Fletcher, J. M., Lyon, G. R., Fuchs, L. S., & Barnes, M. A. (2007). *Learning disabilities: From identification to intervention.* Guilford Press.

Fletcher, J. M., Lyon, G. R., Fuchs, L. S., & Barnes, M. A. (2019). *Learning disabilities in children: Evidence-based interventions.* Guilford Publications.

Foorman, B. R., Coyne, M. D., Denton, C. A., Dimino, J. A., Hayes, L., Justice, L. M., . . . & Wissel, S. (2016). *Foundational skills to support reading for understanding in kindergarten through 3rd grade.* National Center for Education Evaluation and Regional Assistance (NCEE), Institute of Education Sciences, US Department of Education.

Foorman, B. R., Francis, D. J., Fletcher, J. M., Schatschneider, C., & Mehta, P. (1998). The role of instruction in learning to read: Preventing reading failure in at-risk children. *Journal of Educational Psychology, 90,* 37–55. http://dx.doi.org/10.1037/0022-0663.90.1.37

Foorman, B. R., Petscher, Y., & Herrera, S. (2018). Unique and common effects of decoding and language factors in predicting reading comprehension in grades 1–10. *Learning and Individual Differences, 63,* 12–23. https://doi.org/10.1016/j.lindif.2018.02.011

Fountas, I. C., & Pinnell, G. S. (1996). *Guided reading: Good first teaching for all children.* Heinemann.

Fountas, I. C., & Pinnell, G. S. (2009). *Leveled Literacy Intervention.* Portsmouth, NH: Heinemann.

Freeman, A. R., MacKinnon, J. R., & Miller, L. T. (2005). Keyboarding for students with handwriting problems: A literature review. *Physical & Occupational Therapy in Pediatrics, 25*(1/2), 119–147. https://doi.org/10.1080/j006v25n01_08

Frijters, J. C., Tsujimoto, K. C., Boada, R., Gottwald, S., Hill, D., Jacobson, L. A., Lovett, M. W., Mahone, E. M., Willcutt, E. G., Wolf, M., Bosson-Heenan, J., & Gruen, J. R. (2018). Reading-related causal attributions for success and failure: Dynamic links with reading skill. *Reading Research Quarterly, 53*(1), 127–148. https://doi.org/10.1002/rrq.189

Frith, U. (1985). Beneath the surface of developmental dyslexia. In K. Patterson, J. Marshall, & M. Coltheart (Eds.), *Surface dyslexia: Neurological and cognitive studies of phonological reading* (pp. 301–330). Lawrence Erlbaum.

Fry, E., & Kress, J. K. (2006). *The reading teacher's book of lists.* Jossey-Bass.

Fuchs, D., & Fuchs, L. (2017). Critique of the national evaluation of response to intervention: A case for simpler frameworks. *Exceptional Children, 83*(3), 255–268. https://doi.org/10.1177/0014402917693580

Furey, W. M., Marcotte, A. M., Wells, C. S., & Hintze, J. M. (2017). The effects of supplemental sentence-level instruction for fourth-grade students identified as struggling writers. *Reading & Writing Quarterly, 33*(6), 563–578. https://doi.org/10.1080/10573569.2017.1288591

Gabrieli, J. D. E. (2009). Dyslexia: A new synergy between education and cognitive neuroscience. *Science, 325*(5938), 280–283. https://doi.org/10.1126/science.1171999

Gajria, M., Jitendra, A. K., Sood, S., & Sacks, G. (2007). Improving comprehension of expository text in students with LD: A research synthesis. *Journal of Learning Disabilities, 40*(3), 210–225. https://doi.org/10.1177/00222194070400030301

Galazka, M. A., Hadijikhani, N., Sundqvist, M., & Johnels, J. Å. (2021) Facial speech processing in children with and without dyslexia. *Annals of Dyslexia, 71*, 501–524. https://doi.org/10.1007/s11881-021-00231-3

Galuschka, K., Görgen, R., Kalmar, J., Haberstroh, S., Schmalz, X., & Schulte-Körne, G. (2020). Effectiveness of spelling interventions for learners with dyslexia: A meta-analysis and systematic review. *Educational Psychologist, 55*(1), 1–20. https://doi.org/10.1080/00461520.2019.1659794

Gearin, B., Fien, H., & Nelson, N. J. (2018). Mind wandering: A potentially generative idea for understanding the socioeconomic status academic achievement gap. *Translational Issues in Psychological Science, 4*(2), 138–152. https://doi.org/10.1037/tps0000156

Gearin, B., Petscher, Y., Stanley, C., Nelson, N. J., & Fien, H. (2022). Document analysis of state dyslexia legislation suggests likely heterogeneous effects on student and school outcomes. *Learning Disability Quarterly, 45*(4), 267–279. https://doi.org/10.1177/0731948721991549

Gearin, B., Turtura, J., Kame'enui, E. J., Nelson, N. J., & Fien, H. (2020). A multiple streams analysis of recent changes to state-level dyslexia education law. *Educational Policy, 34*(7), 1036–1068. https://doi.org/10.1177/0895904818807328

Georgiou, G., & Parrila, R. (2013). Rapid automatized naming and reading: A review. In H. L. Swanson, K. R. Harris, & S. Graham (Eds.), *Handbook of learning disabilities* (pp. 169–185). Guilford Press.

Gerber, P. (2011). The impact of learning disabilities on adulthood: A review of the evidence-based literature for research and practice in adult education. *Journal of Learning Disabilities, 45*, 31–46. https://doi.org/10.1177/0022219411426858

Gilbert, J., & Graham, S. (2010). Teaching writing to elementary students in grades 4–6: A national survey. *The Elementary School Journal, 110*(4), 494–518.

Gillam, S. L., Vaughn, S., Roberts, G., Capin, P., Fall, A. M., Israelsen-Augenstein, M., Holbrook, S., Wada, R., Hancock, A., Fox, C., Dille, J., Magimairaj, B. M., & Gillam, R. B. (2023). Improving oral and written narration and reading comprehension of children at risk for language and literacy difficulties: Results of a randomized clinical trial. *Journal of Educational Psychology, 115*(1), 99–117. https://doi.org/10.1037/edu0000766

Goldstein, D. (2022, May 22). In the fight over how to teach reading, this guru makes a major retreat. *New York Times*. https://www.nytimes.com/2022/05/22/us/reading-teaching-curriculum-phonics.html

Goodman, K. S. (1967). Reading: A psycholinguistic guessing game. *Journal of the Reading Specialist 6*(4), 126–135. https://doi.org/10.1080/19388076709556976

Goodman, Y. M. (1989). Roots of the whole-language movement. *Elementary School Journal, 90*(2), 113–127. https://doi.org/10.1086/461607

Goodwin, A. P., & Ahn, S. (2010). A meta-analysis of morphological interventions: Effects on literacy achievement of children with literacy difficulties. *Annals of Dyslexia, 60*(2), 183–208. https://doi.org/10.1007/s11881-010-0041-x

Goodwin, A. P., & Ahn, S. (2013). A meta-analysis of morphological interventions in English: Effects on literacy outcomes for school-age children. *Scientific Studies of Reading, 17*(4), 257–285. https://doi.org/10.1080/10888438.2012.689791

Gough, P. B. & Tunmer, W. E. (1986). Decoding, reading, and reading disability. *Remedial and Special Education, 7*, 6–10.

Graham, D., & Walsh, K. (2020). *Teacher prep review: Program performance in early reading instruction.* National Council on Teacher Quality.

Graham, S. (2019). Changing how writing is taught. *Review of Research in Education, 43*(1), 277–303.

Graham, S., & Hebert, M. (2010). *Writing to read: Evidence for how writing can improve reading.* Alliance for Excellent Education.

Graham, S., & Santangelo, T. (2014). Does spelling instruction make students better spellers, readers, and writers? A meta-analytic review. *Reading & Writing, 27*(9), 1703–1743. https://doi.org/10.1007/s11145-014-9517-0

Graham, S., Berninger, V. W., Abbott, R. D., Abbott, S. P., & Whitaker, D. (1997). Role of mechanics in composing of elementary school students: A new methodological approach. *Journal of Educational Psychology, 89*(1), 170–182. https://doi.org/10.1037/0022-0663.89.1.170

Graham, S., Berninger, V., & Fan, W. (2007). The structural relationship between writing attitude and writing achievement in first and third grade students. *Contemporary Educational Psychology, 32*(3), 516–536. https://doi.org/10.1016/j.cedpsych.2007.01.002

Graham, S., Liu, X., Aitken, A., Ng, C., Bartlett, B., Harris, K. R., & Holzapfel, J. (2018). Effectiveness of literacy programs balancing reading and writing instruction: A meta-analysis. *Reading Research Quarterly, 53*(3), 279–304. https://doi.org/10.1002/rrq.194

Graham, S., MacArthur, C., & Schwartz, S. (1995). Effects of goal setting and procedural facilitation on revising behavior and writing performance of students with writing and learning problems. *Journal of Educational Psychology, 87*(2), 230–240. https://doi.org/10.1037/0022-0663.87.2.230

Graham, S., McKeown, D., Kiuhara, S., & Harris, K. R. (2012). A meta-analysis of writing instruction for students in the elementary grades. *Journal of Educational Psychology, 104*(4), 879–896. https://doi.org/10.1037/a0029185

Graves, D. H. (1983). *Writing: Teachers and children at work.* Heinemann.

Greene, V. E., & Enfield, M. L. (1997). *Framing your thoughts: Sentence structure.* Language Circle Enterprises. Hammill, D., & Larsen.

Guskey, T. R. (2010). Lessons of mastery learning. *Educational Leadership, 68*(2), 52.

Guthrie, J. T., Wigfield, A., Humenick, N. M., Perencevich, K. C., Taboada, A., & Barbosa, P. (2006). Influences of stimulating tasks on reading motivation and comprehension. *Journal of Educational Research, 99*(4), 232–246. https://doi.org/10.3200/JOER.99.4.232-246

Habib, M. (2021). The neurological basis of developmental dyslexia and related disorders: A reappraisal of the temporal hypothesis, twenty years on. *Brain Science, 11*(708), 1–32.

Hanford, E. (2017, September 11). Hard to read: How American schools fail kids with dyslexia. *APM Reports*. https://www.apmreports.org/story/2017/09/11/hard-to-read.

Haring, N. G., Lovitt, T. C., Eaton, M. D., & Hansen, C. L. (1978). *The fourth R: Research in the classroom*. Merrill.

Harm, M. W., & Seidenberg, M. S. (2004). Computing the meanings of words in reading: Cooperative division of labor between visual and phonological processes. *Psychological Review, 111*(3), 662–720. https://doi.org/10.1037/0033-295X.111.3.662

Hatcher, P. J., Hulme, C. & Ellis, W. (1994). Ameliorating early reading failure by integrating the teaching of reading and phonological skills: The phonological linkage hypothesis. *Child Development, 65*, 41–57. https://doi.org/10.1111/j.1467-8624.1994.tb00733.x

Hayes, J. R., & Flower, L. S. (1980). Identifying the organization of writing processes. In L. W. Gregg, & E. R. Steinberg (Eds.), *Cognitive processes in writing* (pp. 3–30). LawrenceErlbaum Associates.

Hebert, M., Kearns, D. M., Hayes, J. B., Bazis, P., & Cooper, S. (2018). Why children with dyslexia struggle with writing and how to help them. *Language, speech, and hearing services in schools, 49*(4), 843–863. https://doi.org/10.1044/2018_LSHSS-DYSLC-18-0024

Henderson, L. M., Tsogka, N., & Snowling, M. J. (2013). Questioning the benefits that coloured overlays can have for reading in students with and without dyslexia. *Journal of Research in Special Educational Needs, 13*(1), 57–65. https://doi.org/10.1111/j.1471-3802.2012.01237.x

Henry, M. (2003). *Unlocking literacy*. Brookes Publishing.

Hettleman, K. R. (2003). *The invisible dyslexics: How public school systems in Baltimore and elsewhere discriminate against poor children in the diagnosis and treatment of early reading difficulties*. The Abell Foundation.

Heubeck, E. (2023, February 27). Universal screening for dyslexia isn't enough. *Education Week*. https://www.edweek.org/teaching-learning/universal-screening-for-dyslexia-isnt-enough/2023/02

Hibel, J., Farkas, G., & Morgan, P. L. (2010). Who is placed into special education? *Sociology of Education, 83*(4), 312–332. https://doi.org/10.1177/0038040710383518

Hinshelwood, J. (1900). *Word- and mind-blindness*. Lewis.

Hirsch, E. D. (2019). *Why knowledge matters: Rescuing our children from failed educational theories*. Harvard Education Press.

Hochman, J. C., & Wexler, N. (2017b). One sentence at a time: The need for explicit instruction in teaching students to write well. *American Educator, 41(2)*, 30–43.

Hochman, J., & Wexler, N. (2017a). *The writing revolution: A guide to advancing thinking through writing in all subjects and grades*. Jossey-Bass.

Hock, M. F., Brasseur, I. F., Deshler, D. D., Catts, H. W., Marquis, J. G., Mark, C. A., & Stribling, J. W. (2009). What is the reading component skill profile of adolescent struggling readers in urban schools? *Learning Disability Quarterly, 32*(1), 21–38. https://doi.org/10.2307/25474660

Hoff, E. (2013). Interpreting the early language trajectories of children from low-SES and language minority homes: Implications for closing achievement gaps. *Developmental Psychology, 49*(1), 4–14. https://doi.org/10.1037/a0027238

Hoffman, J. V., & McCarthey, S. J. (1994). So what's new in the new basals? A focus on first grade. *Journal of Reading Behavior, 26*(1), 47. https://doi.org/10.1080/10862969409547836

Hoffman, J. V., Sailors, M., & Patterson, E. U. (2002). Decodable texts for beginning reading instruction: The year 2000 basals. *Journal of Literacy Research, 34*(2), 269–298. https://doi.org/10.1207/s15548430jlr3403_2

Holmes, V. M., & Castles, A. E. (2001). Unexpectedly poor spelling in university students. *Scientific Studies of Reading, 5*(4), 319–350. https://doi.org/10.1207/S1532799XSSR0504_02

Holmes, V. M., Malone, A. M., & Redenbach, H. (2008). Orthographic processing and visual sequential memory in unexpectedly poor spellers. *Journal of Research in Reading, 31*(1), 136–156. https://doi.org/10.1111/j.1467-9817.2007.00364.x

Holmes, V. M., & Quinn, L. (2009). Unexpectedly poor spelling and phonological-processing skill. *Scientific Studies of Reading, 13*(4), 295–317. https://doi.org/10.1080/10888430903001225

Hoover, W. A., & Gough, P. B. (1990). The simple view of reading. *Reading and Writing, 2*(2), 127–160. https://doi.org/10.1007/BF00401799

Hoover, W. A., & Tunmer, W. E. (2020). *The cognitive foundations of reading and its acquisition: A framework with applications connecting teaching and learning.* Springer International Publishing.

Hoover, W. A., & Tunmer, W. E. (2022). The primacy of science in communicating advances in the science of reading. *Reading Research Quarterly, 57*(2), 399–408. https://doi.org/10.1002/rrq.446

Hull, G. A., & Schultz, K. (Eds.). (2002). *School's out: Bridging out-of-school literacies with classroom practice* (Vol. 60). Teachers College Press.

Individuals with Disabilities Education Act, 20 U.S.C. § 1400 et seq. (2004).

International Dyslexia Association (2002). *Definition of dyslexia*. https://dyslexiaida.org/definition-of-dyslexia/

International Dyslexia Association. (2019). *Structured literacy: An introductory guide.*

International Reading Association (1998). Learning to read and write: Developmentally appropriate practices for young children. *Reading Teacher, 52*, 193–214.

Jitendra, A. K., Burgess, C., & Gajria, M. (2011). Cognitive strategy instruction for improving expository text comprehension of students with learning disabilities: The quality of evidence. *Exceptional Children, 77*(2), 135–159. https://doi.org/10.1177/001440291107700201

Johnson, S. (1755) *A dictionary of the English language.* J & P Knapton.

Jones, C. D., & Reutzel, D. R. (2012). Enhanced alphabet knowledge instruction: Exploring a change of frequency, focus, and distributed cycles of review. *Reading Psychology, 33*, 448–464. https://doi.org/10.1080/02702711.2010.545260.

Jones, S., Myhill, D., & Bailey, T. (2013). Grammar for writing? An investigation of the effects of contextualised grammar teaching on students' writing. *Reading & Writing, 26*(8), 1241–1263. https://doi.org/10.1007/s11145-012-9416-1

Joshi, R. M., Binks, E., Hougen, M., Dahlgren, M. E., Ocker-Dean, E., & Smith, D. L. (2009). Why elementary teachers might be inadequately prepared to teach reading. *Journal of Learning Disabilities, 42*(5), 392–402. https://doi.org/10.1177/0022219409338736

Justice, L. M., Pence, K., Bowles, R. B., & Wiggins, A. (2006). An investigation of four hypotheses concerning the order in which 4-year-old children learn the alphabet letters. *Early Childhood Research Quarterly, 21*(3), 374–389. https://doi.org/10.1016/j.ecresq.2006.07.010

Kabuto, B. (2016). The social construction of a reading (dis)ability. *Reading Research Quarterly, 51(3)*, 289–304. https://doi.org/10.1002/rrq.135

Kearns, D. M., & Whaley, V. M. (2019). Helping students with dyslexia read long words: Using syllables and morphemes. *TEACHING Exceptional Children, 51*(3), 212–225. https://doi.org/10.1177/0040059918810010

Kearns, D. M., Hancock, R., Hoeft, F., Pugh, K. R., & Frost, S. J. (2019). The neurobiology of dyslexia. *TEACHING Exceptional Children, 51*(3), 175–188. https://doi.org/10.1177/0040059918820051

Kellum, R. (1983). The influence of Francis Parker's pedagogy on the pedagogy of John Dewey. *Journal of Thought, 18*(1), 77–91. https://www.jstor.org/stable/23801652

Kessler, B., & Treiman, R. (2001). Relationships between sounds and letters in monosyllables. *Journal of Memory and Language, 44*, 562–617. https://doi.org/10.1006/jmla.2000.2745

Kieffer, M. J., & Lesaux, N. K. (2010). Morphing into adolescents: Active word learning for English-language learners and their classmates in middle school. *Journal of Adolescent & Adult Literacy, 54*(1), 47–56. https://doi.org/10.1598/JAAL.54.1.5

Kieffer, M., & Vukovic, R. (2013). Growth in reading-related skills of language minority learners and their classmates: More evidence for early identification and intervention. *Reading & Writing, 26*(7), 1159–1194. https://doi.org/10.1007/s11145-012-9410-7

Kilpatrick, D. A. (2015). *Essentials of assessing, preventing, and overcoming reading difficulties.* John Wiley & Sons.

Kim, Y. S. G., Quinn, J. M., & Petscher, Y. (2021). What is text reading fluency and is it a predictor or an outcome of reading comprehension? A longitudinal investigation. *Developmental Psychology, 57*(5), 718–732. https://doi.org/10.1037/dev0001167

Kim, Y. S. G., Wagner, R. K., & Lopez, D. (2012). Developmental relations between reading fluency and reading comprehension: A longitudinal study from grade 1 to grade 2. *Journal of Experimental Child Psychology, 113*(1), 93–111. https://doi.org/10.1016/j.jecp.2012.03.002

Kintsch, W. (1988). The role of knowledge in discourse comprehension: A construction-integration model. *Psychological Review, 95*(2), 163–182. https://doi.org/10.1037/0033-295X.95.2.163

Kirby, J. R., & Savage, R. S. (2008). Can the simple view deal with the complexities of reading? *Literacy, 42*(2), 75–82.

Kirby, J. R., Georgiou, G. K., Martinussen, R., & Parrila, R. (2010). Naming speed and reading: From prediction to instruction. *Reading Research Quarterly, 45*, 341–362. https://doi.org/10.1598/RRQ.45.3.4

Kirby, P. (2020). Dyslexia debated, then and now: A historical perspective on the dyslexia debate. *Oxford Review of Education, 46*(4), 472–486. https://doi.org/10.1080/03054985.2020.1747418

Kline, E., Moore, D. W., & Moore, S. A. (1987). Colonel Francis Parker and beginning reading instruction. *Reading Research and Instruction, 26*(3), 141–150. https://doi.org/10.1080/19388078709557906

Knowledge Matters Campaign (n.d.). *Statement from the knowledge matters campaign scientific advisory committee.* https://knowledgematterscampaign.org/statement-from-the-knowledge-matters-campaign-scientific-advisory-committee/

Kreiner, D. S., Schnakenberg, S. D., Green, A. G., Costello, M. J., & McClin, A. F. (2002). Effects of spelling errors on the perception of writers. *Journal of General Psychology, 129*, 5–17. https://doi.org/10.1080/00221300209602029

Kurtz, H., Lloyd, S., Harwin, A., Chen, V., & Furuya, Y. (2020). *Early reading instruction: Results of a national survey.* Editorial Projects in Education.

Kussmaul, A. (1877). Word-deafness—word-blindness: Derangements of the impressive or perceptive speech-track in general—Alexia and kindred derangements in the comprehension of the symbols of expression—Apraxia and aphasia. In Dr. H. van Ziemssen (Ed.), *Cyclopeadia of the practice of medicine* (Vol. 14, pp. 770–778).

Labaree, D. F. (2005). Progressivism, schools, and schools of education: An American romance. *Paedagogica Historia, 41*(1), 275–288. https://doi.org/10.1080/0030923042000335583

LaBerge, D., & Samuels, S. J. (1974). Toward a theory of automatic information processing in reading. *Cognitive Psychology, 6*, 293–323. https://doi.org/10.1016/0010-0285(74)90015-2

Lee, J. A. C., & Al Otaiba, S. (2015). Socioeconomic and gender group differences in early literacy skills: A multiple-group confirmatory factor analysis approach. *Educational Research & Evaluation, 21*(1), 40–59. https://doi.org/10.1080/13803611.2015.1010545

Lee, S. A. S., Davis, B., & Macneilage, P. (2010). Universal production patterns and ambient language influences in babbling: A cross-linguistic study of Korean- and English-learning infants. *Journal of Child Language, 37*(2), 293–318. https://doi.org/10.1017/S0305000909009532

Levesque, K. C., Breadmore, H. L., & Deacon, S. H. (2021). How morphology impacts reading and spelling: Advancing the role of morphology in models of literacy development. *Journal of Research in Reading, 44*(1), 10–26. https://doi.org/10.1111/1467-9817.12313

Lewis, W., Walpole, S., & McKenna, M. C. (2014). *Cracking the common core: Choosing and using texts in grades 6–12.* Guilford.

Liberman, I. Y., Shankweiler, D., Fischer, F. W., & Carter, B. (1974). Explicit syllable and phoneme segmentation in the young child. *Journal of Experimental Child Psychology, 18*, 201–212. https://doi.org/10.1016/0022-0965(74)90101-5

Lichtenstein, R. (2019). Parent advocates champion evidence-based practice under the banner of dyslexia—Part 3. *Communiqué, 47*(5), 16–18.

Lovett, M. W., Frijters, J. C., Steinbach, K. A., Sevcik, R. A., & Morris, R. D. (2021). Effective intervention for adolescents with reading disabilities: Combining reading and motivational remediation to improve outcomes. *Journal of Educational Psychology, 113*(4), 656–689. https://doi.org/10.1037/edu0000639.supp

Lovett, M. W., Frijters, J. C., Wolf, M., Steinbach, K. A., Sevcik, R. A., & Morris, R. D. (2017). Early intervention for children at risk for reading disabilities: The impact of grade at intervention and individual differences on intervention outcomes. *Journal of Educational Psychology, 109*(7), 889–914. https://doi.org/10.1037/edu0000181

Lupo, S. M., Berry, A., Thacker, E., Sawyer, A., & Merritt, J. (2020). Rethinking text sets to support knowledge building and interdisciplinary learning. *Reading Teacher, 73*(4), 513–524. https://doi.org/10.1002/trtr.1869

Luscombe, B. (2022). Inside the massive effort to change the way kids are taught to read. *TIME*. https://time.com/6205084/phonics-science-of-reading-teachers/

Lyon, G. R. (2002, June 6). *Learning disabilities and early intervention strategies*. National Institute of Child Health and Human Development.

Mancilla-Martinez, J., & Lesaux, N. K. (2011). The gap between Spanish speakers' word reading and word knowledge: A longitudinal study. *Child Development, 82*, 1544–1560. https://doi.org/10.1111/j.1467-8624.2011.01633.x

Manyak, P. C., Baumann, J. F., & Manyak, A. (2018). Morphological analysis instruction in the elementary grades: Which morphemes to teach and how to teach them. *Reading Teacher, 72*(3), 289–300. https://doi.org/10.1002/trtr.1713

Martin, B., Jr., & Carle, E. (1967). *Brown, bear, brown bear, what do you see?* Doubleday & Company.

Mayer, R. (1989). Systematic thinking fostered by illustrations in scientific text. *Journal of Educational Psychology, 81*(2), 240–246. https://doi.org/10.1037/0022-0663.81.2.240

McArthur, G., & Castles, A. (2017). Helping children with reading difficulties: Some things we have learned so far. *NPJ Science of Learning, 2*(1), Article 7. https://doi.org/10.1038/s41539-017-0008-3

McCarter, P. K., Jr. (1974). Early diffusion of the alphabet. *The Biblical Archaeologist, 37*(3), 54–68.

McCutchen, D., Northey, M., Herrera, B. L., & Clark, T. (2022). What's in a word? Effects of morphologically rich vocabulary instruction on writing outcomes among elementary students. *Reading & Writing, 35*(2), 325–351. https://doi.org/10.1007/s11145-021-10184-z

McGuffey, W. H. (1909). *McGuffey Eclectic Primer* (Revised Ed.). Project Gutenberg. Retrieved August 22, 2022, from https://www.gutenberg.org/files/14642/14642-pdf.pdf.

McGuinness, D. (2004). *Early reading instruction: What science really tells us about how to teach reading*. MIT Press.

McLeod, S., van Doorn, J., & Reed, V. A. (2001). Normal acquisition of consonant clusters. *American Journal of Speech-Language Pathology, 10*(2), 99–110. https://doi.org/10.1044/1058-0360

McNamara, D. S., Graesser, A. C., & Louwerse, M. M. (2013). Sources of text difficulty: Across the ages and genres. In J. P. Sabatini & E. Albro (Eds.), *Assessing reading in the 21st century: Aligning and applying advances in the reading and measurement sciences* (pp. 89–116). R&L Education.

McNeill, B., & Kirk, C. (2014). Theoretical beliefs and instructional practices used for teaching spelling in elementary classrooms. *Reading and Writing, 27*(3), 535–554. https://doi.org/10.1007/s11145-013-9457-0

McShane, M. (2023, January 31). Dispatches from the land of luxury beliefs. *Forbes*. https://www.forbes.com/sites/mikemcshane/2023/01/31/dispatches-from-the-land-of-luxury-beliefs/?sh=3a39e1ea922c

Medina A. L., & Pilonieta, P. (2006). Once upon a time: Comprehending narrative text. In J. S. Schumm (Eds.), *Reading assessment and instruction for all learners* (pp. 222–261). Guilford.

Melby-Lervåg, M., Lyster, S. A. H., & Hulme, C. (2012). Phonological skills and their role in learning to read: A meta-analytic review. *Psychological Bulletin, 138*(2), 322–352. https://doi.org/10.1037/a0026744

Merriam-Webster. (n.d.). *Reluctant*. In Merriam-Webster.com dictionary. Retrieved January 4, 2023, from https://www.merriam-webster.com/dictionary/reluctant.

Mesmer, H. A., Cunningham, J. W., & Hiebert, E. H. (2012). Toward a theoretical model of text complexity for the early grades: Learning from the past, anticipating the future. *Reading Research Quarterly, 47*(3), 235–258. https://doi.org/10.1002/rrq.019

Metropolitan Museum of Art (n.d.). *Proto-Cuneiform tablet reflecting an account of barley distribution*. https://www.metmuseum.org/art/collection/search/329081.

Mitchell, C. (2020, March 3). *Dyslexia is not a bad word, advocates say. Schools should use it. Education Week*. https://www-edweek-org.proxy-remote.galib.uga.edu/teaching-learning/dyslexia-is-not-a-bad-word-advocates-say-schools-should-use-it/2020/03

Moats, L. C. (2000). *Whole language lives on: The illusion of "balanced" reading instruction*. Thomas B. Fordham Foundation.

Moats, L. C. (2005). How spelling supports reading. *American Educator, 29*(4), 12–43.

Moats, L. C. (2014). What teachers don't know and why they aren't learning it: Addressing the need for content and pedagogy in teacher education. *Australian Journal of Learning Difficulties, 19*(2), 75–91. https://doi.org/10.1080/19404158.2014.941093

Moats, L. C. (2020a). *Speech to print: Language essentials for teachers*. Brookes Publishing.

Moats, L. C. (2020b). *Teaching reading is rocket science (2020): What expert teachers of reading should know and be able to do*. American Federation of Teachers.

Monaghan, E. J. (1983). *A common heritage: Noah Webster's blue-back speller*. Archon Books.

Morgan, W.P. (1896). A case of congenital wordblindness. *British Medical Journal, 2*, 1378.

Morris, R. D., Lovett, M. W., Wolf, M., Sevcik, R. A., Steinbach, K. A., Frijters, J. C., & Shapiro, M. B. (2012). Multiple-component remediation for developmental reading disabilities: IQ, socioeconomic status, and race as factors in remedial outcome. *Journal of Learning Disabilities, 45*(2), 99–127. https://doi.org/10.1177/0022219409355472

Mosher, R. M. (1928). Some results of teaching beginners by the look-and-say method. *Journal of Educational Psychology, 19*(3), 185–193. https://doi.org/10.1037/h0070267

Moss, B. (2008). The information text gap: The mismatch between non-narrative text types in basal readers and 2009 NAEP recommended guidelines. *Journal of Literacy Research, 40,* 201–219.

Myers, J., Scales, R. Q., Grisham, D. L., Wolsey, T. D., Dismuke, S., Smetana, L., Yoder, K. K., Ikpeze, C., Ganske, K., & Martin, S. (2016). What about writing? A national exploratory study of writing instruction in teacher preparation programs. *Literacy Research & Instruction, 55*(4), 309–330. https://doi.org/10.1080/19388071.2016.1198442

Myhill, D., Jones, S. M., Lines, H., & Watson, A. (2012). Re-thinking grammar: The impact of embedded grammar teaching on students' writing and students' metalinguistic understanding. *Research Papers in Education, 27*(2), 139–166. https://doi.org/10.1080/02671522.2011.637640

Myhill, D., Jones, S., & Lines, H. (2018). Supporting less proficient writers through linguistically aware teaching. *Language & Education: An International Journal, 32*(4), 333–349. https://doi.org/10.1080/09500782.2018.1438468

Nagro, S. A., Hooks, S. D., & Fraser, D. W. (2019). Over a decade of practice: Are educators correctly using tertiary interventions? *Preventing School Failure, 63*(1), 52–61. https://doi.org/10.1080/1045988X.2018.1491021

Nagy, W. (1988). *Teaching vocabulary to improve reading comprehension.* International Reading Association.

Nagy, W., & Stahl, S. (2002). *Promoting vocabulary development.* Texas Education Agency.

Nation, K., & Cocksey, J. (2009). The relationship between knowing a word and reading it aloud in children's word reading development. *Journal of Experimental Child Psychology, 103*(3), 296–308. https://doi.org/10.1016/j.jecp.2009.03.004

Nation, K., Angell, P., & Castles, A. (2007). Orthographic learning via self-teaching in children learning to read English: Effects of exposure, durability, and context. *Journal of Experimental Child Psychology, 96*(1), 71–84. https://doi.org/10.1016/j.jecp.2006.06.004

National Assessment of Educational Progress (2022). *National achievement-level results: Grade 4.* https://www.nationsreportcard.gov/reading/nation/achievement?grade=4

National Center on Improving Literacy. (2023). *State of dyslexia.* https://improvingliteracy.org/state-of-dyslexia

National Early Literacy Panel. (2008). *Developing early literacy.* National Institute for Literacy. http://www.nifl.gov

National Institute of Child Health and Human Development. (2000). *Report of the National Reading Panel. Teaching children to read: An evidence-based assessment of the scientific research literature on reading and its implications for reading instruction: Reports of the subgroups* (NIH Publication No. 00-4754). U.S. Government Printing Office. https://www.nichd.nih.gov/publications/pubs/nrp/findings

Ng, M. M. R., Bowers, P. N., & Bowers, J. S. (2022). A promising new tool for literacy instruction: The morphology matrix. *PLoS ONE, 17*(1), 1–18. https://doi.org./10.1371/journal.pone.0262260.

O'Connor, R. E., Beach, K. D., Sanchez, V. M., Bocian, K. M., & Flynn, L. J. (2015). Building BRIDGES: A design experiment to improve reading and United States history knowledge of poor readers in eighth grade. *Exceptional Children, 81*(4), 399–425. https://doi.org/10.1177/0014402914563706

O'Connor, R. E., Beach, K. D., Sanchez, V. M., Kim, J. J., Knight-Teague, K., Orozco, G., Jones, B. T., Crawford, L., & Smolkowski, K. (2019). Teaching academic vocabulary to sixth-grade students with disabilities. *Learning Disability Quarterly, 42*(4), 231–243. https://doi.org/10.1177/0731948718821091

OED Online (2022). *Structured*. Retrieved December 1, 2022, from https://oed.com/view/Entry/191897

Olson, D. R. (n.d.). Alphabetic systems. In T. Grant (Ed.), *Encyclopædia Britannica Online.* https://www.britannica.com/topic/writing/Alphabetic-systems

Oxford University Press. (2010). *Primer. Oxford Reference*. Retrieved 2023, from https://www.oxfordreference.com/view/10.1093/acref/9780198606536.001.0001/acref-9780198606536-e-3871

Pan, S. C., Rickard, T. C., & Bjork, R. A. (2021). Does spelling still matter—and if so, how should it be taught? Perspectives from contemporary and historical research. *Educational Psychology Review, 33*(4), 1523–1552. https://doi.org/10.1007/s10648-021-09611-y

Paracchini, S. (2022). The genetics of dyslexia: Learning from the past to shape the future. In M. J. Snowling, C. Hulme, & K. Nation (Eds.), *The science of reading: A handbook* (2nd ed.). Wiley Blackwell.

Parker, F. W. (1902). An account of the work of the Cook County and Chicago Normal School from 1883 to 1889. *Elementary School Teacher and Course of Study, 2*, 752–780. https://doi.org/10.1086/453130

Parker, F. W., & Patridge, L. E. (1883). *Notes of talks on teaching: Given by Francis W. Parker, at the Martha's Vineyard Summer Institute, July 17 to August 19, 1882.* EL Kellogg & Company.

Parker, S. (2019). *Reading instruction and phonics: Theory and practice for teachers* (2nd ed.). Royce-Kotran Publishing.

Paulesu, E., Démonet, J. F., Fazio, F., McCrory, E., Chanoine, V., Brunswick, N., Cappa, S. F., Cossu, G., Habib, M., Frith, C.D., & Frith, U. (2001). Dyslexia: Cultural diversity and biological unity. *Science, 291*, 2165–2167.

Pearson, P. D. (2000). *Reading in the twentieth century. Center for the Improvement of Early Reading Achievement.* Office of Educational Research and Improvement. https://eric.ed.gov/?id=ED479530.

Pennington, B. F. (2006). From single to multiple-deficit models of developmental disorders. *Cognition, 101*(2), 385–413. https://doi.org/10.1016/j.cognition.2006.04.008

Pennington, B. F., Santerre-Lemmon, L., Rosenberg, J., MacDonald, B., Boada, R., Friend, A., Leopold, D. R., Samuelsson, S., Byrne, B., Willcutt, E. G., & Olson, R. K. (2012). Individual prediction of dyslexia by single versus multiple deficit models. *Journal of Abnormal Psychology, 121*(1), 212–224. https://doi.org/10.1037/a0025823

Perfetti, C. A. (1985). *Reading ability.* Oxford University Press.

Perfetti, C. A. (2007). Reading ability: Lexical quality to comprehension. *Scientific Studies of Reading, 11*(4), 357–383. https://doi.org/10.1080/10888430701530730

Perfetti, C. A., & Stafura, J. (2014). Word knowledge in a theory of reading comprehension. *Scientific Studies of Reading, 18*(1), 22–37. https://doi.org/10.1080/10888438.2013

Perfetti, C. A. (2017). Lexical quality revisited. In E. Segers & P. van den Broek (Eds.), *Developmental perspectives in written language and literacy: In honor of Ludo Verhoeven.* John Benjamins.

Perry, C., Ziegler, J. C., & Zorzi, M. (2007). Nested incremental modeling in the development of computational theories: The CDP+ model of reading aloud. *Psychological Review, 114*(2), 273–315. https://doi.org/10.1037/0033-295X.114.2.273

Peterson, R. L., & Pennington, B. F. (2012). Developmental dyslexia. *The Lancet, 379*(9830), 1997–2007. https://doi.org/10.1016/S0140-6736(12)60198-6

Peterson, R. L., & Pennington, B. F. (2015). Developmental dyslexia. *Annual Review of Clinical Psychology, 11*, 283–307. https://doi.org/10.1146/annurev-clinpsy-032814-112842

Piasta, S. B., & Wagner, R. K. (2010a). Developing early literacy skills: A meta-analysis of alphabet learning and instruction. *Reading Research Quarterly, 45*(1), 8–38. https://doi.org/10.1598/RRQ.45.1.2

Piasta, S. B., & Wagner, R. K. (2010b). Learning letter names and sounds: Effects of instruction, letter type, and phonological processing skill. *Journal of Experimental Child Psychology, 105*(4), 324–344. https://doi.org/10.1016/j.jecp.2009.12.008

Pinker, S. (1994). *The language instinct.* W. W. Morrow.

Popp, H. M. (1975). Current practices in the teaching of beginning reading. *Toward a Literate Society*, 101–146.

Powel, B. B. (1991). *Homer and the origin of the Greek alphabet.* Cambridge University Press.

Preciado v. Board of Education of Clovis Municipal Schools, 443 F. Supp. 3d 1289 (D.N.M. 2020).

Ramus, F. (2014). Should there really be a "Dyslexia debate"? *Brain: A Journal of Neurology, 137*, 3371–3374. https://doi.org/10.1093/brain/awu295

Read, C. (1971). Pre-school children's knowledge of English phonology. *Harvard Educational Review, 41*(1), 1–34.

Rehfeld, D. M., Kirkpatrick, M., O'Guinn, N., & Renbarger, R. (2022). A meta-analysis of phonemic awareness instruction provided to children suspected of having a reading disability. *Language, Speech & Hearing Services in Schools, 53*(4), 1177–1201. https://doi.org/10.1044/2022_LSHSS-21-00160

Report of the National Reading Panel. (2000). *Teaching children to read: An evidence-based assessment of the scientific research literature on reading and its implications for reading instruction.* National Institute of Child Health and Human Development, National Institutes of Health.

Rice, M., Erbeli, F., Thompson, C. G., Sallese, M. R., & Fogarty, M. (2022). Phonemic awareness: A meta-analysis for planning effective instruction. *Reading Research Quarterly, 57*(4), 1259–1289. https://doi.org/10.1002/rrq.473

Richlan, F., Kronbichler, M., & Wimmer, H. (2011). Meta-analyzing brain dysfunctions in dyslexic children and adults. *Neuroimage, 56*, 1735–1742. https://doi.org/10.1016/j.neuroimage.2011.02.040

Ridley School District v. M.R., 680 F.3d 260 (3d Cir. 2012).

Roberts, T. A. (2021). Learning letters: Evidence and questions from a science-of-reading perspective. *Reading Research Quarterly, 56*(1), S171–S192. https://doi.org/10.1002/rrq.394

Roediger, H. L., & Karpicke, J. D. (2006). The power of testing memory: Basic research and implications for educational practice. *Perspectives on Psychological Science, 1*(3), 181–210. https://doi.org/10.1111/j.1745-6916.2006.00012.x

Rogich v. Clark County School District, 79 IDELR 252 (D. Nev. 2021).

Romance, N. R., & Vitale, M. R. (2001). Implementing an in-depth expanded science model in elementary schools: Multi-year findings, research issues, and policy implications. *International Journal of Science Education, 23*, 373–404. http://dx.doi.org/10.1080/09500690116738

Rose, J. (2006). *Independent review of the teaching of early reading final report.* U.K. Department for Education and Skills. https://dera.ioe.ac.uk/5551/2/report.pdf

Rose, J. (2009). *Identifying and teaching children and young people with dyslexia and literacy difficulties: An independent report.* https://dera.ioe.ac.uk/id/eprint/14790/7/00659-2009DOM-EN_Redacted.pdf

Rose, T. E., & Zirkel, P. (2007). Orton-Gillingham methodology for students with reading disabilities: 30 years of case law. *Journal of Special Education, 41*(3), 171–185. https://doi.org/10.1177/00224669070410030301

Rosenshine, B. (2009). Systematic instruction (pp. 235–243). In T. L. Good (Ed.), *21st Century education: A reference handbook* (vol. 1). Sage.

Rosenthal, J., & Ehri, L. C. (2008). The mnemonic value of orthography for vocabulary learning. *Journal of Educational Psychology, 100*(1), 175–191. https://doi.org/10.1037/0022-0663.100.1.175

Rousseau, J-J. (2003). *Emile, or, treatise on education* (W. H. Payne, Trans.). Prometheus Books. (Original work published in 1896).

Rozemarijn, v. L. (2015). *Proto-sinaitic-phoenician-latin-alphabet.jpg.* Wikimedia Commons. https://commons.wikimedia.org/wiki/File:Proto-sinaitic-phoenician-latin-alphabet.jpg

Saddler, B. (2012). *Teacher's guide to effective sentence writing.* Guilford Press.

Saddler, B. (2018). Writing a true sentence: Developing syntactical sophistication through sentence-level writing instruction. *Perspectives on Language & Literacy, 44*(2), 23–28.

Saddler, B., Asaro-Saddler, K., Moeyaert, M., & Cuccio-Slichko, J. (2019). Teaching summary writing to students with learning disabilities via strategy instruction. *Reading & Writing Quarterly, 35*(6), 572–586. https://doi.org/10.1080/10573569.2019.1600085

Samuels, S. J., Rasinski, T., & Hiebert, E. H. (2011). Eye movements and reading: What teachers need to know. In S. Jay Samuels & Alan E. Farstrup (Eds.), *What research has to say about reading instruction* (4th ed.). International Reading Association.

Santangelo, T., & Graham, S. (2016). A comprehensive meta-analysis of handwriting instruction. *Educational Psychology Review*, *28*(2), 225–265. https://doi.org/10.1007/s10648-015-9335-1

Savage, R., Georgiou, G., Parrila, R., & Maiorino, K. (2018). Preventative reading interventions teaching direct mapping of graphemes in texts and set-for-variability aid at-risk learners. *Scientific Studies of Reading*, *22*(3), 225–247. https://doi.org/10.1080/10888438.2018.1427753

Sayeski, K. L., & Zirkel, P. A. (2021). Orton Gillingham and the IDEA: Analysis of the frequency and outcomes of case law. *Annals of Dyslexia*, *71*(3), 483–500. https://doi.org/10.1007/s11881-021-00230-4

Sayeski, K. L., Reno, E. A., & Thoele, J. M. (2022). Specially designed instruction: Operationalizing the delivery of special education services. *Exceptionality: A Special Education Journal.* Advance online publication. https://doi.org/10.1080/09362835.2022.2158087

Sayeski, K., Earle, G., Eslinger, R., Whitenton, J. (2017). Teacher candidates' mastery of phoneme-grapheme correspondence: massed versus distributed practice in teacher education. *Annals of Dyslexia*, *67*(1), 26–41. https://doi.org/10.1007/s11881-016-0126-2

Schatschneider, C., & Torgesen, J. K. (2004). Using our current understanding of dyslexia to support early identification and intervention. *Journal of Child Neurology*, *19*(10), 759–765. https://doi.org/10.1177/08830738040190100501

Schumacher, J., Hoffmann, P., Schmäl, C., Schulte-Körne, G., & Nöthen, M. M. (2007). Genetics of dyslexia: The evolving landscape. *Journal of Medical Genetics*, *44*(5), 289–297. https://doi.org/10.1136/jmg.2006.046516

Schwanenflugel, P. J., Hamilton, A. M., Kuhn, M. R., Wisenbaker, J. M., & Stahl, S. A. (2004). Becoming a fluent reader: Reading skill and prosodic features in the oral reading of young readers. *Journal of Educational Psychology*, *96*(1), 119–129. https://doi.org/10.1037/0022-0663.96.1.119

Seidenberg, M. S. (2017). *Language at the speed of sight: How we read, why so many can't, and what can be done about it*. Basic Books.

Seidenberg, M. S., & McClelland, J. L. (1989). A distributed, developmental model of word recognition and naming. *Psychological Review*, *96*(4), 523–568. https://doi.org/10.1037/0033-295X.96.4.523

Serafini, F. (2001). *The reading workshop: Creating space for readers*. Heinemann Publishers.

Shahar, Y. D., & Share, D. L. (2008). Spelling as a self-teaching mechanism in orthographic learning. *Journal of Research in Reading*, *31*(1), 22–39. https://doi.org/10.1111/j.1467-9817.2007.00359.x

Shanahan, T., & Lomax, R. G. (1986). An analysis and comparison of theoretical models of the reading-writing relationship. *Journal of Educational Psychology*, *78*(2), 116–123. https://doi.org/10.1037/0022-0663.78.2.116 https://doi.org/10.1037/0022-0663.78.2.116

Share, D. L. (1995). Phonological recoding and self-teaching: Sine qua non of reading acquisition. *Cognition, 55*(2), 151–218. https://doi.org/10.1016/0010-0277(94)00645-2

Share, D. L. (2008). On the Anglocentricities of current reading research and practice: The perils of overreliance on an "outlier" orthography. *Psychological Bulletin, 134*(4), 584–615. https://doi.org/10.1037/0033-2909.134.4.584

Shaywitz, B. A., Shaywitz, S. E., Pugh, K. R., Mencl, W. E., Fulbright, R. K., Skudlarski, P., Constable, R. T., Marchione, K. E., Fletcher, J. M., Lyon, G. R., & Gore, J. C. (2002). Disruption of posterior brain systems for reading in children with developmental dyslexia. *Biological Psychiatry, 52*(2), 101–110. https://doi.org/10.1016/S0006-3223(02)01365-3

Shaywitz, S. (2020). *Overcoming dyslexia* (2nd ed.). Sheldon Press.

Smith, F. (1994). *Writing and the writer* (2nd ed.). L. Erlbaum Associates.

Smith, F., & Goodman, K. S. (1971). On the psycholinguistic method of teaching reading. *The Elementary School Journal, 71*(4), 177–181. https://doi.org/10.1086/460630

Smith, M. (1973). The perennial problem of illiteracy. *Modern Age, 17*(1), 33–39.

Smith, N. B. (1957). What research says about phonics instruction. *The Journal of Educational Research, 51*(1), 1–9. https://doi.org/10.1080/00220671.1957.10882430

Smith, R., Snow, P., Serry, T., & Hammond, L. (2021). The role of background knowledge in reading comprehension: A critical review. *Reading Psychology, 42*(3), 214–240. https://doi.org/10.1080/02702711.2021.1888348

Snow, C. (2002). *Reading for understanding: Toward an R&D program in reading comprehension*. Rand Corporation.

Snow, P. C. (2021). SOLAR: The science of language and reading. *Child Language Teaching & Therapy, 37*(3), 222–233. https://doi.org/10.1177/0265659020947817

Snowling, M. J. (2019). *Dyslexia: A very short introduction*. Oxford University Press.

Snowling, M. J. (2013). Early identification and interventions for dyslexia: A contemporary view. *Journal of Research in Special Education Needs, 13*, 7–14. https://doi.org/10.1111/j.1471-3802.2012.01262.x

Snowling, M. J. (2000). *Dyslexia* (2nd ed.). Blackwell Publishing.

Snowling, M. J., & Melby-Lervåg, M. (2016). Oral language deficits in familial dyslexia: A meta-analysis and review. *Psychological Bulletin, 142*(5), 498–545. https://doi.org/10.1037/bul0000037

Snowling, M. J., Hayiou-Thomas, M. E., Nash, H. M., & Hulme, C. (2020). Dyslexia and developmental language disorder: Comorbid disorders with distinct effects on reading comprehension. *Journal of Child Psychology and Psychiatry, 61*(6), 672–680. https://doi.org/10.1111/jcpp.13140

Snowling, M. J., Hulme, C., & Nation, K. (2020). Defining and understanding dyslexia: Past, present and future. *Oxford Review of Education, 46*(4), 501–513. https://doi.org/10.1080/03054985.2020.1765756

Snowling, M. J., West, G., Fricke, S., Bowyer, C. C., Dilnot, J., Cripps, D., Nash, M., & Hulme, C. (2022). Delivering language intervention at scale: Promises and pitfalls. *Journal of Research in Reading, 45*(3), 342–366. https://doi.org/10.1111/1467-9817.12391

Snyder, T. (1993). *120 years of American education: A statistical portrait.* National Center for Education Statistics.

Solity, J., & Vousden, J. (2009). Real books vs. reading schemes: A new perspective from instructional psychology. *Educational Psychology, 29*, 469–511. https://doi.org/10.1080/01443410903103657

Spear-Swerling, L. (Ed.). (2022). *Structured literacy interventions: Teaching students with reading difficulties, grades K–6.* Guilford Publications.

Spiel, C. F., Evans, S. W., & Langberg, J. M. (2014). Evaluating the content of individualized education programs and 504 plans of young adolescents with attention deficit hyperactivity disorder. *School Psychology Quarterly, 29*, 452–468. https://doi.org/10.1037/spq0000101

Spinelli, J. (1990). *Maniac Magee.* Harper Trophy.

Stanovich, K. E. (1986). Matthew effects in reading: Some consequences of individual differences in the acquisition of literacy. *Reading Research Quarterly, 21*(4), 360–407. https://doi.org/10.1177/0022057409189001-204

Stanovich, K. E., & Siegel, L. (1994). Phenotypic performance profile of children with reading disabilities: A regression-based test of the phonological-core variable-difference model. *Journal of Educational Psychology, 86*(1), 24–53. https://doi.org/10.1037/0022-0663.86.1.24

Steacy, L. M., Compton, D. L., Petscher, Y., Elliott, J. D., Smith, K., Rueckl, J. G., Sawi, O., Frost, S. J., & Pugh, K. R. (2019). Development and prediction of context-dependent vowel pronunciation in elementary readers. *Scientific Studies of Reading, 23*(1), 49–63. https://doi.org/10.1080/10888438.2018.1466303

Steacy, L. M., Kearns, D. M., Gilbert, J. K., Compton, D. L., Cho, E., Lindstrom, E. R., & Collins, A. A. (2017). Exploring individual differences in irregular word recognition among children with early-emerging and late-emerging word reading difficulty. *Journal of Educational Psychology, 109*(1), 51–69. https://doi.org/10.1037/edu0000113

Steacy, L. M., Wade-Woolley, L., Rueckl, J. G., Pugh, K. R., Elliott, J. D., & Compton, D. L. (2019). The role of set for variability in irregular word reading: Word and child predictors in typically developing readers and students at-risk for reading disabilities. *Scientific Studies of Reading, 23*(6), 523–532. https://doi.org/10.1080/10888438.2019.1620749

Stone, J. E. (1991). Developmentalism: A standing impediment to the design of the "New American School." *Network News and Views, 10*(2), 1–3.

Stone, J. E. (1996). Developmentalism: An obscure but pervasive restriction on educational improvement. *Education Policy Analysis, 4*(8), 1–32. https://doi.org/10.14507/epaa.v4n8.1996

Sun, Y., Shi, A., Zhao, W., Yang, Y., Li, B., Hu, X., Shanks, D. R., Yang, C., & Luo, L. (2022). Long-lasting effects of an instructional intervention on interleaving preference in inductive learning and transfer. *Educational Psychology Review, 34*(3), 1679–1707. https://doi.org/10.1007/s10648-022-09666-5

Sunde, K., Furnes, B., & Lundetræ, K. (2020). Does introducing the letters faster boost the development of children's letter knowledge, word reading and spelling in the first year of school? *Scientific Studies of Reading, 24*(2), 141–158. https://doi.org/10.1080/10888438.2019.1615491

Tannenbaum, K. R., Torgesen, J. K., & Wagner, R. K. (2006). Relationships between word knowledge and reading comprehension in third-grade children. *Scientific Studies of Reading, 10*(4), 381–398. https://doi.org/10.1207/s1532799xssr1004_3

Taylor, J. S. H., Rastle, K., & Davis, M. H. (2013). Can cognitive models explain brain activation during word and pseudoword reading? A meta-analysis of 36 neuroimaging studies. *Psychological Bulletin, 139*(4), 766–791. https://doi.org/10.1037/a0030266

The American primer: Or, an easy introduction to spelling and reading. (1813). Printed and sold by Mathew Carey. https://library.csun.edu/SCA/Peek-in-the-Stacks/primers.

The New England primer. (ca. 1882). https://libwww.freelibrary.org/digital/item/55726

Time. (March 14, 1955). *Education: Why Johnny can't read.*

Torgesen, J. K. (2002). The prevention of reading difficulties. *Journal of School Psychology, 40*, 7–26. http://dx.doi.org/10.1016/S0022-4405(01)00092-9

Torgesen, J. K. (2004). Avoiding the devastating downward spiral: The evidence that early intervention prevents reading failure. *American Educator, 28*, 6–19.

Torgesen, J. K. (2005). Recent discoveries on remedial interventions for children with dyslexia. In M. J. Snowling, C. Hulme (Eds.), *The science of reading: A handbook*, pp. 521–537. Blackwell Publishing.

Torgesen, J. K., Wagner, R. K., Rashotte, C. A., Burgess, S., & Hecht, S. (1997). Contributions of phonological awareness and rapid automatic naming ability to the growth of word-reading skills in second-to fifth-grade children. *Scientific Studies of Reading, 1*(2), 161. https://doi.org/10.1207/s1532799xssr0102_4

Torgesen, J. K., Wagner, R. K., Rashotte, C. A., Rose, E., Lindamood, P., Conway, T., & Garvan, C. (1999). Preventing reading failure in young children with phonological processing disabilities: Group and individual responses to instruction. *Journal of Educational Psychology, 91*, 579–593. http://dx.doi.org/10.1037/0022-0663.91.4.579

Torppa, M., Vasalampi, K., Eklund, K., & Niemi, P. (2022). Long-term effects of the home literacy environment on reading development: Familial risk for dyslexia as a moderator. *Journal of Experimental Child Psychology, 215*. https://doi.org/10.1016/j.jecp.2021.105314

Toste, J. R., Capin, P., Williams, K. J., Cho, E., & Vaughn, S. (2019). Replication of an experimental study investigating the efficacy of a multisyllabic word reading intervention with and without motivational beliefs training for struggling readers. *Journal of Learning Disabilities, 52*, 45–58. https://doi.org/10.1177/0022219418775114

Treiman, R. (1993). *Beginning to spell: A study of first grade children.* Oxford University Press.

Treiman, R., Stothard, S. E., & Snowling, M. J. (2013). Instruction matters: Spelling of vowels by children in England and the US. *Reading & Writing, 26*(3), 473–487. https://doi.org/10.1007/s11145-012-9377-4

Tunmer, W. E., & Chapman, J. W. (2012). Does set for variability mediate the influence of vocabulary knowledge on the development of word recognition skills? *Scientific Studies of Reading, 16*(2), 122–140. https://doi.org/10.1080/10888438.2010.542527

Twain, M., & Neider, C. (2000). *The autobiography of Mark Twain.* Harper Collins.

U.S. Department of Education (2021). *The federal role in education.* https://www2.ed.gov/about/overview/fed/role.html

Understood. (n.d.). *The difference between IEPs and 504 plans.* Understood.org. https://www.understood.org/articles/the-difference-between-ieps-and-504-plans

Vadasy, P. F., & Sanders, E. A. (2021). Introducing phonics to learners who struggle: Content and embedded cognitive elements. *Reading & Writing, 34*(8), 2059–2080. https://doi.org/10.1007/s11145-021-10134-9

Vadasy, P. F., Sanders, E. A., & Peyton, J. A. (2006). Paraeducator-supplemented instruction in structural analysis with text reading practice for second- and third-graders at risk for reading problems. *Remedial and Special Education, 27*, 365–378. https://doi.org/10.1177/07419325060270060601

Vadasy, P. F., Sanders, E. A., Peyton, J. A., & Jenkins, J. R. (2002). Timing and intensity of tutoring: A closer look at the conditions for effective early literacy tutoring. *Learning Disabilities Research & Practice, 17,* 227–241. http://dx.doi.org/10.1111/1540-5826.00048

Van Antwerp, Bragg, & Co. (1885). *The eclectic manual of methods.* Van Antwerp, Bragg, & Co.

van Bergen, E., Hart, S. A., Latvala, A., Vuoksimaa, E., Tolvanen, A., & Torppa, M. (2021). Literacy skills seem to fuel literacy enjoyment, rather than vice versa. *Developmental Science, 26*(3), 1–11. https://doi.org/10.1111/desc.13325

Vander Stappen, C. & Van Reybroeck, M. (2018). Phonological awareness and rapid automatized naming are independent phonological competencies with specific impacts on word reading and spelling: An intervention study. *Frontiers in Psychology, 9*(320), 1–16. https://doi:10.3389/fpsyg.2018.00320

VanDerHeyden, A. M., & Burns, B. K. (2017). Four dyslexia screening myths that cause more harm than good in preventing reading failure and what you can do instead. *Communique, 45*(7), 30–28.

Venezky, R. L. (1999). *The American way of spelling: The structure and origins of American English orthography.* Guilford Press.

Vihman, M. M. (2014). *Phonological development: The first two years* (2nd ed.). Wiley Blackwell.

Wagner, R. K., & Lonigan, C. J. (2022). Early identification of children with dyslexia: Variables differentially predict poor reading versus unexpected poor reading. *Reading Research Quarterly, 1*. https://doi.org/10.1002/rrq.480

Wakely, M. B., Hooper, S. R., de Kruif, R. E. L., & Swartz, C. (2006). Subtypes of written expression in elementary school children: A linguistic-based model. *Developmental Neuropsychology, 29*(1), 125–159. https://doi.org/10.1207/s15326942dn2901_7

Wanzek, J., & Vaughn, S. (2007). Research-based implications from extensive early reading interventions. *School Psychology Review, 36*, 541–561. https://doi.org/10.1080/02796015.2007.12087917

Wanzek, J., Vaughn, S., Scammacca, N. K., Metz, K., Murray, C. S., Roberts, G., & Danielson, L. (2013). Extensive reading interventions for students with reading difficulties after grade 3. *Review of Educational Research, 83*, 163–195. https://doi.org/10.3102/0034654313477212

Washburn, E. K., Joshi, R., & Binks-Cantrell, E. (2011). Are preservice teachers prepared to teach struggling readers? *Annals of Dyslexia, 61*, 21–43. https://doi.org/10.1007/s11881-010-0040-y

Watson, N. (2006). *The literary tourist: Readers and places in romantic & Victorian Britain*. Palgrave Macmillan.

Webster, N. (1783). *A grammatical institute of the English language, Part II*. Young and M'Cullouch.

Webster, N. 1758–1843. (1822). *The American spelling book: Containing the rudiments of the English language, for the use of schools in the United States*. Websters and Skinners.

Weiser, B. L. (2013). Ameliorating reading disabilities early: Examining an effective encoding and decoding prevention instruction model. *Learning Disability Quarterly, 36*(3), 161–177. https://doi.org/10.1177/0731948712450017

Weizman, Z. O., & Snow, C. E. (2001). Lexical input as related to children's vocabulary acquisition: Effects of sophisticated exposure and support for meaning. *Developmental Psychology, 37*(2), 265. https://doi.org/10.1037/0012-1649.37.2.265

Wexler, N. (2019). *The knowledge gap: The hidden cause of America's broken education system and how to fix it*. Avery.

Willcutt, E. G., Doyle, A. E., Nigg, J. T., Faraone, S. V., & Pennington, B. F. (2005). Validity of the executive function theory of attention-deficit/hyperactivity disorder: A meta-analytic review. *Biological Psychiatry, 57*(11), 1336–1346. https://doi.org/10.1016/j.biopsych.2005.02.006

Willingham, D. T. (2009). Three problems in the marriage of neuroscience and education. *Cortex, 45*(4), 544–545. https://doi.org/10.1016/j.cortex.2008.05.009

Willingham, D. T. (2011). Ask the cognitive scientist: Can teachers increase students' self-control? *American Educator, 35*(2), 22–27.

Willingham, D. T. (2019, December 13). On the reality of dyslexia. *Science and Education Blog*. http://www.danielwillingham.com/daniel-willingham-science-and-education-blog/on-the-reality-of-dyslexia

Willingham, D. T., & Lovette, G. (2014). *Can reading comprehension be taught?* Teachers College Record. Teachers College.

Woods, C., Emberling, G., & Teeter, E. (2010). *Visible language: Inventions of writing in the ancient middle east and beyond*. The Oriental Institute of the University of Chicago.

World Health Organization. (2019). International classification of diseases (ICD-10): Version for 2019.

Wright, T. S., & Cervetti, G. N. (2017). A systematic review of the research on vocabulary instruction that impacts text comprehension. *Reading Research Quarterly, 52*(2), 203–226. https://doi.org/10.1002/rrq.163

Yell, M. L., Collins, J., Kumpiene, G., & Bateman, D. (2020). The individualized education program: Procedural and substantive requirements. *TEACHING Exceptional Children, 52*(5), 304–318. https://doi.org/10.1177/0040059920906592

Youman, M., & Mather, N. (2018). Dyslexia laws in the USA: A 2018 update. *Perspectives on Language and Literacy, 44,* 37–41.

Yudin, M. (2015). *Guidance on dyslexia.* https://sites.ed.gov/idea/files/policy_speced_guid_idea_memosdcltrs_guidance-on-dyslexia-10-2015.pdf

Ziegler, J. C., & Goswami, U. (2005). Reading acquisition, developmental dyslexia, and skilled reading across languages. *Psychological Bulletin, 131,* 3–29. https://doi.org/10.1037/0033-2909.131.1.3

Zirkel, P. (2022). Dyslexia: State laws and court decisions. *Communique, 50*(7), 20–21.

Index

academic word list (AWL), 137
advanced phonics patterns, *100*, *101*, 108
advocacy, for dyslexia, 13, 161–74
affixes: phonics instruction and, *100*, 105–6. *See also* prefixes; suffixes
affluence, dyslexia and, 4
affricates, 94
Alexander the Great, 16n4
alphabet/alphabetic principle: challenges of teaching, 25–26; connected texts and, 115–16; consonants in, 22–23, *23*; dyslexia and, 6n1, 13, 19–20; in English orthography, 19–20, 25–26, 27; of Greeks, 22, 23; invention of, 21–22; in Latin, 23–24, *24*; letter names instruction for, 89–90; one-letter-per-sound instruction for, 97; in orthographic mapping, 65–66; of Phoenicians, 22–23, *23*, *24*; phonemes in, 26, 41; phonemic awareness and, 88; phonics instruction for, 97; structured literacy and, 84; vowels in, 22, 23; word-reading skills and, 67–68. *See also* letter-sound relationship
Alphabet Method, in *The Eclectic Manual of Methods for Assistance of Teachers*, 36
The American Primer, 32

American Psychiatric Association (APA). *See Diagnostic and Statistical Manual*
aphasia, 1
Are You My Mother? (Eastman), 114–15
articulatory gestures, 92
AWL. *See* academic word list

background knowledge, for language comprehension, 122, 123, *138*, 138–39
backward reading myth, 14
balanced literacy, 55–57, 113
basal reading programs, 51–55
bases/base elements: morphemes as, 69, 106, *133*; morphology matrices and, 134–38, *136*
Beck, I., 125, 127
Berlin, Rudolf, 1
blends, phonics instruction and, *100*, 101, 102, 107
blocked practice, 103
Blue-Back Speller (Webster), 34, *34*
bound morphemes, 133, *133*
Broca's area, 76
Brown, M. W., 114
Brown Bear, Brown Bear (Martin), 29, 115
Byrne, B., 98–99

209

California, English-Language Arts Framework of, 53
Calkins, Lucy, 54, 56
Carle, Eric, 53
Carnegie Corporation, 47
Catts, H. W., 162
Chall, Jeanne, 46–48, 51
Chaucer, 41
Christie, Agatha, 138
Chunky Monkey, 57
Clay, Marie, 54
closed syllables, 107
Cobble's Knot, 16
code-emphasis reading, 47–48; basal reading programs and, 52, 54
cognitive load, 139–41
coherence, 139–40
cohesion, 139
Coltheart, M., 71n6
Combined Method, in *The Eclectic Manual of Methods for Assistance of Teachersf*, 36
A Compendious Dictionary of the English Language (Webster), 35
complex multisyllabic words, *100, 101*, 106–8
computational models, of word reading, 74
concentration, in dyslexia, 7
concepts of print, 115
connected text: encoding, *86, 87*; fluency with, 112; for language comprehension, 123–24; word reading of, 111–16; in writing workshops, 155–57
connectionist model, of word reading, *73*, 73–74
Connor, C. M., 146
consonant blends, 102, 107
consonant clusters, 102
consonants: in alphabets, 22–23, *23*; phonics instruction and, *100*, 100–102; in primers, 32; pronunciation of, 91–95, *93*; sound-spelling relationship and, 132–33

consonant-vowel-consonant (CVC), 100, *100*; interleaving of, 103
consonant-vowel syllables (CV), 32
context, for word recognition, 68–69
continuants (stops), 92, 94, 95, 101
continuous blending, 101
continuous review, 103–4
Core Knowledge curriculum, 146
Coxhead, A., 137
cumulative review, in vocabulary instruction, 128
cuneiform, of Sumer, 20–21, *21*
CV. *See* consonant-vowel syllables
CVC. *See* consonant-vowel-consonant

decodable texts: in basal reading programs, 51; connected texts as, 113
decoding, 61, 111, 174; dyslexia and, 9, 11; fluency and, 113, 125; morphemes and, 132; in multi-syllabic words, 108; in *The Simple View of Reading*, 62–63; for spelling, 117; universal screening for, 164; vocabulary and, 125; word recognition and, 63, 87. *See also* reading
deficit-based orientation, of dyslexia, 4–5
derivational morphemes, 133, *133*
developmental disorders, multiple deficit model of, *78*, 78–79
developmental dyslexia, 2
developmentalism, 39
developmental learning disorder with impairment in reading, in ICD, 10
Dewey, John, 39–41
Diagnostic and Statistical Manual (DSM-5), 6, 8–10
Dick and Jane primers, 42–43; basal reading programs and, 51, 54; Flesch and, 46; irregular words and, 109, 110
A Dictionary of the English Language (Johnson), *24*, 25

digraphs: phonics instruction and, *100*, 101–2; vowel, 24, 35, 67, 104, 109
diphthongs, 96, *100*, 105
discourse writing, 122, 124, 147–48
Dismal Dozen, 52
Dolch, Edward, 109–10
DRC. *See* dual-route cascaded model
DSM-5. *See Diagnostic and Statistical Manual*
dual-route cascaded model (DRC), for word-reading, 71–73, *72*
dyslexia: as acquired, 7; advocacy for, 13, 161–74; affluence and, 4; alphabetic principle and, 6n1, 13, 19–20; clinical threshold for, 15; complex behavior of reading and, 1–16; co-occurrences with, 7; current situation with, 15; debates over use of term, 3–11; deficit-based orientation of, 4–5; defined, 5–11; as developmental, 6–7; early intervention for, 14, 162, 166–67; English orthography and, 17–30; external causal factors of, 80–81; as familial and hereditary, 79; first descriptions of, 1–3; genetics and, 79; IDEA and, 11–12, 167–71; IEP for, 12, 169–70; internal causal factors of, 79–80; medical model for, 4–5; multifactorial causal models of, 77–81, *78*; myths and misconceptions about, 14; neuroimaging and, 74–77, *75*, *76*; non-special education service options for, 171–73; oral language and, 80; orthographic mapping and, 66; persistent difficulty in, 8, 10; phonemic awareness and, 80; phonological awareness in, 7, 13, 15; reality of, 15; RTI for, 167–68; service options for, 167–73; *The Simple View of Reading* and, 62–63, 173–74; special education services for, 168–71; as specific learning disorder, 8–10, 11–12; state legislation on, 13; teacher training for, 13, 162–64; in triangle model of word reading, 74; unexpectedness in, 8; universal screening for, 164–66; word reading and, 80; word recognition and, 9, 11, 63–64; writing workshops and, 150
Dyson, H., 69

Eagle Eye, 56
Eastman, P. D., 114–15
The Eclectic Manual of Methods for Assistance of Teachers, 36–37
Ehri, Linnea, 64
Einstein, Albert, 16, 145n4
Emile, or On Education (Rousseau), 38
encoding, 65, 111, 174; connected text, *86*, *87*. *See also* spelling
English-Language Arts Framework, of California, 53
English orthography: alphabet in, 19–20, 25–26, 27; borrowed words in, 19, 25; code representation in, 19–20; *A Dictionary of the English Language* and, *24*, 25; dyslexia and, 17–30; history of written language and, 20–25, *21*, *23*, *24*; lack of knowledge of, 26–29; as opaque language, 26; phonemic awareness in, 27–28; phonics instruction and, 98; reading *vs.* language comprehension with, 17–20; spelling in, 19, 22–25, 37; Webster and, 33–35, *34*; word reading and, 85–86
explicit vocabulary instruction, 125, 129–32, *130*
expository texts, 140; in writing workshops, 154
expression (prosody), 141–42

FAPE. *See* free, appropriate public education
First-Grade Studies, 47, 48
504 plan, 171–72
Flesch, Rudolf, 45–46, 52, 57, 96–97

fluency, 6; with connected text, 112; decoding and, 113, 125; in developmental learning disorder, 10; language comprehension and, 134, *138*, 141–42; morphology and, 134; oral reading, 112, 164, 165, 169; phonics and, 114; word recognition and, 86, 87, *87*, 91; word sorting and, 102
fMRI. *See* functional magnetic resonance imaging
Fountas, Irene, 55
free, appropriate public education (FAPE), 168, 170–71
free morphemes, 133, *133*
fricatives, 94
Fröbel, Friedrich, 38
Fry, Edward, 109–10
functional magnetic resonance imaging (fMRI), 75

Galuschka, K., 119
genetics, dyslexia and, 79
glides, 94
Goodman, Kenneth, 48–49
Goodnight Moon (Brown), 114
Gordian knot, 16, 16n4
Gough, P. B., 62–63
Graham, S., 119
grammar: Goodman on, 49; in writing workshops, 151–52. *See also* morphology; phonology; semantics; syntax
Grammatical Institute of the English Language, 34, *34*
grapheme-phoneme correspondence, 174; in decodable texts, 113; irregular words and, 110; in orthographic mapping, 65, 66; phoneme pronunciation and, 91–96, *93*, *95*; phonics instruction and, 98; spelling and, 119; in triangle model of word reading, 74; word recognition and, 85–116, *87*
Graves, Donald, 54

Gray, William S., 42–43
The Great Debate (Chall), 51
The Great Vowel Shift, 41
Greeks, alphabet of, 22, 23
guided reading, 54–55, 114

handwriting, in writing workshops, 152–54
heart-word instruction, *110*, 110–11, *111*
Herbart, Johann Friedrich, 38
heteronyms, 68n4, 111
high-frequency irregular words, 110
high-quality words, 127
Hinshelwood, James, 3
Hirsch, E. D., 144
Hochman, J. C., 157
Hoffman, J. V., 53
Hogan, T., 162
Houghton Mifflin, 52
Huey, Edmund Burke, 46

ICD. *See International Classification of Diseases*
IDA. *See* International Dyslexia Association
IDEA. *See* Individuals with Disabilities Education Act
IEP. *See* individualized education program
independent reading: in basal reading programs, 53, 54, 55; of decodable texts, 113; orthographic mapping and, 66, 67; of predictable texts, 115; vocabulary and, 125
individualized education program (IEP): for dyslexia, 12, 169–70; in 504 plans, 172; IDEA and, 12; SDI and, 169
Individuals with Disabilities Education Act (IDEA): dyslexia and, 11–12, 167–71; FAPE in, 168, 170–71; 504 plans in, 172; RTI in, 167–68; special education services and, 168–71
inferences, 138

inferior frontal gyrus, 76
inflectional morphemes, 133, *133*
integration, in vocabulary instruction, 127–28
intellectual disability, 10
interleaving, 103–4, 113
International Classification of Diseases (ICD), 6, 10–11
International Dyslexia Association (IDA), 6; on structural literacy, 83–84
invented spelling, 117–18
IQ tests, 7
irregular words, 109–11, *110*, *111*

Johnson, Samuel, *24*, 25, 26n3

Key to Pronunciation, 35
knowledge-building: for language comprehension, 142–47; writing workshops for, 148–59
Knowledge Matters Campaign, 146–47
Kussmaul, Adolph, 1, 7

LaBerge, D., 141
language comprehension: background knowledge for, 122, 123, *138*, 138–39; cognitive load in, 139–41; connected text for, 123–24; discourse writing for, 122, 124, 147–48; fluency and, 134, *138*, 141–42; knowledge-building for, 142–47; morphology and, 122, 123, 132–38, *135*, *136*; reading and, 17–20; semantics and, 122, 124–47; *The Simple View of Reading* and, 62–63, 122, *122*, 159; structured literacy and, 121–59; vocabulary and, 122–32, *130*; working memory and, *138*, 139, 140–42; writing workshops for, 148–59
Latin: alphabet in, 23–24, *24*; primers for, 31
learning difference, 5
Learning to Read (Chall), 47

letter-sound relationship, 55, 59; orthographic mapping and, 66n3; phonics instruction and, 98; spelling and, 88–90; word recognition and, 88–91
Leveled Literacy Intervention (LLI), 56
leveled texts, 113–14
lexical quality, 124–25
lexicon, 65, 66–67, 68, 125
liquids, pronunciation of, 94
LLI. *See Leveled Literacy Intervention*
logographs, 20–21, 22
long vowels, 96, *100*, 104–5
"Look and Listen," 52
look-say readers, 42–44; basal reading programs and, 54; Flesch and, 46; irregular words and, 109. *See also* primers
Lovette, G., 143
luxury beliefs, 5
Lyon, Reid, 162

Maniac Magee (Spinelli), 16
Manyak, P. C., 134
Marks of a Readable Style (Flesch), 45
Martin, B., Jr., 29, 115
mathematics, dyslexia and, 7, 8, 10
The Matthew Effect, 139
McClelland, J. L., 73
McGuffey primers, 35–37, *37*; basal reading programs and, 54
McGuffey's Eclectic Primer, 35–36, *36*
meaning-emphasis reading, 47–48
meaningful use, in vocabulary instruction, 128
medical model, for dyslexia, 4–5
mental calculation, in dyslexia, 7
mental lexicon, 65, 66–67, 68, 125
Middle English, pronunciation of, 41
mnemonics, 91
Morgan, W. Pringle, 2, 4
morphemes: in affixes, 106; classification of, 133, *133*; decoding and, 132; word recognition and, 69–70, 87

morphological awareness, 69–70, 80
morphological word families, 132
morphology: affixes and, 105–6; fluency and, 134; instruction in, 134; language comprehension and, 122, 123, 132–38, *135*, *136*; lexical quality and, 124; matrices, 134–38, *135*, *136*; spelling and, 117, 132–47; vocabulary and, 132; word recognition and, 132
Mosher, R. M., 43–44
motor coordination, in dyslexia, 7
MTSS. *See* multi-tiered system of support
multiple deficit model, of developmental disorders, *78*, 78–79
multi-tiered system of support (MTSS), 167, 168, 173
Murder on the Orient Express (Christie), 138

NAEP. *See* National Assessment of Educational Progress
Nagy, W. E., 127
naming speed, 80
narrative texts, 140; in writing workshops, 154
nasals, 94
National Assessment of Educational Progress (NAEP), 60
National Center for Learning Disabilities, 10–11
National Institute of Child Health and Human Development, 55
National Reading Panel, 55–57
neuroimaging, dyslexia and, 74–77, *75*, *76*
neuroplasticity, 77
"The New England Primer," *33*

Office of Civil Rights (OCR), 172
Old English, 24, *24*
opaque languages, 26
Open Court basal series, 52
oral language, dyslexia and, 80
oral reading fluency, 112, 164, 165, 169
oral vocabulary, for word recognition, 68–69
orthographic mapping, for word recognition, 64–67
orthography: lexical quality and, 124; in spelling, 117; in structured literacy, 85; in triangle model of word reading, 73, *73*, 73–74. *See also* English orthography
Orton, 84

Parker, Francis W., 38–39
pedagogy, 31
Pennington, Bruce, 78–79
permanently irregular words, 109
persistent difficulty, in dyslexia, 8, 10
personal narratives, 154
personal organisation, in dyslexia, 7
Pestalozzi, Johann Henrich, 38
Phoenicians, alphabet of, 22–23, *23*, 24
phonemes: in alphabet, 26, 41; orthographic mapping of, 64–65; pronunciation of, 91–96, *93*, *95*; spelling and, 117; in triangle model of word reading, 74; Webster and, 26, 41. *See also* consonants; vowels
phonemic awareness: alphabet/alphabetic principle and, 88; dyslexia and, 80; in English orthography, 27–28; for orthographic mapping, 65; phonics and, 88; for spelling, 88; in triangle model of word reading, 74; word recognition and, 87–91
phonetically regular words, 64
Phonic Method, in *The Eclectic Manual of Methods for Assistance of Teachers*, 36
phonics/phonics instruction: advanced phonics patterns and, *101*, 108; affixes and, *100*, 105–6; for alphabet, 97; balanced literacy and, 55–57; basal reading programs and, 52, 54; complex multisyllabic words and, *101*, 106–8; consonants and,

100, 100–102; CVC and VC and, 100, *100*; diphthongs and, *100*, 105; English orthography and, 98; Flesch and, 45–46; fluency and, 114; grapheme-phoneme correspondence and, 98; irregular words and, 109–11, *110*, *111*; letter-sound relationship and, 98; long vowels and, *100*, 104–5; in look-say readers, 43; myths about, 93, *94*; for orthographic mapping, 66; phonemic awareness and, 88; prefixes and, *100*, 105–6; progressivism and, 98; r-controlled vowels and, *100*, 105; resistance to, 97–98; structured literacy and, 84–85; suffixes and, *100*, 105–6; for word recognition, 84–85, *87*, 87–91, 96–116

phonological/phonemic awareness: in dyslexia, 7, 13, 15; spelling and, 117

phonological recoding, for word recognition, 64–67

phonology: affixes and, 105; spelling and, 105, 132; in triangle model of word reading, 73, *73*, 73–74

Pinnell, Gay Su, 55

PLAAFP. *See* present levels of academic achievement and functional performance

pleiotropy, 78

poverty, 81

predictable texts, 114–15

prefixes: derivational morphemes as, 133, *133*; lexical quality and, 124; morphology and, 132; morphology matrices and, 134–38; phonics instruction and, *100*, 105–6

present levels of academic achievement and functional performance (PLAAFP), 169; in 504 plans, 172

"The Primary-Education Fetich" (Dewey), 40

primers: for reading and spelling, 31–33, *32*, *33*. *See also* Dick and Jane primers; McGuffey primers

progressivism: Dewey and, 39–41; Parker and, 38–39; phonics instruction and, 98; on reading, 37–42, 57–59; Rousseau and, 38

pronunciation: of consonants, 91–95, *93*; in explicit vocabulary instruction, 129; lexical quality and, 124; morphology matrices and, 136; of phonemes, 91–96, *93*, *95*; spelling and, 41, 116; syllables for, 32; of vowels, *95*, 95–96, 108; Webster on, 35, 41. *See also* sound-spelling relationship

prosody (expression), 141–42

The Psychology and Pedagogy of Reading (Huey), 46

punctuation: dyslexia and, 9; in structured literacy, 120; in writing workshops, 150, 155

Quincy Method, 39

rapid automatized naming (RAN), 80

r-controlled vowels, 96, *100*, 105

Read, Charles, 117

reading: background knowledge for, *138*, 138–39; balanced literacy for, 55–57; basal reading programs for, 51–55; Chall and, 46–48; as code-based endeavor, 18–19; code-emphasis, 47–48; Dewey and, 39–41; *Dick and Jane* primers for, 42–43, 46; Flesch and, 45–46; Goodman and, 48–50; individual differences in, 61–81; instruction in United States, 31–60; language comprehension and, 17–20; look-say readers for, 42–44, 46; McGuffey primers for, 35–37, *37*; meaning-emphasis, 47–48; Parker and, 38–39; primers for, 31–33, *32*, *33*; progressivism on, 37–42, 57–59; Rousseau and, 38; Smith and, 48–50; spelling and, 29; teacher training for, 59; Webster and, 33–35, *34*; whole-language

instruction for, 48–51; whole-word instruction for, 39, 44, 46; word recognition and, 61–74. *See also specific topics*
Reading (Goodman), 48–49
Reading and Writing Workshop, 54, 55
reading difficulty. *See* dyslexia
Reading Recovery, 54
Reading Research Quarterly, 47
Rehabilitation Act of 1973, 171
A Report of the National Reading Panel, 55–57
response-to-intervention (RTI), 167–68
root words, 22, 69
Rose, Jim, 7, 9, 162–63
Rose Report, 7, 10
Rousseau, Jean-Jacques, 38
RTI. *See* response-to-intervention

Samuels, S. J., 141
Santangelo, T., 119
Scott-Foresman basal program, 51
Scripps National Spelling Bee, 19
SDI. *See* specially designed instruction
Seidenberg, M. S., 73
self-regulation, 143
self-teaching hypothesis, orthographic mapping and, 66–67
semantics: language comprehension and, 122, 124–47; RAN and, 80; in structured literacy, 85; in triangle model of word reading, 73, 73–74, 80
set for variability, 68–69
Shakespeare, William, 24n2, 41
Share, David, 64
Sharp, Zerna, 42–43
short vowels, 96, 103
sight-word instruction, 28; balanced literacy and, 57; for irregular words, 109; look-say readers and, 42; orthographic mapping and, 64, 65, 65n2, 66
The Simple View of Reading: dyslexia and, 62–63, 173–74; language comprehension and, 62–63, 122, *122*, 159; word recognition and, 62–63, 86, 132
skill lessons, in basal reading programs, 52
Skippy Frog, 56
Smith, Frank, 48–49
socioeconomic status, 81
sound-spelling relationship, 41, 46; balanced literacy and, 55; code-emphasis reading and, 52; consonants and, 132–33; English orthography and, 28; phonemic instruction and, 93; vowels and, 132–33
spaced practice, 103–4
special education services, for dyslexia, 168–71
specially designed instruction (SDI), 168–69, 171
specific language disorder, 10
specific learning disorder: dyslexia as, 8–10, 11–12; in IDEA, 11–12; RTI for, 167; special education services for, 168
spellers, 33
spelling: connected texts and, 116; decoding for, 117; in *A Dictionary of the English Language*, 25; dyslexia and, 9, 11; in English orthography, 19, 22–25, 37; in explicit vocabulary instruction, 129; irregular words and, 110; letter-sound relationship and, 88–90; lexical quality and, 124; McGuffey primers for, 35–37, *37*; morphology and, 117, 132–47; in multi-syllabic words, 108; orthography in, 117; phonemes and, 117; phonemic awareness for, 88; phonological/phonemic awareness and, 117; phonology and, 105, 132; primers for, 31–33, *32*, *33*; pronunciation and, 41, 116; reading and, 29; structured literacy and, 116–20; Webster and, 33–35,

34; in whole-word instruction, 46; word recognition and, 86–87, *87*; in writing workshops, 149, 152–54. *See also* sound-spelling relationship
Spinelli, J., 16
Stanovich, K. E., 139
statistical learning, 116
stops (continuants), 92, 94, 95, 101
strategic instruction, 55
stressed syllables, 35
structured literacy, 60; alphabet and, 84; defined, 85; as descriptive, 84; language comprehension and, 121–59; phonics instruction and, 84–85; spelling and, 116–20; word recognition and, 83–120
student-centered instruction, 38–42, 58
student-friendly explanation, in explicit vocabulary instruction, 129–31
subject-verb agreement, 152
sublexical processing, 71, 71n6
suffixes: derivational morphemes as, 133, *133*; lexical quality and, 124; morphology and, 132; morphology matrices and, 134–38, *135*; phonics instruction and, *100*, 105–6
Sumer, cuneiform of, 20–21, *21*
syllabification, 107–8
syllables: closed, 107; complex multisyllabic words, *100*, *101*, 106–8; consonant clusters in, 102; CV, 32; CVC, 100, *100*, 103; in leveled text, 113; production speed of, 26; for pronunciation, 32; stressed and unstressed, 35; VC, 32
syntax, 48; logographs and, 20; predictability with, 53; RAN and, 80; in structured literacy, 85, 120; in writing workshops, 150, 151–52
synthetic phonics, 36, 47, 52, 53, 59

target text, 146
teacher training: for dyslexia, 13, 162–64; for reading, 59
temporarily irregular words, 109

testing effects, 118
trade texts, 115
transcription skills, 153–54; in structured literacy, 120
transparent languages, 26
triangle model, of word reading, *73*, 73–74, 80
Tryin' Lion, 56
Tunmer, W. E., 62–63
Twain, Mark, 19, 25

unexpectedness, in dyslexia, 8
Units of Study, 56
unstressed syllables, 35

VC. *See* vowel-consonant syllables
verbal efficiency theory, 141
verbal memory, in dyslexia, 7
verbal processing speed, in dyslexia, 7
The Very Hungry Caterpillar (Carle), 53
visual and auditory impairments, 10
visual impairment myth, 14
visual word form area (VWFA), 76–77
vocabulary: elements of effective instruction, 125–29; Goodman on, 49; language comprehension and, 122–32, *130*; morphology and, 132; morphology matrices and, 137
vowel-consonant syllables (VC), 32, 100, *100*
vowel digraphs, 24, 35, 67, 104, 109
vowels: in alphabets, 22, 23; long, 96, *100*, 104–5; in multi-syllabic words, 108; in primers, 32; pronunciation of, *95*, 95–96, 108; r-controlled, 96, *100*, 105; short, 96, 103; sound-spelling relationship and, 132–33
Vowel Valley, *95*, 95–96
VWFA. *See* visual word form area

Webster, Noah, 60; *Blue Black Speller* of, 34, *34*; English orthography and, 33–35, *34*; *Grammatical Institute of the English Language* of, 34, *34*; Johnson and, 26n3; phonemes and,

26, 41; on pronunciation, 35, 41; reading and spelling and, 33–35, *34*; structured literacy and, 84
Wexler, N., 157
whole-language instruction: basal reading programs and, 52–55; leveled texts in, 113; for reading, 48–51; spelling and, 117–18
whole-word instruction: of Flesch, 46; orthographic mapping and, 65; of Parker, 39; for reading, 39, 44, 46; word recognition in, 63
Why Johnny Can't Read (Flesch), 45–46
wide reading, 145
Willingham, D. T., 143, 144–45
word blindness, 1, 3
word dictation, spelling and, 119
word mapping, 119
Word Method, in *The Eclectic Manual of Methods for Assistance of Teachers*, 36
word reading: computational models of, 74; of connected text, 111–16; DRC for, 71–73, *72*; dyslexia and, 80; English orthography and, 85–86; models for, 70–74, *72*, *73*; skills, 67–68; triangle model of, *73*, 73–74, 80
word recognition: in basal reading programs, 54; context for, 68–69; decoding and, 63, *87*; defined, 63; dyslexia and, 9, 11, 63–64; fluency and, *86*, 87, *87*, 91; grapheme-phoneme correspondence and, 85–116, *87*; letter-sound relationship and, 88–91; in look-say readers, 42; morphemes and, 69–70, 87; morphology and, 132; oral vocabulary for, 68–69; orthographic mapping for, 64–67; phoneme pronunciation and, 91–96, *93*, *95*; phonemic awareness and, 87–91; phonics instruction for, 84–85, *87*, 87–91, 96–116; phonological recoding for, 64–67; reading and, 61–74; set for variability and, 68–69; *The Simple View of Reading* and, 62–63, *86*, 132; spelling and, 86–87, *87*; structured literacy and, 83–120; VWFA and, 76–77; in whole-word instruction, 63; word-reading skills and, 67–68
word sorting: fluency and, 102; spelling and, 119
working memory: language comprehension and, *138*, 139, 140–42; phonics and, 66
workshops, for writing, 54, 55, 148–59
World Health Organization (WHO). *See* International Classification of Diseases
writing: discourse, 122, 124, 147–48; dyslexia and, 3, 8, 10, 16; English orthography and, 17; history of, 20–25, *21*, *23*, *24*; morphology for, 137–38; process of, 155–57; structured approach to, 147, 157–59; workshops for, 54, 55, 148–59
The Writing Revolution (Hochman and Wexler), 157

About the Author

Kristin Sayeski is an associate professor in the Department of Communication Sciences and Special Education at the University of Georgia (UGA). Dr. Sayeski received her doctorate in special education from the University of Virginia in 2000. Prior to joining the faculty at UGA, Dr. Sayeski held appointments at the University of Nevada—Las Vegas, the University of Virginia, and Vanderbilt University. Her professional and research interests include identifying exemplary practices related to teacher development and determining effective instructional practices for students with high-incidence disabilities, particularly in the area of reading instruction and intervention.

www.ingramcontent.com/pod-product-compliance
Lightning Source LLC
Chambersburg PA
CBHW051116230426
43667CB00014B/2605